The Rough

Singapore

written and researched by

Mark Lewis

with additional contributions by

Richard Lim and Gemma Sharkey

ROUGH
GUIDES

www.roughguides.com

Contents

Colour section — 1

Introduction 4
What to see............................... 5
When to go 9
Things not to miss 10

Basics — 17

Getting there 19
Arrival 23
City transport........................... 25
The media................................ 29
Health 30
Travel essentials 31

The City — 37

① The Colonial District and
   Marina Bay......................... 39
② Chinatown and the Central
   Business District 52
③ Bras Basah, Little India and
   the Arab Quarter 66
④ Orchard Road 78
⑤ Northern Singapore............ 83
⑥ Eastern Singapore 91
⑦ Western Singapore............. 98
⑧ Sentosa and the southern
   isles 105

Listings — 111

⑨ Accommodation................ 113
⑩ Eating............................... 121

⑪ Nightlife............................ 140
⑫ Entertainment and
   the arts............................. 146
⑬ Festivals........................... 150
⑭ Shopping 153
⑮ Sports 159
⑯ Kids' Singapore................ 163

Contexts — 165

History 167
Religion................................... 173
Singaporean recipes 177
Singapore in literature............ 181
Books 188
Glossary................................. 192

Travel store — 193

Small print & Index — 197

Festive Singapore
colour section
following p.48

Singapore food colour
section following p.144

Singapore
Zoological
Gardens &
Night Safari
Colour maps following
p.208

◄◄ Colourful shutters in Little India ◄ Chinatown at dusk

Introduction to
Singapore

Singapore is certainly the handiest and most marvellous city I ever saw, as well planned and carefully executed as though built entirely by one man. It is like a big desk, full of drawers and pigeonholes, where everything has its place, and can always be found in it.

W. Hornaday, 1885

Despite the immense changes that the twentieth century wrought upon the tiny island of Singapore, this succinct appraisal by the natural historian William Hornaday is as valid today as it was in 1885. Over the past half-century, the city-state has been transformed from an endearingly chaotic colonial port, one that embodied the exoticism of the East, into a pristine, futuristic shrine to consumerism. In the process, the city acquired a reputation for soullessness, but these days Singapore has taken on a more relaxed and intriguing character, one that achieves a healthier and more enjoyable balance between Westernized modernity and the island's traditional cultures and street life.

The foundation for Singapore's prosperity was its designation as a tax-free port by Sir Stamford Raffles, who set up a British trading post here in 1819. The port plays a key role in the economy to this day, though the island now also thrives on high-tech industry, financial services and tourism, all bolstered by a super-efficient infrastructure. None of this could have been achieved without major compromise, with the people accepting heavy-handed management by the state over most aspects of life in exchange for levels of affluence that would have seemed unimaginable a couple of generations ago. Thus it is that since independence much of the population has been resettled from downtown slums and outlying kampongs (villages) into new towns, and the city's old quarters have seen historic buildings and streets bulldozed to make way for shopping malls.

Yet while Singapore lacks much of the personality of some Southeast Asian cities, more than enough alluring temples, fragrant medicinal shops and grand colonial buildings survive to captivate visitors. Much of Singapore's fascination springs from its **multicultural population**, a mixture

Fact file

• For nearly 100 years, Singapore was governed as a **British Crown Colony**. In 1959 it attained full internal self-government before briefly entering into an unhappy union with **Malaysia** in 1963. Singapore became **independent** in its own right in 1965.

• Including outlying islands, the country has an **area** of 710 square kilometres – about half the size of Greater London and slightly smaller than New York City.

• The **population** is around five million, of whom over a million are migrant workers. Of the settled population, nearly three-quarters are ethnic Chinese, fourteen percent are Malay and nine percent are of Indian descent. There are four official **languages**: English, Mandarin Chinese, Malay and Tamil. In practice English dominates both in government and in business.

• Singapore is a **republic** with an elected president as head of state, though most power rests with the prime minister.

of Chinese, Malay and Indian, which can make a short walk across town feel like a hop from one country to another, and whose mouthwatering cuisines are a major highlight of any visit. The city also boasts a clutch of fine historical **museums** that offer a much-needed perspective on the many successes and sacrifices that made Singapore what it is today, plus a lively **arts scene** featuring no shortage of international talent and local creativity.

What to see

Shaped like a diamond, Singapore's main island is 42km from east to west and 23km from north to south, compact enough to explore in just a few days. The southern corner of the diamond is home to the main part of the city – "downtown" or just "town" to locals – which centres on the **Singapore River**, the creek where Raffles first landed on the island in 1819. For visitors, the main draws are undoubtedly the city's historic ethnic

The financial district

enclaves, particularly **Little India**, a couple of kilometres north of the river. Packed with gaudy Hindu temples, curry houses and stores selling exotic produce and spices, the district retains much of its original character, as does the **Arab Quarter** nearby, dominated by the golden domes of the **Sultan Mosque**. South of the river, **Chinatown** is a little sanitized though it still has a number of appealing shrines, an immaculately restored Chinese mansion, the **Baba House**, plus a heritage centre documenting the hardships experienced by generations of Chinese migrants to Singapore.

Wherever you wander in these old quarters, you'll see rows of the city's characteristic **shophouses**, compact townhouse-like buildings that traditionally had a shop below and residential space above, though their most striking feature is that the facade at ground level is set back from the road to create a **five-foot way**, a shaded corridor serving as a pavement walkway.

Flower garlands for sale in Little India

Singlish

You wouldn't guess that English is the dominant language of government and education in Singapore from the chatter you might overhear in the street, where Singlish, or Singaporean English, takes pride of place. Entertaining, not to say often baffling, Singlish is a mash-up of English with the grammatical patterns and vocabulary of Chinese and Malay. Pronunciation is staccato, with final consonants often dropped – so "cheque book" would be rendered "che-boo". In two-syllable words the second syllable is lengthened and stressed by a rise in pitch: ask a Singaporean what they've been doing, and you could be told "slee-PING".

Conventional English syntax is twisted and wrung, and tenses and pronouns discarded. If you ask a Singaporean if they've ever seen a *Harry Potter* film, you might be answered "I ever see", while enquiring whether they want to go out to buy something might yield "Go, come back already". Responses are almost invariably reduced to their bare bones, with words often repeated for stress; request something in a shop and you'll hear "have, have", or "got, got".

Exclamations drawn from Malay and Hokkien Chinese complete this pidgin, the most ubiquitous being the Malay suffix "lah", used to add emphasis to replies, as in: "Do you think we'll get in for free?" "Cannot lah!" If Singlish has you totally confused, try raising your eyes to the heavens and crying "ay yor" (with a drop of tone on "yor") – an expression of annoyance or exasperation.

Of course, the British left their distinctive imprint on the island as well, most visibly just north of the Singapore River in the **Colonial District**, around whose grand Neoclassical buildings – including City Hall, Parliament House and the famed **Raffles Hotel** – the island's British residents used to promenade. Also here are the excellent **National Museum**, showcasing Singapore's history and culture, and **Fort Canning Hill**, a lush park that's home to a few historic remains. From here, it's a five-minute stroll to the eastern end of **Orchard Road**, whose entire length is a veritable metropolis of shopping malls. Just beyond is the finest park on the whole island, the **Botanic Gardens**, featuring a little bit of everything that makes Singapore such a verdant city, though most tourists make a beeline for the ravishing orchid section.

Downtown Singapore is probably where you'll spend most of your time, but the rest of the state has

◄ Macaques in Bukit Timah Nature Reserve

its attractions too. North of downtown is the island's last remaining pocket of primary rainforest, the **Bukit Timah Nature Reserve**, and the splendid **zoo**, where the animals are confined in naturalistic enclosures rather than cages. There's more fauna of the avian kind on show in the west of the island at the excellent **Jurong Bird Park**, while eastern Singapore is home to some sandy beaches and a museum recalling the infamous **Changi Prison**, where so many soldiers lost their lives in World War II. Among the many smaller islands and islets that lie within Singapore waters, the only one that is close to being a must-see is **Sentosa**. Linked to the main island by causeway and cable car, it boasts Southeast Asia's only Universal Studios theme park and several slick beach hotels.

When you're spent after a full day's sightseeing, the top place to unwind is undoubtedly down by the **Singapore River**, where the warehouses that

Historical roots: the layout of Singapore

The basic skeleton plan of Singapore's central streets and districts has changed little since the British assembled it in the first half of the nineteenth century. Singapore's founder, **Sir Stamford Raffles**, established the huge green expanse called the Padang as the nucleus of European life as early as 1819, and the edifices of colonial power were constructed around it in subsequent decades. Elsewhere, "native divisions" were established: an 1820s map of Singapore shows **Chinatown** and the **Arab Quarter** in the positions they occupy now. In the same decade, Indian immigrants started to gravitate towards the brick kiln and livestock industries that were developing along Serangoon Road – the spine of today's **Little India**.

Singapore seems never to stand still, and neither does its coastline. Way back in 1823, the south bank of the Singapore River was clawed back from the swamp that covered it to form the site of modern-day Raffles Place in the Financial District. This was the earliest example of a programme of **land reclamation** that has substantially remoulded and extended the contours of Singapore, most notably in the recent creation of **Marina Bay** by pushing three parcels of land out around the mouth of the Singapore River. The new areas are now home to the prestigious Esplanade theatre complex, the giant observation wheel that is the Singapore Flyer and one of the island's two new casino resorts.

once serviced the port are now home to a wide variety of buzzing restaurants and bars. You can take in all manner of **entertainment** – anything from an indie gig to homegrown theatre – at a plethora of venues, none finer than the **Esplanade** complex near the Colonial District.

When to go

Singapore is just 136km north of the equator, so be prepared for a hot and sticky time whenever you visit: temperatures at night hardly ever dip below 20°C (68°F), while the typical daytime maximum temperature of 31°C (88°F) in the shade can feel truly uncomfortable with the sun beating down amid constantly high humidity. Winds are lighter around April and September, making these times of year feel especially sultry. At least spells of rain and sharp tropical downpours year-round bring a welcome respite from the heat, with November to January – the so-called **rainy season** – particularly wet.

Singapore climate

	Jan	Feb	Mar	Apr	May	Jun	Jul	Aug	Sep	Oct	Nov	Dec
Average daily temperature												
max/min (°C)	30/23	31/24	32/24	32/24	32/25	31/25	31/25	31/24	31/24	31/24	31/24	30/23
max/min (°F)	86/74	88/75	90/75	90/75	90/77	88/77	88/77	88/75	88/75	88/75	88/75	86/74
Average rainfall												
mm	244	162	185	179	172	162	158	176	170	194	256	289

things not to miss

Unless you're in town for a while, it's not possible to see everything Singapore has to offer in one trip. What follows is a selective taste of the city-state's highlights – the most vibrant neighbourhoods, best museums and most captivating events. They're all arranged in five colour-coded categories so you can find the very best things to see, do and experience. All highlights have a page reference to take you straight into the Guide, where you can find out more.

01 Chinatown Page **52** • Chinatown's once characterful shophouses have been rendered improbably perfect by restoration, but the area is still home to authentic shrines and shops specializing in Chinese food, medicine and other products.

02 Clubbing at Zouk Page **144** • Some of the world's most happening DJs guest at Singapore's hippest nightspot, set in a converted warehouse beside the river.

03 The Singapore skyline Page **50** • The towers of the Financial District are amazing viewed from nearby Marina Bay or, if you don't mind a mild dose of vertigo, from right beneath.

04 **Bukit Timah Nature Reserve** Page **85** • This pocket of primary rainforest offers an authentic jungle experience, with several easy trails and opportunities to come face to face with hyperactive macaques.

05 **The arts scene** Page **146** • From ballet in the ultramodern Esplanade complex to street performances of Chinese opera, Singapore's entertainment scene has something for everyone.

06 The Thian Hock Keng Temple Page 53

Gilt altars, Eastern deities, chanting monks, praying worshippers and incense smoke – stroll into the courtyard and soak up the atmosphere.

08 National Museum Page 47

Take stock of Singapore's achievements at this showpiece museum, where the exhibits and displays are enlivened by plenty of oral-history clips.

07 Thimithi See *Festive Singapore* colour section

The annual fire-walking festival is centred on the Sri Mariamman temple, a Hindu shrine that, in true multicultural Singapore style, happens to be in the heart of Chinatown.

09 An Orchard Road shopping spree Page 154

Think Oxford Street, 5th Avenue or Ginza: Orchard Road has famous brands enough to impress even the most jaded shopaholic.

10 Food
See

Singapore food colour section • Best sampled at the food markets called hawker centres, Singapore's food is simply dazzling, ranging from south Indian dosa and Malay curries to a bewildering variety of Chinese noodle dishes.

12 Changi Prison Museum
Page **94** • A hushed and moving memorial to the horrors perpetrated in Singapore during World War II.

11 Universal Studios Page **107**
• Packed with hair-raising rollercoaster rides and fantastic re-creations of everything from big-city America to ancient Egypt.

13 The Botanic Gardens Page **81** • This superb garden features everything from jungle and ornamental tropical trees and shrubs to a fine collection of orchids.

14 Arab Quarter Page **75** • Centred on the golden-domed Sultan Mosque, the Arab Quarter is a fascinating mix of carpet-sellers, curio shops and alternative boutiques, and its informal Arab and Malay restaurants are a great place to chill out in the evening.

16 Zoo and night safari Page **88** • Spot orang-utans and Malayan tigers at this excellent zoo; one section is entirely devoted to nocturnal animals and open, appropriately, at night.

15 A Singapore Sling at the Raffles Hotel Page **141** • No Singapore trip is complete without a swig of this famous cherry brandy cocktail, created at the hotel in the 1910s.

15

18 Little India Page **70** • This most atmospheric of Singapore's historic quarters is an assault on the senses, with its colourful south Indian-style shrines, spice shops and outlets blaring Tamil music.

17 The Baba House Page **60** • This stunningly restored Chinese mansion features beautiful antiques and offers a glimpse into the Chinese-Malay hybrid culture of Singapore's Baba-Nonya minority.

19 Boat Quay Page **65** • Alfresco dining at its best, with bars and restaurants galore, their reflected lights dancing on the waters of the Singapore River by night.

Basics

Basics

Getting there 19

Arrival 23

City transport 25

The media 29

Health 30

Travel essentials 31

Getting there

Reaching Singapore by air is straightforward: the island is one of the main air hubs of Southeast Asia and is often a stopover on one of the world's busiest long-haul routes, between Europe and Australasia, so fares can be much more competitive than you might expect. There are also budget flights linking the country with the rest of Southeast Asia, with southeastern Chinese cities including Hong Kong, with India and with many cities in Australia.

If you want to see more of Southeast Asia on your trip to Singapore you could consider buying an **open-jaw** ticket which allows you, for example, to fly into Bangkok, travel overland to Singapore and then fly home from there. There's also the option of a **round-the-world ticket** (RTW); some travel agents can sell you an "off-the-shelf" RTW ticket that will have you touching down in about half a dozen cities worldwide (Singapore is on many itineraries). Alternatively, it's not hard to book a **package trip** offering several days in Singapore, either in its own right or in combination with an excursion through Malaysia.

Whether you book your flight from a regular or an online travel agent or with the airline directly, it pays to buy it as far in advance as possible. Fares shoot up for travel during **high season** – from mid-June to early September, and over Christmas and New Year. It's also a little more expensive to fly at the weekend; the sample fares below are for midweek travel.

Flights from the UK and Ireland

There are daily flights to Singapore from the UK. Singapore Airlines, British Airways and Qantas all offer **nonstop** flights out of London Heathrow, a journey time of twelve to thirteen hours, with Singapore Airlines also flying several times a week from Manchester via Munich. Many European, Middle Eastern and Asian airlines offer **indirect** flights to Singapore, which involve a change of plane at their hub airport en route and thus take at least a couple of hours longer, though they are generally also cheaper if you're starting from one of the London airports. Conveniently, a few airlines, such as Air France, KLM or Lufthansa, can also get you to Singapore from a UK regional airport or from Ireland. Finally, there's also the option of flying with the budget carrier AirAsia X from London Stansted to Kuala Lumpur, then picking up an AirAsia flight on to Singapore, but note that the connections may be tight and that if you miss your onward flight, you're probably best off spending a night in KL and continuing to Singapore by bus the next day. Furthermore, you may not save much this way, particularly if travelling during low season, unless you get an exceptional fare by booking early.

Fares from London to Singapore start at around £500 during low season, but climb to at least £600 in high season, when fares of £800 are not uncommon if you book just a few months in advance. If you're flying from a UK regional airport, it may cost you very little extra to go via a hub in mainland Europe rather than London; otherwise reckon on an extra £100 or so. Fares from the Republic of Ireland come in at around €500 in low season, while in high season you're doing well if you're quoted €800. All prices mentioned here include taxes. A good time to book your tickets is during the winter as this tends to be when the airlines advertise promotional fares, valid for travel within the next six to nine months and shaving at least ten percent off regular prices.

Flights from the US and Canada

Singapore is roughly halfway around the world from North America, which means that whether you head east or west towards Southeast Asia you have a long journey

Six steps to a better kind of travel

At Rough Guides we are passionately committed to travel. We feel strongly that only through travelling do we truly come to understand the world we live in and the people we share it with – plus, tourism has brought a great deal of **benefit** to developing economies around the world over the last few decades. But the extraordinary growth in tourism has also damaged some places irreparably, and of course **climate change** is exacerbated by most forms of transport, especially flying. This means that now more than ever it's important to **travel thoughtfully** and **responsibly**, with respect for the cultures you're visiting – not only to derive the most benefit from your trip but also to preserve the best bits of the planet for everyone to enjoy. At Rough Guides we feel there are six main areas in which you can make a difference:

- Consider what you're contributing to the **local economy**, and how much the services you use do the same, whether it's through employing local workers and guides or sourcing locally grown produce and local services.
- Consider the **environment** on holiday as well as at home. Water is scarce in many developing destinations, and the biodiversity of local flora and fauna can be adversely affected by tourism. Try to patronize businesses that take account of this.
- Travel with a purpose, not just to tick off experiences. Consider **spending longer** in a place, and getting to know it and its people.
- Give thought to how often you **fly**. Try to avoid short hops by air and more harmful night flights.
- Consider **alternatives to flying**, travelling instead by bus, train, boat and even by bike or on foot where possible.
- Make your trips "**climate neutral**" via a reputable carbon offset scheme. All Rough Guide flights are offset, and every year we donate money to a variety of charities devoted to combating the effects of climate change.

ahead. Setting off from the west coast, you'll invariably fly west across the Pacific; it's faster to fly the transatlantic route if you're departing from the east coast, though sometimes you may pay less to fly via the Pacific.

Unsurprisingly, the most comprehensive service is provided by Singapore Airlines, which operates daily **direct flights** from New York (nonstop from Newark – the longest scheduled passenger flight in the world at 19hr – or from JFK via Frankfurt), Los Angeles (18hr nonstop, or via Tokyo) and San Francisco (via Seoul), plus several flights a week from Houston (via Moscow). **Indirect flights** on other airlines might not add more than a couple of hours to your journey if you're lucky with connections, and will generally cost less.

From **New York**, you'll pay $1100 return in low season, but at least $1500 in high season; fares from the west coast tend to be slightly lower. From Canada, the best fares are from **Vancouver** – Can$1200 in low season, rising by just ten percent or so in high

season; fares from other Canadian airports are twenty to fifty percent higher depending on the time of year you want to travel.

Flights from Australia and New Zealand

The **budget carriers** JetStar and Tiger Airways offer some of the best deals **from Australia** to Singapore; JetStar serves most of the major Australian cities while Tiger Airways only flies directly between Singapore and Perth, though it offers connections to Melbourne. There are no budget flights **from New Zealand**, but it's possible to fly with JetStar from Auckland or Christchurch to an east-coast Australian city and change to an onward JetStar flight to Singapore. Otherwise, the usual full-cost airlines, including quite a few Southeast Asian carriers, operate flights to Singapore from major cities. Flights from Auckland to Singapore are just over ten hours nonstop, while from Sydney and Perth the journey takes eight and five hours respectively.

Fares in high season are generally a tenth to a third higher than in low season. In general, a low-season return ticket from Sydney to Singapore is typically around Aus$700 on JetStar including taxes and baggage charges, while the same ticket on a full-cost airline costs around Aus$1000. From Auckland, you're looking at fares of around NZ$1600 in low season.

Flights from South Africa

There are nonstop flights **from Johannes-burg** to Singapore with both Singapore Airlines and South African Airways, taking around eleven hours. These tend to be expensive though, costing around twenty percent more than indirect flights with a Middle Eastern carrier like Emirates or Qatar Airways, or with Malaysia Airlines, for which you can expect to pay around R6800 in low season, R9000 in high season.

From Southeast Asia

Thanks to the **low-cost airlines**, it's easier than ever to visit Singapore as part of a Southeast Asian trip taking in two or more cities. JetStar Asia and Tiger Airways, between them, cover most of Southeast Asia's major cities and several beach destinations, and you can also choose to fly via Kuala Lumpur on AirAsia, or take advantage of a multitude of flights on full-cost airlines. There's also Berjaya Air, which connects Singapore with the Malaysian resort islands of Redang and Tioman, and Malaysia Airlines' offshoot Firefly, which operates between Singapore and several Malaysian towns.

Travelling overland into Singapore might seem more interesting in terms of sight-seeing, but there are hardly any direct transport connections other than with Peninsular Malaysia. **Buses** provide the most comprehensive services, with no major town in Peninsular Malaysia more than 12 hours from Singapore; Kuala Lumpur to Singapore takes six hours. There's a plethora of Malaysian bus companies, the largest being Transnasional, which is both reliable and good value. Other companies that stand out from the crowd are the premium operators Aeroline, Plusliner and Singapore's Transtar, which mainly serve the largest Malaysian cities, including Kuala Lumpur and Penang. Finally, there are also buses from Hat Yai in southern Thailand, a fourteen-hour slog.

Unfortunately, the Malaysian **rail** network is inefficient and actually slower than the buses, but there are daily services to Singapore down both coasts of Peninsular Malaysia. One starts from Butterworth, near Penang, and heads south via Kuala Lumpur; another starts just south of Butterworth at Ipoh, and takes the same route down; and then there's a service which begins near Kota Bharu, close to the Thai border, soon leaving the east coast to take you south through jungle backwaters. These trains are complemented by a couple more services from Kuala Lumpur. And if you've got money to burn, you could embark on the luxurious Eastern & Oriental Express from Bangkok (see below).

Disappointingly, Singapore has no long-distance international **ferry** services at all; the only ferries sail from nearby Indonesian islands, including Bintan and Batam, plus the

---

The Eastern & Oriental Express

Unlike some luxury trains in other parts of the world, the **Eastern & Oriental Express** (®www.orient-express.com) isn't a re-creation of a colonial-era rail journey, but a sort of fantasy realization of how such a service might have looked had it existed in the Far East. Employing 1970s Japanese rolling stock, given an elegant old-world cladding with wooden inlay work and featuring Thai and Malay motifs, the train departs Bangkok on certain Sundays, bound for Singapore. En route there are extended stops at Kanchanaburi for a visit to the infamous bridge over the River Kwai, and at Butterworth, where there's time for a half-day tour of Georgetown. An observation deck at the rear of the train makes the most of the passing scenery.

The trip takes four days and three nights (three days and two nights if done from Singapore) and costs around £1250/US$1900 per person in swish, en-suite Pullman accommodation, including meals.

small southern Malaysian town of Kampung Pengerang in Johor, all of which are mainly visited from Singapore rather than being on the tourist trail in their own country. You can get a reasonable overview of Indonesian ferry services on ⊛www.singaporecruise.com.

Airlines, agents and operators

The airlines listed below either fly to Singapore or can provide connections with code-share partners who do.

Aer Lingus ⊛www.aerlingus.com
AirAsia/AirAsia X ⊛www.airasia.com
Air Canada ⊛www.aircanada.com
Air France ⊛www.airfrance.com
Air India ⊛www.airindia.com
Air New Zealand ⊛www.airnz.co.nz
All Nippon Airways (ANA) ⊛www.anaskyweb.com
American Airlines ⊛www.aa.com
Bangkok Airways ⊛www.bangkokair.com
Berjaya Air ⊛www.berjaya-air.com
British Airways ⊛www.ba.com
Cathay Pacific ⊛www.cathaypacific.com
Continental Airlines ⊛www.continental.com
Delta ⊛www.delta.com
Emirates ⊛www.emirates.com
Etihad Airways ⊛www.etihadairways.com
EVA Air ⊛www.evaair.com
Firefly ⊛www.fireflyz.com.my
Garuda Indonesia ⊛www.garuda-indonesia.com
Gulf Air ⊛www.gulfair.com
JAL ⊛www.jal.com
JetStar/JetStar Asia ⊛www.jetstar.com
KLM ⊛www.klm.com
Korean Air ⊛www.koreanair.com
Lufthansa ⊛www.lufthansa.com
Malaysia Airlines ⊛www.malaysiaairlines.com
Northwest ⊛www.nwa.com
Qantas Airways ⊛www.qantas.com
Qatar Airways ⊛www.qatarairways.com
Royal Brunei ⊛www.bruneiair.com
Silk Air ⊛www.silkair.com
Singapore Airlines ⊛www.singaporeair.com
SriLankan Airlines ⊛www.srilankan.lk
Swiss ⊛www.swiss.com
Thai Airways ⊛www.thaiair.com
Tiger Airways ⊛www.tigerairways.com
Turkish Airlines ⊛www.thy.com
United Airlines ⊛www.united.com

Agents and operators

Asialuxe Holidays US ☎1-800/742-3133, ⊛www.asialuxeholidays.com. Singapore city breaks.

Bestway Tours US and Canada ☎1-800/663-0844, ⊛www.bestway.com. A handful of cultural tours featuring Singapore as part of a wider itinerary.

Eastravel UK ☎01473/214305, ⊛www.eastravel.co.uk. A small range of Singapore trips.

Emerald Global UK ☎020/7312 1708, ⊛www.etours-online.com. Singapore flight and hotel deals.

Explorient US ☎1-800/785-1233, ⊛www.explorient.com. Singapore in its own right or combined with Malaysia or cities elsewhere in East Asia.

Flight Centre Australia ☎133 133, Canada ☎1-877/967-5302, New Zealand ☎0800/243544, South Africa ☎0860/400 727, UK ☎0870/499 0040, US ☎1-877/992-4732; ⊛www.flightcentre.com. Budget travel specialist.

Lee's Travel UK ☎0800/811 9888, ⊛www.leestravel.com. Southeast Asia specialist, particularly good for discounted flight offers.

North South Travel UK ☎01245/608 291, ⊛www.northsouthtravel.co.uk. Friendly, competitive travel agency whose profits partly go into support projects in the developing world.

Pentravel South Africa ☎0860/106264, ⊛www.pentravel.co.za. Budget flights and hotel deals.

Premier Holidays UK ☎0844/493 7080, ⊛www.premierholidays.co.uk. Singapore city breaks combined with a few days in Malaysia.

Rex Air UK ☎020/7439 1898, ⊛www.rexair.co.uk. Specialist in discounted flights to the Far East, with a few package tours to boot.

Silverbird UK ☎020/8875 9090, ⊛www.silverbird.co.uk. Tailor-made Far Eastern trips, plus hotel deals.

STA Travel Australia ☎134 782, New Zealand ☎0800/474 400, South Africa ☎0861/781 781, UK ☎0871/230 0040, US ☎1-800/781-4040; ⊛www.statravel.co.uk. Worldwide specialists in independent travel; also student ID, travel insurance, car rental, rail passes, and more.

Tailormade Trips UK ☎0800/840 0850. Customized Southeast Asian tours.

Thompsons Tours South Africa ☎0861/846 677, ⊛www.thompsons.co.za. Flights and various packages to Southeast Asia.

Trailfinders Australia ☎1300/780 212, Ireland ☎01/677 7888, UK ☎0845/058 5858; ⊛www.trailfinders.com. One of the best-informed and most efficient agents for independent travellers.

Travel CUTS Canada ☎1-866/246-9762, US ☎1-800/592-2887; ⊛www.travelcuts.com. Canadian youth and student travel firm.

USIT Ireland ☎01/602 1906, Northern Ireland ☎028/9032 7111; ⊛www.usit.ie. Ireland's main student and youth travel specialists.

Bus, rail and ferry contacts

Aeroline ⓦ www.aeroline.com.my
Batam Fast Ferries ⓦ www.batamfast.com
Bintan Resort Ferries ⓦ www.brf.com.sg
Indofalcon Ferries ⓦ www.indofalcon.com.sg

Malaysian Railways ⓦ www.ktmb.com.my
Penguin Ferry Services ⓦ www.penguin.com.sg
Plusliner ⓦ www.plusliner.com.my
Transnasional ⓦ www.transnasional.com.my
Transtar ⓦ www.transtar.com.sg

Arrival

Singapore's Changi International Airport is gleaming, modern and ridiculously efficient – Singapore in microcosm. Arriving by bus or train is a slightly less streamlined experience thanks to border formalities and occasional jams at the two causeways connecting Singapore to the southernmost Malaysian state of Johor. Wherever you arrive, the island's well-oiled infrastructure means that you'll have no problem getting into the centre.

By air

Changi Airport (ⓦ www.changiairport.com) is at the eastern tip of Singapore, 16km from the city centre. There are four terminals: terminals 1 to 3 are part of the same complex and are linked by transit trains; the remaining building is the so-called Budget Terminal, 1500m to the southwest and connected to Terminal 2 by a shuttle bus. Confusingly, the Budget Terminal doesn't have a monopoly on the low-cost airlines – JetStar and AirAsia actually use Terminal 1.

The three main terminals each has a **tourist office** (daily 6am–2am) which can make hotel bookings, plus separate hotel reservation counters which represent the major hotels (but not establishments at the cheaper end). There are also the usual exchange facilities/ATMs and plenty of shops, restaurants and food courts. But chances are you'll not linger long – baggage comes through so quickly that you can be heading to the city centre within twenty minutes of arrival.

The airport's **MRT** (metro) station is beneath terminals 2 and 3. While trains run between 5.30am (6am on Sun) and midnight daily, the last train downtown leaves around 11.15pm, and at certain times of day you may need to change at Tanah Merah station to continue into the centre. A one-way ticket for the half-hour downtown trip costs just under $2, though unless you buy a stored-value card you will also have to pay a $1

Finding an address

Premises within high-rise towers, shopping complexes and other buildings generally have an address containing two numbers preceded by #, as in "#xx-yy". While xx refers to the floor (ground level is 01, the next floor up 02, and so on) while yy refers to the unit number. So a restaurant whose address includes #04-08 can be found in unit 8 on the building's fourth storey. It's also worth noting that all buildings within municipal housing estates have a block number displayed prominently on the side, rather than a number relating to their position on the street on which they're located.

If you want to look up an address on a **map**, you can enter the street, building name or six-digit postal code into ⓦ www.streetdirectory.com and will usually get a fairly precise fix on the location.

deposit which is refunded at your destination station when you return the ticket. All the three main terminals are served by the **#36 bus** (every 10min, 6am–midnight; under $2), which passes through the suburb of Katong and Marina Centre before heading to the Orchard Road area. For more on the public transport system and the complexities of ticketing, see opposite.

Whether you take the MRT or a bus, lack of room for luggage (especially on the bus) may be a hindrance. To get round the problem, consider taking the **Airport Shuttle** bus ($9/$6), which calls at downtown hotels, or a **taxi** (reckon on at least $20 to get downtown), though note that airport departures command a $3 surcharge (Fri–Sun 5pm–midnight $5). For more on taxi rates, see p.27.

While practically all flights land at Changi, Berjaya Air flights from Malaysia use tiny **Seletar airport**, part of a former British military base in the north of the island. From here, bus #103M (2 hourly) runs to the Serangoon MRT station, while a taxi into town will cost around $20 including the $3 airport surcharge, with an additional booking fee to pay if you end up having to book a taxi on the phone (see p.27 for reservation numbers).

By bus

Most buses from Malaysia and Thailand use the main causeway to reach Singapore from Johor, and terminate at one of three locations. Local buses from **Johor Bahru** (JB) in **Malaysia** arrive at the Ban San Terminal at the junction of Queen and Arab streets, from where a two-minute walk along Queen Street and a left turn along Rochor Road takes you to Bugis MRT station. Buses from elsewhere in Malaysia and from **Thailand** mostly terminate at the Lavender Street Terminal, at the corner of Lavender Street and Kallang Bahru (and a 5min walk from Lavender MRT) or at the Golden Mile Complex on Beach Road. Bus #100 southwest along Beach Road will get you close to City Hall and Esplanade MRT stations. The exception to this picture is luxury buses, which tend to use the faster second crossing from Johor to Tuas and either have their own terminals or will drop passengers at a particular hotel or shopping complex.

Leaving Singapore

Leaving Singapore presents no special issues, though if you're flying from Changi (flight enquiries ☎1800/5424422 or on ⊛www.changiairport.com) during rush hour, be sure to set off early to allow for traffic. Tickets can be purchased directly from the airlines or from a travel agent such as STA Travel, 534A North Bridge Road (near Bugis MRT; ☎67377188, ⊛www.statravel.com.sg), Chan Brothers, 150 South Bridge Road (Chinatown; ☎64388880, ⊛www.chanbrothers.com) or Zuji (⊛www.zuji.com .sg). For details of budget airlines serving East Asia and Australia, see pp.20–21.

If you want to travel to or from Malaysia, be sure to book well in advance if your trip coincides with either a major festival (see p.34) or the school holidays (see p.34). Bus companies worth contacting include Transnasional, which has the most comprehensive services (☎62947034), Konsortium (☎63923911) and Transtar (☎62999009). If you simply want to pop across to Malaysia briefly, perhaps to get a fresh visa upon your return or take advantage of much lower prices in the shops, the easiest way is to head to **Johor Bahru** on the local #170 bus, the Singapore–Johor Express bus or a yellow Causeway Link #CW2 service; all of these leave fairly frequently from the Ban San Terminal on Queen Street and tickets cost only $2–3 single. Having cleared Malaysian formalities at the causeway, you can head into the city on foot rather than get back on the bus unless you wish to end up at the Larkin Terminal outside the centre, from where there are buses to all parts of the country. You can head back on the #170 or #CW2 at the causeway.

Train tickets can be bought at ⊛www.ktmb.com.my or from the railway station (daily 8.30am–8.30pm; ☎62225165), unless you want to ride the sumptuous Eastern & Oriental Express (see p.21), in which case you can book at their office at Shaw Towers #32-01/03, 100 Beach Road (☎63950678).

Arriving at the causeway, you will have to get off the bus on the Malaysian side to clear immigration and customs, then get back on board – if you're on a local #170 bus, hang on to your ticket and use it to continue on any vehicle on this route – to reach the Singapore side of the bridge, where you go through the same rigmarole.

By train

For decades **trains** from Malaysia have used the Art Deco Singapore Railway Station on Keppel Road, southwest of Chinatown, but in mid-2011 the terminus will move to a building next to the Causeway immigration complex in Woodlands. From here, bus #170 or #170X will get you to Kranji MRT nearby, with the #170 continuing all the way to Little India. From the old station, bus #10 or #97 head east and west respectively to Tanjong Pagar and HarbourFront stations, while bus #57 will get you to Little India.

By sea

Boats from Indonesia's **Riau archipelago** dock either at the HarbourFront Centre, off Telok Blangah Road at the southern tip of Singapore, or at the Tanah Merah Ferry Terminal in the east of the island. The former is the southern terminus of the MRT's North East line, while the latter is linked by bus #35 to Tanah Merah and Bedok MRT stations. Most ferries from the resort island of Batam end up at HarbourFront Centre, though a few of these boats plus all services from the other resort island, Bintan, use the Tanah Merah terminal. If you see a reference to "RFT" in schedules, it means the HarbourFront Centre.

The only ferry service from **Malaysia** comprises humble "bumboats" from Kampung Pengerang just east of Singapore in the Straits of Johor. These moor at Changi Point, beyond the airport, from where bus #2 travels to Tanah Merah MRT station and on to Geylang, Victoria Street and New Bridge Road in Chinatown.

City transport

Downtown Singapore is best explored on foot and is compact enough to be tackled this way: for example, Orchard Road is only just over 2km end to end, and it's a similar distance from the Padang to the middle of Chinatown. Of course you'll need a high tolerance for muggy heat to put in the legwork, and tourists tend instead to rely on the underground MRT trains. At some point you may also end up taking a bus, which are just as efficient as the trains but a little bewildering, such is the profusion of routes. Both trains and buses are reasonably priced, as are taxis.

For public transport information, contact either **SBS Transit** (☎1800/2255663, ⓦwww.sbstransit.com.sg) – historically a bus company, though it's now responsible for one of the MRT lines – or **SMRT** (☎1800/3368900, ⓦwww.smrt.com.sg), for information on its MRT lines and bus services.

The MRT

With its slick air-conditioned trains, the MRT (Mass Rapid Transit) system is something of an engineering marvel, the underground tunnels having been carved out of Singapore's soft subsoil with the threat of collapse a constant danger during construction. The system has four lines. The **East–West** line runs from Boon Lay in the western town of Jurong to Pasir Ris in the far east via the colonial district, with a branch serving Changi Airport; the **North–South** line runs a vaguely horseshoe-shaped route from Marina Bay to the colonial district

Ez-Link cards and tourist passes

You can avoid the rigmarole of buying tickets for every bus or MRT ride by purchasing a stored-value **Ez-Link card** (⊛ www.ezlink.com.sg), available at MRT stations and bus interchanges. Besides offering convenience, the card shaves 10–25 percent off the cost of every trip, and a journey involving up to three transfers – from MRT to bus or vice versa or from one bus to another – is treated as one extended trip if you use the card, again resulting in a slight saving. Cards start at $15, for which you get $10 of credit ($5 covers the cost of the card itself). The cost of each journey you make is automatically deducted from the card when you hold it over a reader at a bus exit door or an MRT exit gate. Cards can be topped up with additional credit at ticket offices or ticket machines, and stay valid for five years.

Alternatively, you can buy the **Singapore Tourist Pass** (⊛ www.thesingapore touristpass.com), which costs $8 per day (plus a $10 deposit, refunded along with remaining credit when you return the card) and valid for up to three days' travel. Used in the same way as Ez-Link cards, the passes are sold at Changi Airport MRT plus a few downtown MRT stations, and can be topped up at MRT ticket offices for additional days' travel.

and Orchard Road, then up to the north of the island and down again to Jurong; the **North–East** line links the HarbourFront Centre and VivoCity mall on the south coast with Punggol in the northeast via Chinatown and Little India; and the **Circle** line does another horseshoe from HarbourFront along the west coast, up through Holland Village and then across to various eastern suburbs, before it curls back downtown to the Orchard Road area. Trains run on average around every five minutes from 6am until midnight, but, as you'll soon discover, overcrowding is a problem downtown, not just during rush hour, and the last trains leave downtown as early as 11.30pm – which puts paid to getting back by train after an extended session of drinking or clubbing.

The easiest and cheapest way of getting about is to buy an **Ez-Link card** (see box above), though note that you must have at least $3 on the card to be able to get on a train. Otherwise, single **tickets** cost between $1 and $2, and can be bought from ticket counters or from automated machines at stations. Annoyingly, all single tickets require you to pay an additional $1 deposit, refunded when you return the ticket to the ticket counter or a ticket machine at the end of your journey. There's a strict prohibition on eating, drinking and smoking, and platform signs indicate a ban on bringing durians onto trains – hardly surprising, as you wouldn't want the smell permeating a confined space.

Buses

Singapore's **bus network** is slightly cheaper to use than the MRT system for short trips, and covers practically all of downtown's nooks and crannies, not to mention most of the island. Most buses operate from 6am, with services tailing off between 11.30pm and 12.30am, and the majority are air-conditioned. Both double- and single-decker buses are in use, and you always board at the front.

Fares rise in small steps with the distance travelled (cash fares are always between $1 and $2), so if you're paying cash you may well have to consult the driver on the precise fare for your destination. Cash should be dropped down the metal chute next to the driver; change isn't given, so have plenty of coins to hand to avoid frittering money away – or buy an Ez-Link card or tourist pass, though note that you must touch the card on the electronic reader not only on entering but also **at the exit**, otherwise the maximum fare will be deducted.

A few buses have **fixed fares**, chiefly services within new towns, limited premium services (which run express for much of their route, always have route numbers of the form "5xx" and cost $3 or $3.50) and **night buses**, which operate late on Fridays, Saturdays and before a public holiday and connect downtown with the new towns. SMRT's night buses (11.30pm–4.30am; $3.50) start from Resorts World Sentosa, while SBS night buses (midnight–2am; $4) operate from Marina Centre; they can be useful for downtown travel after the MRT shuts, but note that they may run express in certain parts of town.

Both the SBS Transit and SMRT websites (see p.25) have detailed breakdowns of the bus routes they operate, including journey planners and maps. A pocket-sized guide to the network, variously called *TransitLink Guide* or *Singapore Bus Guide*, is also available from bookshops for a few dollars.

Taxis

Singapore's **taxis** are seemingly without number and they keep on proliferating; indeed some locals joke that in uncertain economic times the authorities probably license yet more taxis to keep jobless figures down. While this means flagging down a taxi generally isn't a problem, it can be tricky downtown, particularly at night or during a storm. If you have difficulty getting a cab, it can be best to head to the nearest mall to join the queue at a taxi rank.

Taxis come in various colours, but all are clearly marked "TAXI" and have a sign or display on top indicating if they are available for hire. Regular cabs (as opposed to premium/"limousine" vehices) charge $2.80 for the first kilometre and 20c for every 385 metres travelled, with a slightly lower tariff

kicking in after you've gone 10km. However, there are **surcharges** to bear in mind: a third extra on journeys during rush hour (which, for taxis, means Mon–Fri 7–9.30am & 5–8pm, plus Sat 5–8pm), and fifty percent extra between midnight and 6am. There are also charges arising from Singapore's **electronic road pricing (ERP)** scheme, which means a $3 surcharge on taxi journeys starting from the ERP zone downtown (Mon–Sat 5pm–midnight) *plus* passengers being liable for the actual ERP charge their trip has incurred (shown on the driver's ERP card reader). Journeys from Changi Airport incur a $3 surcharge ($5 Fri–Sun 5pm–midnight), trips from Sentosa $3, and there's a fee of $2.50–5 to **book** a taxi over the phone. Should you need to do this, you can try Comfort/City Cab (☎65521111), Silvercab/Premier Taxi (☎63636888) or SMRT Taxis (☎65558888).

On the whole, Singaporean taxi drivers are friendly and honest but their English isn't necessarily good, so it's worth having your **destination written down** (in English) if you are heading off the beaten track. If a taxi displays a destination sign or "Changing shift" above, it means the driver is about to head home or that a new driver is about to take over the vehicle, and that passengers will be accepted only if they are going in the right direction for either to happen.

Useful bus routes

Below is a selection of handy bus routes. Note that one-way systems downtown mean that services that use Orchard Road and Bras Basah Road in one direction return via Stamford Road, Penang Road, Somerset Road and Orchard Boulevard; buses up Selegie and Serangoon roads return via Jalan Besar and Bencoolen Street; and services along North and South Bridge roads return via Eu Tong Sen Street and Hill Street.

#2 From Eu Tong Sen Street in Chinatown all the way to Changi Prison and Changi Beach, via the Arab Quarter and Geylang Serai.

#7 From Holland Village to the Botanic Gardens and on to Orchard Road, Bras Basah Road and Victoria Street (for the Arab Quarter), continuing to Geylang Serai.

#36 Orchard Road to Changi Airport via Marina Centre and the Singapore Flyer.

#56 Little India to Marina Centre via *Raffles Hotel*.

#65 Orchard Road to Little India and then up Serangoon Road.

#170 From the Ban San Terminal at the northern end of Queen Street to Johor Bahru in Malaysia, passing Little India, the Newton Circus food court, the northern end of the Botanic Gardens, Bukit Timah Nature Reserve and Kranji War Cemetery on the way.

#174 Runs between the Botanic Gardens and Baba House in Neil Road, via Orchard Road, the Colonial District, Boat Quay and Chinatown.

Renting cars and bikes

Given the efficiency of public transport, there's hardly any reason to **rent a car** in Singapore, especially when it's a pricey business. Major disincentives to driving are in place in order to combat traffic congestion, including large fees for a permit to own a car and tolls to drive into and within a large part of downtown, encompassing Orchard Road, Chinatown and the financial district, plus more tolls to use various highways. This being Singapore, it's all done in the most hi-tech way using electronic road pricing **(ERP)**: all Singapore cars have a gizmo installed that reads a stored-value card or Ez-Link card, from which the toll is deducted as you drive past an ERP gantry. **Parking** can be expensive, though at least every mall has a car park (displays all over town will tell you how many spaces are left at nearby buildings) and many car parks offer the convenience of taking the fee off your ERP card, failing which you will have to purchase coupons from a licence booth, post office or shop. If you are still keen to rent in Singapore itself, you can contact Avis (W www.avis .com.sg) or Hertz (W www.hertz.com), both of which have offices at Changi Airport – and note that in Singapore, you drive on the left.

Though largely flat, Singapore is hardly ideal cycling country. Main roads have few bike lanes and furious traffic, though this doesn't put off the few dedicated locals and expats whom you'll see pedalling equally furiously along suburban thoroughfares such as Bukit Timah Road. Cycling downtown isn't such a great idea though, and bicycles aren't allowed at all on expressways. Where bikes come into their own is in out-of-town recreational areas and nature parks, which are linked by a park connector network that it's possible to cycle; for more on this, check the Visitors' Guide section of the National Parks Board website (W www.nparks.gov.sg). The East Coast Park, on the southeast shore of the island, has a popular cycle track with rental outlets along the way (expect to pay $5–8 an hour for a mountain bike, and have some form of ID handy). It's also possible to cycle at Bukit Timah Nature Reserve (see p.85), on Sentosa (see p.105) and Pulau Ubin (see p.96). Wherever you cycle, you'll need a high tolerance for getting very hot and sweaty – or drenched if you're caught in a downpour.

Organized tours and trips

If you're pushed for time, consider taking a **sightseeing tour**. Four-hour city tours typically take in Orchard Road, Chinatown and Little India, and cost around $40; specialist tours are also available – on such themes as Singapore by night, World War II sights and Peranakan culture. For details of current offerings, contact the STB (see p.35) or check their website. It's also possible to arrange a tour with one of the country's registered tourist guides, each of whom will have their own fees and specializations; again, contact STB for details.

Among the more popular tours are boat trips along the **Singapore River**, many of which use tarted-up versions of traditional bumboats (daily 9am–11pm; every 15min; T 63366111, W www.rivercruise.com.sg). You can choose from the **Singapore River Experience** ($15/$8), which takes in Clarke Quay, Boat Quay and Marina Bay, and the **New River Experience** ($20/$10), which adds Robertson Quay. There are several ticket booths along the river, and you can board the boats at any of them. Alternatively there are **HiPPO river cruises** on simple modern craft with a large awning for shade (daily 9am–10pm; $15/$9); tickets can be bought from their booth at Clarke Quay.

Harbour cruises (information and bookings on T 65339811 or W www.water tours.com.sg; 2hr) offer views of the Financial District and the Singapore Flyer, and supposedly evoke the spirit of journeys made by the fifteenth-century Chinese mariner Cheng Ho, though the boats used look not so much like a traditional junk as a miniature Chinese palace stuck on top of a floating platform. Boats depart daily from the Marina South Pier, 1500m southeast of Marina Bay MRT station, with prices starting at $27 including light refreshments and free pick-up from the station or a few downtown hotels; there are also pricier, longer trips with tea or dinner thrown in.

Trishaws – three-wheeled cycle rickshaws – were once a practical transport option in Singapore, though these days they provide a sort of novelty sightseeing ride to tourists lasting 45 minutes or so. Many drivers congregate in Chinatown behind the Buddha Tooth Relic Temple, and on or around Queen Street (near Bugis MRT station). Note that there are no official prices, so you'll have to bargain with the driver to agree on a suitable payment.

One final option – and one kids will love – is the **Singapore Ducktour**, an amphibious craft dating from the Vietnam War, which provides hour-long, land- and sea-bound tours (hourly 10am–6pm; $33/$17; ☏63386877, Ⓦwww.ducktours.com.sg) of the Colonial District and Marina Bay. Tours start at the Suntec City Mall in Marina Centre.

The media

Singapore boasts plenty of newspapers, TV channels and radio stations serving up lively reportage of events, sports and entertainment in the four official languages, though don't expect to come across hard-hitting or healthily sceptical coverage of domestic politics. The media are kept on their toes by a legal requirement that they must periodically renew their licence to publish, and most newspapers have actually been herded into a conglomerate in which the state has a major stake. Likewise radio and TV are dominated by Mediacorp, a company which is effectively stated-owned; satellite dishes are banned, and, while many international broadcasters are available on cable, the sole cable provider is a company in which Mediacorp is a major shareholder.

While a wide range of foreign newspapers and magazines are available from bookstores like Borders and Kinokuniya, there are occasional bans on editions containing pieces that displease the authorities, and Singapore's leaders have a long history of winning defamation suits against foreign publications in the island's courts. Given these circumstances, it's no surprise that in the 2009 World Press Freedom Index, issued by the pressure group Reporters Without Borders, Singapore was far down the rankings at no. 133 – some way below much poorer nations not exactly noted as exemplars of free speech, such as Indonesia and Kenya.

If this seems an unremittingly bleak picture, it should be said that the advent of **independent news websites** and **blogs** has been a breath of fresh air in recent years – to the extent that in the run-up to Singapore's 2006 general elections, the government attempted to ban blogging by opposition politicians or indeed anyone writing about political matters. Elsewhere in cyberspace, it's possible to turn up various YouTube clips

of discussion forums and interviews with activists, offering an alternative take on local issues.

Newspapers, magazines and online news

Straits Times Ⓦwww.straitstimes.com. This venerable broadsheet was founded in 1845, though, sadly, its pedigree isn't matched by the candour of its journalism; not so bad on foreign news, however.

Talking Cock Ⓦwww.talkingcock.com. Satirical website which takes a sardonic look at local news and social issues.

Today Ⓦwww.todayonline.com. A free paper from the state-owned broadcaster Mediacorp, Today is slightly less bland than the Straits Times and carries worthwhile arts reviews at the weekend.

Temasek Review Ⓦwww.temasekreview .com. Escaping official censure or worse so far, this audacious website delivers insightful analysis of political machinations in Singapore.

Radio and TV

BBC World Service Ⓦwww.bbcworldservice .com. 88.9FM, 24hr.

Channel News Asia ⓦ www.channelnewsasia .com. Mediacorp's CNN-like diet of rolling TV news, via cable.
Channel 5 ⓦ www.5.mediacorptv.sg. The main terrestrial channel for English programming, with plenty of imported shows.

Mediacorp Radio ⓦ www.mediacorpradio.sg. Several English-language radio stations, including the speech-based 938 LIve (93.8FM) and Symphony (92.4FM) for classical music.

Health

The levels of hygiene and medical care in Singapore are higher than in much of the rest of Southeast Asia. Tap water is drinkable throughout the island and all food for public consumption is prepared to exacting standards.

No inoculations are required for visiting Singapore, although the immigration authorities may require proof of a yellow fever vaccination (administered within the last ten years) if you've visited an endemic country within the last six days. However, it's a wise precaution to visit your doctor no later than four weeks before you leave to check that you are up to date with your polio, typhoid, tetanus and hepatitis A inoculations.

It pays to use mosquito repellant in Singapore, particularly if you're in a nature reserve or beach area. This isn't because Singapore is malarial – it isn't – but because mosquitoes may carry **dengue fever**, an illness which is seldom fatal but can be debilitating while it lasts. Note that DEET-based repellants are not available in Singapore, so if you prefer these you will have to buy them at home.

Travellers unused to tropical climates periodically suffer from **sunburn** and **dehydration**. The easiest way to avoid this is to restrict your exposure to the sun, use high-factor sunscreens, drink plenty of water, and wear sunglasses and a hat. Heat stroke is more serious: it is indicated by a high temperature, dry red skin and a fast pulse and can require hospitalization. If you require emergency aid dial ☏995, or get to one of the following state **hospitals**: Singapore General, Outram Rd (☏62223322), Alexandra Hospital, Alexandra Rd (☏64722000), and National

University Hospital, Kent Ridge (☏67795555), or the more central, but private, Raffles Hospital 585 North Bridge Road (☏63111111). You can find a list of dentists in the Singapore Buying Guide (equivalent to the Yellow Pages).

Medical services in Singapore are excellent, with staff almost everywhere speaking good English. Pharmacies are well stocked with familiar brand-name drugs and pharmacists can offer advice on minor complaints. Guardian pharmacy has over forty outlets, including ones at Centrepoint, 176 Orchard Rd; Raffles City Shopping Centre, 252 North Bridge Rd; and Clifford Centre, 24 Raffles Place. Usual hours are 9am–6pm, but some stay open until 10pm.

Private clinics are found throughout the city including most shopping centres. Both the Tanglin Shopping Centre (19 Tanglin Rd) and Paragon (290 Orchard Rd) have clinics. A visit costs from $50, not including the cost of any prescribed medication. Don't forget to keep any receipts for insurance claim purposes.

Medical resources for travellers

Australia, New Zealand and South Africa

The Travel Doctor – TMVC ☏1300/658 844, ⓦ www.tmvc.com.au. Lists travel clinics in Australia, New Zealand and South Africa.

US and Canada

Canadian Society for International Health
☏ 613/241-5785, ⓦ www.csih.org. Extensive list of travel health centres.
CDC ☏ 1-800/232 4636, ⓦ www.cdc.gov/travel. Official US government travel health site.
International Society for Travel Medicine
☏ 1-404/373-8282, ⓦ www.istm.org. Has a full list of travel health clinics.

UK and Ireland

Hospital for Tropical Diseases Travel Clinic
☏ 020/7388 9600, ⓦ www.thehtd.org.
MASTA (Medical Advisory Service for Travellers Abroad) ☏ 0870/606 2782, ⓦ www .masta.org for the nearest clinic.
Travel Medicine Clinic Northern Ireland
☏ 028/9031 5220.
Tropical Medical Bureau Ireland
☏ 1850/487 674, ⓦ www.tmb.ie.

Travel essentials

Costs

Singapore is one of the more expensive Asian cities, especially for accommodation. **Bargaining** can save you money here and there but is only possible in smaller family-owned shops and hotels.

If money is no object, you'll be able to take advantage of hotels, restaurants and shops as sumptuous as any in the world. On the other hand, with budget dormitory accommodation in plentiful supply, and both food and internal travel cheap, you could survive on less than £20/US$30 a day. Where two prices are given for a museum or other attraction in this book, the second price is for a child ticket unless otherwise stated.

Note that Singapore has a seven percent Goods and Services Tax **(GST)**, which involves all companies except small businesses. Prices in shops include GST (see p.153 for details of refunds for tourists), but it's not uncommon for hotels and restaurants to leave it out, quoting prices with **"++"** at the end. In this case, the first plus indicates that they levy a ten percent **service charge** (as all mid-range and upmarket hotels and restaurants do) and the second plus indicates GST slapped on the combined cost of the room or food and the service charge, that is, a 17.7 percent surcharge in total.

Crime and personal safety

If you lose something in Singapore, you're more likely to have someone running after you with it than running away. Nevertheless, you shouldn't become complacent – muggings have been known to occur and theft from dormitories by other tourists is a common complaint.

It's very unwise to have anything to do with **drugs** of any description in Singapore. The penalties for trafficking drugs in or out of the country are severe in the extreme – foreigners have been executed in the past – and if you are arrested for drugs offences you can expect no mercy and little help from your consular representatives. Singapore's police, who wear dark blue, keep a fairly low profile, but are polite and helpful when approached.

Singapore is known locally as **fine city**. There's a fine of up to $1000 for smoking in public places such as cinemas, trains, lifts, air-conditioned restaurants (non-air-conditioned restaurants normally have a

Emergency numbers

Police ☏ 999/Freephone police hotline ☏ 1800-2550000
Ambulance and Fire Brigade ☏ 995

smoking section) and shopping malls, and within a five-metre radius of entrances. There's also a $20 fine for "jaywalking" – crossing a main road within 50m of a pedestrian crossing or bridge, with repeat offenders risking a $1000 fine and a three-month jail term. Littering carries a $300 fine and eating and drinking on the MRT could cost you $500.

Other fines include those for urinating in lifts (some lifts are fitted with urine detectors) and not flushing a public toilet. Chewing gum is also illegal here ($500 fine), except when prescribed for medical reasons.

Electricity

Singapore's **power supply** is at 230 V/50 Hz, and British-style sockets – taking plugs with three square pins – are the standard.

Entry requirements

British citizens, and those of the Republic of Ireland, the United States, Canada, Australia, New Zealand and South Africa, don't need a visa to enter Singapore. Regulations change from time to time, though, so check with the embassy before departure. You'll normally be stamped in for thirty days.

Extending your stay for up to three months is perfectly possible, at the discretion of the Immigration Department (10 Kallang Rd; Mon–Fri 8am–5pm, Sat 8am–1pm; ☏63916100); extensions beyond three months are not unknown, but are less common. If you have any problems with extending your stay, there's always the option of taking a bus up to Johor Bahru, across the border in Malaysia, and then coming back in again.

Embassies and consulates in Singapore

Australia 25 Napier Rd ☏68364100.
Canada 11-01, One George St ☏68545900.
Ireland Ireland House, 541 Orchard Rd, 08-00 Liat Towers ☏62387616.
New Zealand Ngee Ann City Tower A, 15-06/10 391A Orchard Rd ☏62359966.
South Africa 331 North Bridge Rd, 15th floor Odeon Towers ☏63393319.
UK 100 Tanglin Rd ☏64244200.
US 27 Napier Rd ☏64769100.

Singaporean embassies and consulates abroad

Australia 17 Forster Crescent, Yarralumla, Canberra, ACT 2600 ☏02/62712000.
Canada Suite 1820, 999 West Hastings St, Vancouver, V6C 2W2 ☏604/669-5115.
Ireland Contact UK embassy.
New Zealand 17 Kabul St, Khandallah, Wellington, PO Box 13-140 ☏04/470-0850.
South Africa 80-982 Schoeman St, Arcadia, Pretoria 0083 ☏012 430 6035.
UK 9 Wilton Crescent, London SW1X 8SP ☏020/7235 9852.
US 3501 International Place NW, Washington, DC 20008 ☏202/537-3100; 231 East 51st St, New York, NY 10022 ☏212/223-3331.

Customs

Upon entry from anywhere other than Malaysia you can bring into Singapore one litre each of spirits, wine and beer **duty-free**; duty is payable on all tobacco. For up-to-the-minute customs information, go to Ⓦwww.customs.gov.sg.

Many goods for sale in Singapore are duty-free, including electronic and electrical items, cosmetics, cameras, clocks, watches, jewellery, and precious stones and metals, but you should bear in mind how much you are allowed to import into your own country with you free of charge. Tourists can reclaim the Goods and Services Tax (GST) of seven percent under certain conditions; for more on the red tape this involves, see p.135.

Festivals

As there are so many ethnic groups and religions in Singapore, your visit could easily coincide with a **festival**. Bear in mind that the major festival periods will make traffic on the island heavier and crossing into Malaysia much slower. Some (though not all) festivals are also public holidays – see p.34 for details of these. For full details on Singapore's festivals see p.150 and the "*Festive Singapore*" colour section.

Insurance

Since there are no reciprocal agreements between Singapore and any other country, the cost of medical services must be borne by the visitor. Consequently, it's essential to

Rough Guides travel insurance

Rough Guides has teamed up with WorldNomads.com to offer great **travel insurance** deals. Policies are available to residents of more than 150 countries, with cover for a wide range of **adventure sports**, 24-hour emergency assistance, high levels of medical and evacuation cover and a stream of **travel safety information**. Roughguides.com users can take advantage of their policies online 24/7, from anywhere in the world – even if you're already travelling. And since plans often change when you're on the road, you can extend your policy and even claim online. Roughguides.com users who buy travel insurance with WorldNomads.com can also leave a positive footprint and donate to a community development project. For more information go to Ⓦ**www.roughguides.com/shop**.

arrange **travel insurance** before you leave home, which will cover you for medical expenses incurred, as well as for loss of luggage, cancellation of flights and so on.

A typical travel insurance policy usually provides cover for the **loss of baggage**, tickets and – up to a certain limit – cash or cheques, as well as cancellation or curtailment of your journey. Most of them exclude so-called dangerous sports unless an extra premium is paid. When securing baggage cover, make sure that the per-article limit – typically under £500 – will cover your most valuable possession. If you need to make a claim, you should keep receipts for medicines and medical treatment, and in the event that you have anything stolen, you must obtain an official statement from the police.

Internet access

The best place to look for **internet cafés** is Little India, where they are ubiquitous and charge around $3/hr. They can be relatively hard to find elsewhere downtown, though, and prices can be as high as $6/hr when you do come across them. As you might expect, many café chains offer wi-fi access.

Mail

Singapore's **postal system** is predictably efficient, with letters and cards often reaching their destination within three days. Stamps are available at post offices and some stationers and hotels. Airmail letters to Europe and the USA cost from $1.10, and postcards cost 50c to send. You'll find fax and telex facilities at all major post offices, too.

The **GPO** (Mon–Fri 8am–6pm, Sat 8am–2pm) is beside Paya Lebar MRT

station. There are more than sixty other post offices across the state, with usual opening hours of Monday to Friday 8.30am to 5pm and Saturday 8.30am to 1pm. In addition, postal services are available until 9pm at the Comcentre on Killiney Road.

Maps

The **maps** in this book should be sufficient for most of your exploration, and you can back them up with the various free maps of downtown available from the Singapore Tourism Board. The best map available to buy is the *Singapore Street Directory*, a street atlas for drivers; it comes in various sizes and is available from bookstores (standard edition $13), with an online version at Ⓦwww.streetdirectory.com. Any printed map soon goes out of date given the speed with which parts of town can be reshaped according to the planners' latest schemes, so the online street directory is in fact your best bet for accurate maps of any part of the island.

Money

The **currency** is the Singapore dollar, written simply as $ and divided into 100 cents. Notes are issued in denominations of $2, $5, $10, $20, $50, $100, $500, $1000 and $10,000; coins are in denominations of 1, 5, 10, 20 and 50 cents, and $1. At the time of writing, the exchange rate was around $2.10 to £1 and $1.40 to US$1. All prices given in the guide are in Singapore dollars, unless otherwise stated.

Singapore **banking hours** are generally Monday to Friday 9.30am to 3pm (although some open until 6pm), Saturday 9.30am to

12.30pm. Major branches on Orchard Road are open Sunday 9.30am to 3pm. Outside of these hours, currency exchange is available at moneychangers where rates are as good as you'll find in banks and don't charge any transaction fees. Major hotels also offer currency exchange but don't expect the rates to be as attractive. ATMs are plentiful around Singapore and accept most types of debit and credit card, usually charging a nominal fee for each withdrawal. All major credit cards are widely accepted, with MasterCard being the most common, and there are often adverts in the press offering discounts on shopping and meals if you pay with your card. Travellers' cheques in either US dollars or sterling are another convenient and safe way to conduct transactions in Singapore. You can exchange them at banks or moneychangers and some shops and restaurants accept them as direct payment.

Opening hours and public holidays

Shopping centres are open daily 10am to 9.30pm, while offices generally work Monday to Friday 8.30am to 5pm and sometimes on Saturday mornings (see p.33 for banking hours). In general, Chinese temples open daily from 7am to around 6pm, Hindu temples 6am to noon and 5pm to 9pm, and mosques 8.30am to noon and 2.30 to 4pm.

Singapore has numerous **public holidays**, reflecting its mix of cultures. Dates for some of these vary; with Muslim festivals, we've given the months in which they fall during 2011–13. It's also worth noting local **school holidays**, at which time Sentosa and other places of interest to kids can be inordinately crowded; schools take a break for one week in March and September, throughout June and from mid-November until the end of December.

Public holidays

January 1 New Year's Day
January/February Chinese New Year (2 days)
March/April Good Friday
May 1 Labour Day
May Vesak Day
August 9 National Day

August Hari Raya Puasa (the end of Ramadan)
October/November Deepavali (or Diwali)
October/November Hari Raya Haji (also called Eid al-Adha)
December 25 Christmas Day

Phones

Local calls from private phones in Singapore cost next to nothing; calls from public phones cost 10c for three minutes. All phone numbers have eight digits (except for free or premium-rate numbers, which start with 1800 or 1900 respectively). Landline numbers always begin with a 6 and mobile numbers with an 8.

If you plan on using your **mobile phone** abroad, you may need to contact your provider before you depart to activate roaming. It may be worth buying a local SIM card (from any 7/11 store or Singtel/Starhub shop for around $20; bring your passport). Note that in Singapore, receiving calls and texts on your mobile incurs a charge.

Time

Singapore is eight hours ahead of Universal Time (GMT) year-round, and therefore two hours behind Sydney (when daylight saving time is not in effect there) and thirteen hours ahead of Eastern Standard Time.

Tipping

There are a few cases where you might want to tip someone offering you a personal service, for example a hairdresser or barber, but these are the exception rather than the rule – tipping is seldom the custom in Singapore. The better restaurants add a ten

Dialling codes

To call home **from Singapore**, dial ✆00 plus the relevant country code (see below), then the number (omitting any initial zero).
Australia ✆61
New Zealand ✆64
Ireland ✆353
South Africa ✆27
UK ✆44
US & Canada ✆1

percent service charge to the bill anyway, and the inexpensive *kopitiam*-type diners don't expect tips, nor do taxi drivers.

Tourist information

In a place as organized and wired-up as Singapore, it's usually straightforward to get hold of accurate and comprehensive information of use to travellers: everything from public transport to sales taxes is extensively documented online, some companies provide toll-free ☎1800 helplines, and many restaurants and shops have websites that are kept up to date.

The **Singapore Tourism Board** (STB; information line daily 8am–9pm ☎1800/736 2000, ⓦwww.yoursingapore.com) has offices abroad and operates Visitors' Centres at Changi Airport and downtown. The main downtown location is smack in the middle of Orchard Road, at the junction with Cairnhill Road (daily 9.30am–10.30pm); there are also much smaller Visitors' Centres on the ground floor of the Ion Orchard mall (above Orchard MRT; daily 10am–10pm), and on Cheng Yan Place (near Bugis MRT; daily 11am–10pm).

A number of **publications** offer listings of entertainment events plus reviews of restaurants and nightlife. The best of these are the weeklies *I-S* (ⓦis-magazine.com; free) and *8 Days* ($1.50); and the monthly *Time Out* (ⓦwww.timeoutsingapore.com.sg; $4). Other freebie publications available from Visitors' Centres and hotels contain similar information, and the "Life!" section of the *Straits Times* also has a decent listings section. Geared towards the large expat community (though with some information of interest to tourists) are *The Finder*, a free monthly magazine available at some downtown bars and restaurants, and the website ⓦwww.expatsingapore.com. Other useful websites for hotel booking, restaurant reviews and so on are mentioned in the relevant listings chapters.

Singapore tourist offices abroad

Australia Level 11, AWA Building, 47 York St, Sydney ☎02/9290 2888, ⓔstb-syd@stb-syd .org.au.
UK Grand Buildlings, 1–3 Strand, London ☎020/7484 2710, ⓔstb_london@stb.gov.sg.

US 1156 Avenue of the Americas, Suite 702, New York ☎212/302-4861; 5670 Wiltshire Blvd Suite 1550, Los Angeles ☎323/677-0808, ⓦwww .visitsingapore-usa.com.

Government websites

Australian Department of Foreign Affairs ⓦwww.dfat.gov.au.
British Foreign & Commonwealth Office ⓦwww.fco.gov.uk.
Canadian Department of Foreign Affairs ⓦwww.international.gc.ca.
Irish Department of Foreign Affairs ⓦwww.foreignaffairs.gov.ie.
New Zealand Ministry of Foreign Affairs ⓦwww.mfat.govt.nz.
South African Department of Foreign Affairs ⓦwww.dfa.gov.za.
US State Department ⓦwww.travel.state.gov.

Travellers with disabilities

Singapore is an **accessible** city for **travellers with disabilities**, as hefty tax incentives are provided for developers who include access features for the disabled in new buildings. However, life is made a lot easier if you can afford to pay for more upmarket hotels and to shell out for taxis. Similarly, the more expensive international airlines tend to be better equipped to get you there in the first place: MAS, British Airways, KLM and Qantas all carry aisle wheelchairs and have at least one toilet adapted for disabled passengers. One local tour operator, the Asia Travel Group (03-68 People's Park Centre, 101 Upper Cross St; ☎64380038, ⓦwww .asiatravelgroup.com.sg), offers customized tours of the region in minibuses that accommodate those with disabilities.

The best resource for pre-trip advice is the Disabled People's Association of Singapore, 25 International Business Park, 04-77 German Centre (☎68991220, ⓦwww.dpa .org.sg) or the Singapore Tourism Board STB (see above).

Access is improving all the time, and most hotels now make some provision for disabled guests, though often there will be only one specially designed bedroom in an establishment – always call first for information, and book in plenty of time. Getting around the city is relatively straightforward:

each MRT station has a lift and ramps to aid access, and a limited number of buses also offer disabled access. In addition, SMRT (☎65558888) has a fleet of wheelchair-accessible taxis, and two private taxi companies, Comfort Cab and CityCab (☎65521111) have drivers that will assist a wheelchair-bound passenger in embarking and disembarking from their cabs. There are acoustic signals at most street crossings.

Contacts

In the UK and Ireland

Irish Wheelchair Association Blackheath Drive, Clontarf, Dublin 3 ☎01/818 6400, ⓦwww.iwa .ie. Useful information about travelling abroad with a wheelchair and/or mobility impairment.
Tourism for All c/o Vitalise, Shap Road Industrial Estate, Kendal, Cumbria, LA9 6NZ ☎0845 124 9971 or 0845 124 9973 (Reservations) ⓦwww .tourismforall.org.uk. An independent charity that provides free lists of accessible accommodation abroad – European, American and long-haul destinations – plus a list of accessible attractions in

the UK. Information on financial help for holidays is also available.

In the US and Canada

Access-Able ⓦwww.access-able.com. Online resource for travellers with disabilities.
Mobility International USA 132 E. Broadway, Suite 343, Eugene, Oregon ☎541/343-1284, ⓦwww.miusa.org. Information and referral services, access guides, tours and exchange programmes.
Society for the Advancement of Travelers with Handicaps (SATH) 347 5th Ave, New York, NY 10016 ☎212/447-7284, ⓦwww.sath.org. Non-profit educational organization that has actively represented travellers with disabilities since 1976.

In Australia and New Zealand

Disabled Persons Assembly 4/173–175 Victoria St, Wellington, New Zealand ☎04/801 9100, ⓦwww.dpa.org.nz. Resource centre with lists of travel agencies and tour operators for people with disabilities.
National Disability Services ☎02/6282 4333, ⓦwww.nds.org.au. Provides lists of travel agencies and tour operators for people with disabilities.

The City

The City

1 The Colonial District and Marina Bay 39

2 Chinatown and the Central Business District 52

3 Bras Basah, Little India and the Arab Quarter 66

4 Orchard Road 78

5 Northern Singapore 83

6 Eastern Singapore 91

7 Western Singapore 98

8 Sentosa and the southern isles 105

The Colonial District and Marina Bay

The British left Singapore an impressive legacy in the stately nineteenth-century piles of the **COLONIAL DISTRICT**, abutting the north bank at the mouth of the Singapore River. The heart of the district is the immaculately groomed grass of the **Padang** ("field" in Malay), to the south of which are the **Empress Place Building**, **Old Parliament House** and the **Singapore Cricket Club** – the epitome of the colonizers' stubborn refusal to adapt to their surroundings – while just to the north is grand old **Raffles Hotel**. Heading west from the Padang, you pass **City Hall**, the **former Supreme Court** and its new, Norman Foster-designed replacement, before you reach the verdant slopes of **Fort Canning Hill**. For all the historical edifices cluttering the area, there are just a few sights that require an extended visit. The **National Museum** and **Peranakan Museum**, both just beneath Fort Canning Hill, and the **Asian Civilisations Museum** within the Empress Place Building, are all excellent, and **St Andrew's Cathedral**, in its own grounds just west of the Padang, also deserves a visit.

It's another of Singapore's many quirks that one of the oldest parts of town sits next to some of the newest, built on the reclaimed land framing **Marina Bay**. A massively ambitious piece of civil engineering, the bay is fed by the Singapore and Kallang rivers and has a barrage closing off its southern end. The result is a seaside freshwater reservoir with a crucial role in reducing Singapore's dependence on Malaysian water supplies. For visitors the main attractions are, close to the Padang at **Marina Centre**, the **Theatres on the Bay** arts complex, with its bug's-eye roof, plus the oversized ferris wheel that is the **Singapore Flyer**; and, south of the bay, the **Marina Bay Sands** casino resort. In September, Singapore's night-time **Formula One Grand Prix** sees crash barriers sprout in both the Colonial District and Marina Centre, whose main roads form the event's racetrack.

The Padang

The **Padang**, earmarked by Raffles as a recreation ground shortly after his arrival, is the very essence of colonial Singapore. Such is its symbolic significance that its borders have never been encroached upon by speculators and it remains much as it was in 1907, when G.M. Reith wrote in his *Handbook to Singapore*: "Cricket, tennis, hockey, football and bowls are played on the plain…beyond the carriage drive on the other side, is a strip of green along the sea wall, with a footpath, which affords a cool and

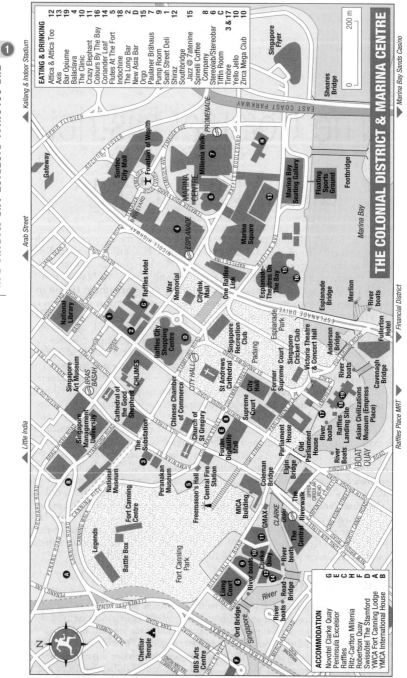

THE COLONIAL DISTRICT & MARINA CENTRE

EATING & DRINKING	
Attica & Attica Too	12
Axis	13
Bar Opiume	19
Balaclava	4
The Clinic	10
Crazy Elephant	11
Colours By The Bay	16
Coriander Leaf	14
Flutes At The Fort	5
Indochine	18
The Long Bar	2
New Asia Bar	D
Orgo	15
Paulaner Brähaus	7
Pump Room	9
Seah Street Deli	1
Shiraz	12
Southbridge	15
Jazz @ 7atenine	
Spinelli Coffee	8
Company	
Stereolab/Stereobar	C
Tiffin Room	3 & 17
Timbre	
Yello Jello	10
Zirca Mega Club	10

ACCOMMODATION	
Novotel Clarke Quay	G
Peninsula Excelsior	E
Raffles	C
Ritz-Carlton Millenia	H
Robertson Quay	F
Swissôtel The Stamford	D
YWCA Fort Canning Lodge	A
YMCA International House	B

pleasant walk in the early morning and afternoon." Once the last over of the day had been bowled, the Padang assumed a more social role: the image of Singapore's European community hastening to the corner once known as Scandal Point to catch up on the latest gossip is pure Somerset Maugham. Today the Padang is kept as pristine as ever by a bevy of gardeners mounted on state-of-the-art lawnmowers.

The brown-tiled roof, whitewashed walls and green blinds of the **Singapore Cricket Club**, at the southwestern end of the Padang, have a nostalgic charm. Founded in the 1850s, the club was the hub of colonial British society and still operates a "members only" rule, though there's nothing to stop you watching the action from the Padang itself. The Singapore Rugby Sevens are played here, as well as a plethora of other big sporting events and parades; a timetable of forthcoming events is available at the club's reception. Eurasians, who were formerly ineligible for membership of the Cricket Club, founded their own establishment in 1883, the **Singapore Recreation Club**, which lies across on the north side of the Padang. The current grandiose, colonnaded clubhouse dates back to an overhaul completed in 1997.

The Supreme Court buildings and City Hall

Just to the west of the Cricket Club, Singapore's erstwhile **Supreme Court** was built in Neoclassical style between 1937 and 1939, and sports a domed roof of green lead and a splendid, wood-panelled entrance hall. Formerly the site of the exclusive *Hotel de L'Europe*, whose drawing rooms allegedly provided Somerset Maugham with inspiration for many of his Southeast Asia short stories, the building has itself been upstaged by Sir Norman Foster's **New Supreme Court** just behind on North Bridge Road – mainly thanks to its impressive, flying saucer-shaped upper tier.

Next door to the former Supreme Court is the older **City Hall**. Its uniform rows of grandiose Corinthian columns lend it the austere air of a mausoleum and reflect its role in Singapore's wartime history: it was on the steps of the building that Lord Louis Mountbatten (then Supreme Allied Commander in Southeast Asia) announced Japan's surrender to the British in 1945. Fourteen years later, Lee Kuan Yew chose the same spot from which to address his electorate at a victory rally celebrating self-government for Singapore. For now, newlyweds still line up to have their big day captured in front of one of Singapore's most imposing buildings, but both City Hall and the old Supreme Court have been vacated and are being renovated to jointly comprise the prestigious new National Art Gallery of Singapore (Ⓦwww.nationalartgallery.sg), due to open in 2013.

The Victoria Concert Hall and Theatre

Across from the southern end of the Padang are two more fine examples of colonial architecture, the **Victoria Concert Hall** and adjoining **Victoria Theatre**, still the venues for some of Singapore's most prestigious cultural events. The theatre was completed in 1862 as Singapore's town hall, while the concert hall was added in 1905 as a memorial to the monarch's reign. During the Japanese occupation, the clock tower was altered to Tokyo time, while the statue of Raffles that once stood in front of the tower narrowly escaped being melted down. The newly installed Japanese curator of the National Museum (where the statue was sent) hid the statue and reported it destroyed. A copy can be seen by the river here at **Raffles' landing site**, where, in January 1819, the great man apparently took his first steps on Singaporean soil. Sir Stamford now stares contemplatively across the river towards the financial district.

Sir Stamford Raffles

Despite living and working in a period of imperial arrogance and land-grabbing, Sir Stamford Raffles maintained an unfailing concern for the welfare of the people under his governorship, and a conviction that British colonial expansion was for the general good. He believed Britain to be, as Jan Morris says in her introduction to Maurice Collis's biography of Raffles, "the chief agent of human progress…the example of fair Government".

Fittingly for a man who was to spend his life roaming the globe, Thomas Stamford Raffles was born at sea on July 6, 1781 on the *Ann*, whose master was his father Captain Benjamin Raffles. By his fourteenth birthday, the young Raffles was working as a clerk for the **East India Company** in London, his schooling curtailed because of his father's debts. Even at this early age, Raffles' ambition and self-motivation was evident as he stayed up through the night to study and developed a hunger for knowledge which would later spur him to learn Malay, amass a vast treasure-trove of natural history artefacts and write his two-volume *History of Java*.

Raffles' diligence and hard work showed through in 1805, when he was chosen to join a team going out to Penang, then being developed as a British entrepôt. Once in Southeast Asia, he enjoyed a meteoric rise: by 1807 he was named **chief secretary to the governor in Penang**. Upon meeting Lord Minto, the governor general of the East India Company in India, in 1810, Raffles was appointed **secretary to the governor general in Malaya**, a promotion quickly followed by the **governorship of Java** in 1811. Raffles' rule of Java was liberal and compassionate, his economic, judicial and social reforms transforming an island bowed by Dutch rule.

Post-Waterloo European rebuilding saw the East Indies returned to the Dutch in 1816 – to the chagrin of Raffles. He was transferred to the **governorship of Bencoolen** in Sumatra, but not before he had returned home for a break. While in England he met his second wife, Sophia Hull (his first, Olivia, had died in 1814), and was knighted. Raffles and Sophia sailed to Bencoolen in early 1818. Once in Sumatra, Raffles found the time to study the region's flora and fauna as tirelessly as ever, discovering **Rafflesia arnoldii** – "perhaps the largest and most magnificent flower in the world" – on a field trip. By now, Raffles felt strongly that Britain should establish a base in the Straits of Melaka and in late 1818, he was given leave to pursue this possibility. The following year he duly sailed to the southern tip of the Malay Peninsula, where his securing of **Singapore** was a daring masterstroke of diplomacy.

For a man whose name is inextricably linked with Singapore, Raffles spent a remarkably short time on the island. His last visit was in 1822; by August 1824, he was back in England. Awaiting news of a possible pension award from the East India Company, he spent his time founding the London Zoo. But the new life Raffles had planned never materialized. Days after hearing that a Calcutta bank holding £16,000 of his capital had folded, his pension application was refused; worse still, the Company was demanding £22,000 for overpayment. Three months later, in July 1826, the brain tumour that had caused Raffles headaches for several years took his life. He was buried at Hendon in north London with no memorial stone – the vicar had investments in slave plantations in the West Indies and was unimpressed by Raffles' friendship with William Wilberforce. Only in 1832 was Raffles commemorated, with a statue in Westminster Abbey.

The old and new parliament houses

North of the statue, up Parliament Lane, the dignified white Victorian building ringed by fencing is the **Old Parliament House**, built as a private dwelling for a rich merchant by Singapore's pre-eminent colonial architect, the Irishman George Drumgould Coleman. Relieved of its legislative duties, the building is now home to a contemporary arts centre called **The Arts House** and includes a shop stocking literature, DVDs and other works by home-grown talent. The bronze elephant in front of Old Parliament House was a gift to Singapore from King Rama V of Thailand (whose father was the king upon whom *The King and I* was based) after his trip to the island in 1871 – the first foreign visit ever made by a Thai monarch. Just across Parliament Lane from its predecessor is the back of the rather soulless **New Parliament House**, where it is possible to watch parliamentary debates in progress; check Ⓦ www.parliament.gov.sg for details.

Empress Place and Cavenagh Bridge

The **Empress Place Building**, very close to the mouth of the Singapore River, is a robust Neoclassical structure named after Queen Victoria and completed in 1865. Having long housed government offices, it is now home to the fine **Asian Civilisation Museum** (Mon 1–7pm, Tues–Thurs, Sat & Sun 9am–7pm, Fri 9am–9pm; $8/$4 or $11/$5.50 joint ticket with the Peranakan Museum – see p.46; ☎63327798), tracing the origins and growth of Asia's many and varied cultures, from Islamic West Asia through South and Southeast Asia to China. A bit of a misfit here, though most apt given the museum's location, is the excellent Singapore River gallery. It has displays of sampans and other river craft, and a diorama of a timber dwelling for coolies that recalls the grim lodging houses that once featured in London's docklands, but best of all are fascinating oral history clips featuring people who once worked on and lived by the river. In keeping with the river's renaissance as a major area for wining and dining, Empress Place also houses several posh riverside restaurants, chiefly run by the all-conquering *Indochine* chain (see p.139).

The elegant suspension struts of **Cavenagh Bridge** are an irresistible draw next to the museum. Named after Major General Orfeur Cavenagh, governor of the Straits Settlements from 1859 to 1867, the bridge was constructed in 1869 by Indian convict labourers using imported Glasgow steel. Times change, but not necessarily here, where a police sign maintains: "The use of this bridge is prohibited to any vehicle of which the laden weight exceeds 3cwt and to all cattle and horses." Cross the bridge to reach Singapore's former GPO (now the

▲ Boats on the Singapore River

The Singapore River

The Singapore River is really little more than a glorified creek, now cut off from the sea by the Marina Bay barrage. Once the river was clogged with the traditional cargo boats known as **bumboats**, with painted eyes on their prows as though they could see where they were going; the boats ferried coffee, sugar and rice to the warehouses called **godowns**, where coolies loaded and unloaded sacks. Inevitably, a series of **bridges** were built across the river too and these have survived, most of them endearingly oldfangled.

Walk along the river now, lined with trendy restaurants and bars, some occupying the few surviving godowns, and it's hard to imagine that in the 1970s this was still a working river. It was also filthy, and the river's present status as one of *the* nightlife centres of Singapore originates in the successful **Clean River Project** launched in 1977, which saw the river's commercial traffic moved west to Pasir Panjang within the space of a few years. Several museums have sections exploring the role the river once played and the pros and cons of its transformation, with a particularly good discussion at the Asian Civilisations Museum, which states frankly: "[the project] also washed away … [the river's] vibrant history as a trade waterway. Its newly cleaned waters now appeared characterless and sterile." At least today various **boat rides** offer a view of the riverside restaurants and city skyline (see p.28).

splendid *Fullerton Hotel*; see p.65), with Boat Quay (see p.65) and Raffles Place MRT just a couple of minutes' walk away.

St Andrew's Cathedral

Gleaming even brighter than the rest is the final building of note close to the Padang, **St Andrew's Cathedral**, adjoining Coleman Street and North Bridge Road. Using Indian convict labour the third church to be built on this site, the cathedral was constructed in high-vaulted, and neo-Gothic style, and was consecrated by Bishop Cotton of Calcutta on January 25, 1862. Its exterior walls were plastered using Madras *chunam* – an unlikely composite of eggs, lime, sugar and shredded coconut husks which shines brightly when smoothed – while the small cross behind the pulpit was crafted from two fourteenth-century nails salvaged from the ruins of Coventry Cathedral in England, which was destroyed during World War II. During the Japanese invasion of Singapore, the cathedral became a makeshift hospital, with the vestry serving as an operating theatre and the nave as a ward. Today, closed-circuit TVs have been installed to allow the whole congregation to view proceedings up at the altar – a reflection of the East Asian fascination with all things high-tech, since the cathedral's size hardly requires it. For more on the cathedral's history and architectural features, try to join one of the free **guided tours** led by volunteers (Mon–Sat 10.30am–noon & 2.30–4pm; 20min); enquire at the small, modern visitor's centre on North Bridge Road.

Raffles City and Raffles Hotel

Dwarfing St Andrew's Cathedral is **Raffles City**, a huge development occupying a block between Bras Basah and Stamford roads and comprising two enormous hotels – one of which is the 73-storey **Swissôtel** – and a shopping mall. The complex was designed by Chinese-American architect I.M. Pei (the man behind the Louvre's glass pyramid) and required the highly contentious demolition of the venerable Raffles Institution, a school established by Raffles himself and built in 1835 by George Drumgould Coleman. The *Swissôtel* holds an annual vertical marathon, in which hardy athletes attempt to run up to the top floor in as short a time as possible: the current record stands at under seven minutes. Lifts transport lesser mortals to admire the view from the sumptuous bars and restaurants on the top floors. The imposing **Singapore War Memorial** stands on the open land east of Raffles City; comprising four seventy-metre-high white columns, it's known locally as the "chopsticks".

Across the way from what was, for a time, the world's tallest hotel is one of the most famous. The lofty halls, restaurants, bars, and peaceful gardens of the legendary **Raffles Hotel**, almost a byword for colonialism, prompted Somerset Maugham to remark that it "stood for all the fables of the exotic East". Oddly, though, this most inherently British of hotels started life as a modest seafront bungalow belonging to an Arab trader, Mohamed Alsagoff. After a spell as a tiffin house, the property was bought in 1886 by the enterprising Armenian Sarkies brothers, who eventually controlled a triumvirate of quintessentially colonial lodgings: the *Raffles*, the *Eastern and Oriental* in Penang, Malaysia, and the *Strand* in Rangoon, Burma.

Raffles Hotel opened for business on December 1, 1887 and quickly attracted some impressive guests. Despite a guest list heavy with politicians and film stars over the years, the hotel is proudest of its **literary connections**: Joseph Conrad, Rudyard Kipling, Herman Hesse, Somerset Maugham, Noël Coward and Günter Grass all stayed here, and Maugham is said to have written many of his Asian tales under a frangipani tree in the garden.

The hotel enjoyed its real heyday during the first three decades of the last century, when it established its reputation for luxury – it was the first building in Singapore with electric lights and fans. In 1902, a little piece of Singaporean history was made at the hotel, according to a (probably apocryphal) tale, when the last tiger to be killed on the island was shot inside the building. Thirteen years later bartender Ngiam Tong Boon created another *Raffles* legend, the Singapore Sling cocktail.

During World War II, the hotel became the officers' quarters for the Japanese, and after the Japanese surrender in 1945, *Raffles* was a transit camp for liberated Allied prisoners. Postwar deterioration earned it the affectionate but melancholy soubriquet "grand old lady of the East" and the hotel was little more than a shabby tourist diversion when the government finally declared it a national monument in 1987. A hugely expensive facelift followed and the hotel reopened in 1991. Though the place retains much of its colonial grace, the modern arcade on North Bridge Road lacks finesse. If you do pop in, as most tourists do, you may find that the grand reception on Beach Road is only open to residents, but there is a free **museum** (daily 10am–7pm) upstairs at the North Bridge Road end of the complex, and you can partake of a Singapore Sling in the *Long Bar* for the princely sum of $28.

Hill and Coleman streets

From Stamford Road, Hill Street heads south to the river, flanking the eastern side of Fort Canning Park. The **Singapore Chinese Chamber of Commerce**, at 47 Hill Street, a brash, Chinese-style building from 1964 featuring a striking pagoda roof, lies 30m down on the left. Along its facade are two large panels, depicting nine intricately crafted porcelain dragons. The tiny **Armenian Church** of St Gregory the Illuminator, diagonally across the road, was designed by George Drumgould Coleman in 1835 (which makes it one of the oldest buildings in Singapore). Inside is a single, circular chamber, fronted by a marble altar and a painting of the Last Supper. Among the white gravestones and statues in the church's frangipani-scented gardens is the tombstone of Agnes Joaquim, a nineteenth-century Armenian resident of Singapore, after whom the national flower, the delicate, purple Vanda Miss Joaquim Orchid, is named; she discovered the orchid in her garden and had it registered at the Botanic Gardens.

The **Central Fire Station**, a stone's throw from the Armenian Church, across Coleman Street at 62 Hill Street, is a splendid red-and-white striped edifice. When it was first built in 1908 the watchtower was the tallest building in the region and made it easy for firemen to scan the area for fires. Though the station remains operational, part of it is now taken up by the **Civil Defence Heritage Gallery** (T63322996; Tues–Sun 10am–5pm; free), which traces the history of fire-fighting in Singapore from the formation of the first Voluntary Fire Brigade in 1869. The galleries display old helmets, extinguishers, hand-drawn escape ladders and steam fire engines, all beautifully restored. Of more interest, though, are the accounts of some of the island's most destructive fires. One, not far from Chinatown in 1961, ripped through a shanty district and claimed sixteen thousand homes, a disaster which led directly to a public housing scheme that spawned Singapore's new towns. Nine years later a short circuit caused a blaze that gutted Robinson's department store, then in Raffles Place, with the loss of nine lives.

On Coleman Street directly behind the Central Fire Station is Singapore's **Freemason's Hall** – it's worth noting that Raffles was apparently a mason – with its colonial facade of moulded garlands and protractors. Next door, the **Singapore Philatelic Museum** (Mon 1–7pm, Tues–Sun 9am–7pm; $3/$2; T63373888) occupies Singapore's former Methodist book rooms, which date back to 1906. Although clearly a niche destination, it manages to use its stamp collection imaginatively to highlight facets of the multicultural history and heritage of Singapore. Just beyond is the **National Archives Building** (Mon–Fri 9am–5.30pm, Sat 9am–1.30pm; free; T63327973), which houses enough documents, maps and photographs to keep amateur historians busy for weeks. The oral history collection allows access to fascinating interviews on such subjects as vanishing Singaporean trades, the Japanese occupation and traditional performing arts.

The Peranakan Museum

Dating from 1910, the beautifully ornamented three-storey building at 39 Armenian Street, just west of Hill Street, was once the Tao Nan School, the first school in Singapore to cater for new arrivals from China's Fujian province. Today it houses the worthy **Peranakan Museum** (daily 9.30am–7pm except Mon from 1pm, Fri until 9pm; $6/$3 or $11/$5.50 joint ticket with Asian Civilisations Museum – see p.43; details of free guided tours on T63327591). While the museum boasts that the island's Peranakans are "fully integrated into Singapore's globalized society", in reality they are at best keeping a low profile, and in a country where ethnicity is stated on everyone's ID, "Peranakan" isn't recognized as a valid category – meaning they are inevitably lumped together with the wider Chinese community. The museum should whet your appetite not only for the Baba House (see p.60) but also the Peranakan heritage of the Katong area (see p.93).

Singaporeans Peranakans are **Baba–Nonyas**, and the galleries focus on their posses-sions (theirs was largely a material culture) and customs, in particular the traditional twelve-day wedding. Early on you reach one of the most memorable displays, showing the classic entrance into a Peranakan home, overhung with lanterns and with a pair of *pintu pagar* – tall swing doors; you'll see something similar if you visit the Baba House. Elsewhere, look out for artefacts such as the ornate, tiered "pagoda trays" used in the wedding ceremony, furniture inlaid with mother-of-pearl, and beautiful repoussé silverware, including betel-nut sets and "pillow ends", coaster-like objects which for some reason were used as end-caps for bolsters. It's also worth attending to the video interviews with members of the community, who speak eloquently about matters such as being a hidden minority, whether or not to "marry out" and the prognosis for the Baba-Nonya identity.

The Baba-Nonyas

From the sixteenth century onwards, male Chinese immigrants came to settle in the Malay Peninsula, chiefly in Malacca, Penang (both in what is now Malaysia) and Singapore, and often married Malay women. The male offspring of such unions were termed **Baba** and the females **Nonya** (or Nyonya), though the community as a whole is also sometimes called **Straits Chinese** or simply **Peranakan**, an umbrella term denoting a culture born both of intermarriage and of communities living side by side over generations.

Baba-Nonya society adapted and fused elements from both its parent cultures, and had its own dialect of Malay and unique style. The Babas were often wealthy and were not afraid to flaunt this fact in their lavish **townhouses** featuring furniture inlaid with mother-of-pearl and hand-painted tilework. The Nonyas wore Malay-style batik-printed clothes and were accomplished at crafts such as **beadwork**, with beaded slippers a particular speciality. However it is their **cuisine**, marrying Chinese cooking with contrasting flavours from spices, tamarind and coconut milk, that is the culture's most celebrated legacy.

During the colonial era, many Baba-Nonyas acquired an excellent command of English and so prospered. Subsequently, however, they came under pressure to assimilate into the mainstream Chinese community despite often not speaking much Chinese (the Baba-Nonyas were sometimes labelled "OCBC" after the name of a local bank, though in their case the acronym meant "*orang Cina bukan Cina*", Malay for "Chinese [yet] not Chinese"). It was partly as a result of this assimilation that many of their traditions have gone into serious decline.

The National Museum

On Stamford Road just around the corner from Armenian Street is the eye-catching dome, seemingly coated with silvery fish scales, of the **National Museum of Singapore** (daily 10am–8pm, History Gallery until 6pm; $10/$5; ℡63323659). Its forerunner, the Raffles Museum and Library, opened in 1887 and soon acquired a reputation for its natural history collection. In the 1960s, following independence, the place was renamed the National Museum and subsequently altered its focus to local history and culture, an emphasis retained after a recent overhaul that saw the original Neoclassical building gain a hangar-like rear extension larger than itself. That extension houses the mainstay of the new-look museum, the History Gallery, while the old building is home to the Living Galleries, focusing on various aspects of Singapore culture and society. If you have no interest in seeing the History Gallery, note that after it shuts there's **free admission** to the rest of the museum.

The History Gallery

The History Gallery requires at least a couple of hours to see, thanks to the novel presentation with hardly any labelling; instead, textual descriptions and audio clips of extended commentaries or oral history are all stored on the "Companion", a device like a jumbo iPod which every visitor receives. The sound clips do enliven a collection of artefacts that is in part mundane, but they also take a frustrating amount of time to get through.

Things begin unpromisingly with a two-storey rotunda through which you descend on a spiral ramp while watching a 360° film projection of Singapore scenes that's accompanied by a bombastic choral soundtrack. Thankfully, you're soon into the first gallery proper, which focuses on Temasek (as the Malays called Singapore) before the colonial era. Pride of place here goes to the mysterious

Singapore Stone, all that survives of an inscribed monolith which once stood near where the *Fullerton* hotel is today, though more memorable is beautiful gold jewellery excavated at Fort Canning in 1926 and thought to date from the fourteenth century. There's another film installation here, a cryptic affair depicting fourteenth-century conflict in Temasek.

From here the displays are split into a chronological **Events Path** and a human-interest-driven **Personal Path**, covering the same developments in parallel; you can switch from one to the other as you please. The Personal Path is often more entertaining, featuring, for example, a video reminiscence by a revue performer from Shanghai who arrived to perform in postwar Singapore and ended up staying. It's also worth keeping an eye out for the few items which the museum designates national treasures, some of which are truly worthy of the label, such as the gold jewellery mentioned above and some gorgeous Chinese watercolours depicting hornbills and tropical fruit, acquired by William Farquhar.

Two aspects of the twentieth-century coverage are worthy of special attention: the dimly lit, claustrophobic area dealing with the Japanese occupation and the horrors of Operation Sook Ching (see p.86), and the sections on postwar politics in Singapore – even if most of the cast of characters is unfamiliar. From today's perspective it seems hard to believe that up until around the early 1970s, much was still up for grabs in Singapore politics, and the museum deserves credit for tackling the postwar period and devoting some space to former figures from the opposition.

The Living Galleries

The most accessible of the museum's four Living Galleries focuses on **street food**, covering the history of and variations in local favourites such as *laksa* and *char kuay teow*, and displaying soft drinks and kitchenware that generations of Singaporeans remember from their childhood. Also appealing is the **photography** gallery which, under the banner of "Framing the Family", displays many Singapore family portraits made over the past 100 years, enriched with yet more oral history clips. It includes some interesting commentary on the prevalence of polygamy – not, as you might assume, in Muslim families but among the Chinese. The most edifying gallery tackles **film and wayang** (street opera) and includes plenty of memorabilia of the Malay-language film industry which took off in Singapore in the middle of the last century; it's a sign of how the times have changed since the divorce from Malaysia that this cinematic flowering is news to many non-Malay Singaporeans today. Finally, there's the **fashion** gallery, using trends in women's clothing over the years as a bellwether of the changing status of Singapore women.

Fort Canning Park and around

When Raffles first caught sight of Singapore, **Fort Canning Park** was known locally as Bukit Larangan (Forbidden Hill). Malay annals tell of the five ancient kings of Singapura, said to have ruled the island from this point six hundred years ago, and artefacts unearthed here prove it was inhabited as early as the fourteenth century. The last of the kings, Sultan Iskandar Shah, reputedly lies here, and it was out of respect for and fear of his spirit that the Malays decreed the hill forbidden. Singapore's first Resident (British administrator), William Farquhar, displayed typical colonial tact by promptly having the hill cleared and building a bungalow, Government House, on the summit. It was replaced in 1859 by a fort named after Viscount George Canning, governor general of India, but of this only a gateway, guardhouse and adjoining wall remain. An early European **cemetery** survives, however, upon whose stones are engraved intriguing epitaphs to nineteenth-century sailors, traders and residents, among them the pioneering colonial architect, George Coleman.

Festive Singapore

There's something reassuring in the fact that ancient celebrations and traditions still survive on an island that has apparently embraced all the trappings of the modern world. With so many ethnic groups and religions present in Singapore, you'll be unlucky if your trip doesn't coincide with at least one of the many religious and secular festivals, whether it's an exuberant, family-oriented pageant or a blood-curdlingly gory display of devotion.

Procession during Thaipusam ▲

Dragon Boat Festival ▼

Hindu festivals

Would you walk over a bed of hot coals to prove the strength of your faith? According to Hindu legend, that's exactly what the Goddess Draupadi did to prove her innocence and fidelity to her husband. In Chinatown's Sri Mariamman temple, hundreds of Hindu devotees honour the goddess' efforts each October by fire-walking at the festival of **Thimithi**. An even more gruesome display of faith takes place in January or February, when the **Thaipusam Festival** sees penitents process from Serangoon Road to Tank Road carrying portable shrines (*kavadis*) that are attached to their bodies by assorted hooks and barbs. Other penitents opt to skewer their tongues and cheeks with metal spikes, while along the route, supporters sing and dance in encouragement. The most important date in the Hindu calendar though, is **Deepavali** (or Diwali) the Hindu festival of lights, when devotees mark the victory of light over darkness by lighting small, earthenware oil lanterns and by offering prayers at temple. There's no better time to experience Little India's colourful Serangoon Road, which is decked with lights during the period and hosts cultural performances.

Dragon Boat Festival

Singapore's **Dragon Boat Festival** recalls the legend of a Chinese scholar who cast himself into the sea to protest against corrupt politicians. The subsequent flotilla of boats that set out to save him is remembered in June or July each year when scores of long, dragon-headed rowing boats race one another on Bedok Reservoir. The scholar's would-be rescuers threw rice dumplings into the waters to throw giant fish off his scent, and to this day, Singaporeans eat rice dumplings wrapped in banana leaves in memory of their vain efforts.

Mooncakes and lanterns

Singaporeans mark the **Mid-Autumn Festival** and the autumn full moon by eating mooncakes — pastries traditionally filled with sweet bean paste — and by parading through the Chinese Gardens at night carrying brightly coloured lanterns.

Ramadan

The Muslim fasting month of **Ramadan** represents an annual test of faith through abstinence — a sort of detox for the soul — and for the whole of the ninth month of the Islamic calendar, Muslims forgo food, drink, tobacco and sex during the hours of daylight. Every evening, once darkness falls, they come together to break their fast in the food markets that spring up in Geylang and the Arab Quarter, while the most lavish feast is saved for the night of **Hari Raya Puasa**, which marks the end of Ramadan.

▲ Floating candles during the Moon Festival

▼ Young boys celebrating Hari Raya

▼ Chinese lanterns

Festival City

Modern Singapore may have inherited many age-old religious festivals, but it has also created a few secular celebrations of its own. In April, the **Singapore International Film Festival** thrills cinephiles, while the annual **Arts Festival** in May and June features performances in various genres and draws participants from across the world. July sees the nation's mania for eating celebrated in the **Singapore Food Festival**, while the following month, on August 9, the entire country comes to a standstill to celebrate **National Day**, an annual outburst of civic pride that is marked by pyrotechnics and parades.

Temple-goers during Chinese New Year ▲

Dancer in the Chingay Parade ▼

Chinese New Year

Three-quarters of Singapore's population are ethnic Chinese, making Chinese New Year, which falls in January or February, the biggest festival in the calendar. The run-up to the event is always hectic, as people throng to shops across the island to stock up on assorted treats such as pineapple-jam tarts and bak kwa (sweet barbecued pork slices) to be served up to visiting guests.

It's at this time of year that Chinatown is at its most charismatic, the streets hemmed with stalls selling pussy willow, signifying future prosperity, and mandarin oranges, considered auspicious gifts as the pronunciation for them is "gam", the same as for the Chinese for "gold". Things quieten down considerably during the eve and first day of the New Year, when people get together with close family and will often share a meal of yee sang – a raw fish and noodle salad – for good luck.

Chinese New Year is accompanied by two major organized events. The Chingay Parade was once a public street procession featuring traditional acrobats and lion and dragon dances (which you can also see being performed spontaneously at downtown temples during the period), but these days the event has morphed into a grand ticketed carnival-like affair, featuring local and foreign performers, some from as far afield as Brazil.

The other major event is the River Hong Bao Festival, *hong bao* being the red envelopes containing small amounts of money that all children look forward to receiving during the festival. The event itself is a riot of fireworks, amusements and performances at Marina Bay.

Fort Canning Park itself is verdant and breezy, and offers respite from Singapore's crowded streets. The most obvious of several routes up the hill begins by the National Museum, but it's also possible to use the long flight of steps that starts on Hill Street by the MICA Building. If you use the museum route, you enter the park down the slope from the slightly incongruous **Fort Canning Centre**, once a British army barracks and now housing a dance company, culinary school and other organizations; an information point here has **maps** of the park. Turn left to reach a *keramat* (auspicious place), the supposed site of Iskandar Shah's grave, which attracts a trickle of Muslims. Continue round the hill and you meet the staircase from Hill Street at **Raffles Terrace**, with replicas of a colonial flagstaff and a lighthouse. From here paths swing northwest, with the Singapore River and River Valley Road below, to the far side of the hill where another former military building, now called **Legends**, houses a private club and a couple of restaurants.

Just uphill from Legends and behind the Fort Canning Centre are the Fort Gate – the surviving gateway to Canning's fort – and the 1939 underground bunker from which the Allied war effort in Singapore was masterminded. The bunker is now billed as the **Battle Box** (daily 10am–6pm, last admission at 5pm; $8/$5), which uses audiovisual effects and animatronics to bring to life the events leading up to the decision by British officers to surrender Singapore to the Japanese on February 15, 1942.

Along River Valley Road

Fort Canning Park's southern boundary is defined by **River Valley Road**, which skirts below the park from Hill Street. At its eastern end is the **MICA Building** – formerly the Hill Street Police Station, but now home to the Ministry of Information, Communications and the Arts, with shuttered windows in bright colours; its central atrium houses several galleries majoring in Asian artworks. Close to the Coleman Bridge here is **GMAX** (Mon–Thurs 2pm–1am, Fri 2pm–3am, Sat 1pm–3am, Sun 1pm–1am, $45; ☎63381146), billed as a reverse bungy jump though it's really more like a metal cage suspended from steel cables, allowing several screaming passengers to be tossed around in the air at once. It's best sampled before you settle into one of the many bars and restaurants of **Clarke Quay**, a chain of nineteenth-century godowns, or warehouses, transformed into a nightlife complex complete with futuristic but rather ugly shelters. Most places here are somewhat overpriced, though, and nearby Boat Quay (see p.65) remains a better bet. Further up the road is **Robertson Quay**, rather quieter than either of these though it has a few entertainment venues of its own.

Northeast of Robertson Quay is what is often still called the **Chettiar Temple** (officially the Sri Thendayuthapani Temple; daily roughly 8.30am–12.30pm & 5.30–8.30pm). The shrine, with a large, attractive *gopuram*, was built in 1984 to replace a nineteenth-century temple constructed by Indian *chettiars* (moneylenders) and is dedicated mainly to the worship of the Hindu deity Lord Murugan. It's also the target of every participant in the procession that accompanies the annual Thaipusam Festival (see p.150 and "*Festive Singapore*" colour section).

Marina Centre

Marina Centre is the name generally applied to the large triangle of reclaimed land immediately east of the Padang and *Raffles Hotel*, which has robbed Beach Road of its seafront. The area still has a somewhat artificial feel, with no residential areas or traditional places of worship; instead it is dominated by the Marina Square and Suntec City malls, the Suntec Convention Centre, several blocks of plush offices and expensive hotels. Visitors who come here do so mainly to enjoy the **views** of the Singapore cityscape across Marina Bay, with the Esplanade or the Singapore Flyer as vantage points.

Esplanade – Theatres on the Bay

Singapore's skyline seems to change almost by the day, but rarely has a building caused such ripples as the **Esplanade – Theatres on the Bay** project, adjacent to the Padang. Opinion is split over whether the two huge, spiked shells that roof the complex are peerless modernistic architecture or plain kitsch. They have variously been compared to hedgehogs, kitchen sieves, even durians (the preferred description among locals) after the spiky, smelly fruit, though they are perhaps best described as resembling two giant insect eyes.

Opened in 2002, Esplanade includes a concert hall, theatres, gallery space and, on level 3, a library with a good range of arts-related resources (daily 11am–9pm). It's possible to take a self-guided **iTour** of the building (daily 10am–6pm; $10/$8) based around multimedia content stored on a handheld gizmo, but what lures most casual visitors are the excellent **views** across the bay to the financial district from the south side, where you'll also find a cluster of restaurants and bars.

The Singapore Flyer

Ten minutes' walk east of the Theatres on the Bay, the **Singapore Flyer** (daily 8.30am–10.30pm; $29.50; ☏63333311) stands a lofty 165 metres tall – as high as the summit of Bukit Timah, the island's highest point, and about thirty metres taller than the London Eye. While not lacking in altitude, the Flyer does fall slightly flat as an attraction because of its location. From here, the most atmospheric areas of old Singapore, including the remaining rows of shophouses in Chinatown and Little India, are largely obscured by a forest of jagged and somewhat interchangeable towers; you may well find you get better views from your hotel room if it's high up.

The flight initially has you looking east over the Kallang district, where Singapore's grand new Sports Hub stadium complex is due to be completed in 2012. Also visible is the golf course of mundane Marina East, the lobe of land east of Marina Bay, south of which lies the narrow barrage allowing the bay to be used as a reservoir. In the distance beyond the shipping lanes is Indonesia's Riau archipelago, so close and yet somehow in a different realm, thanks to the 1824 Anglo-Dutch treaty under which the British let the islands south of Singapore slip into the Dutch sphere of influence. Looking north, it's much more exciting to pick out the golden domes of the Sultan Mosque and the shophouses of Arab Street beyond the twin Gateway buildings on Beach Road. As your capsule reaches maximum height, you might just make out the low hump of Bukit Timah, topped with a couple of radio masts, on the horizon beyond Theatres on the Bay.

The descent affords great views of Marina South and the financial district. Originally, the ride began with views of the area, but the wheel's direction of rotation was soon reversed in line with feng shui considerations (apparently having the capsules ascend pointing towards the banks' towers was channelling good luck up and away from the area). The floating platform you see close by on the north side of the bay is a sports arena, large enough for soccer matches.

Marina South

For years, the huge chunk of reclaimed land that is **Marina South** had all the makings of a folly, seeming to have little purpose other than to house the so-so Marina City Park and serve as a conduit for part of the East Coast Parkway highway. But by the time you read this the area will have been transformed by the emergence

▲ The durian-like roof of Esplanade – Theatres on the Bay

of the enormous **Marina Bay Sands** hotel and casino (☎66888868, Ⓦwww
.marinabaysands.com), run by Las Vegas Sands, which previously ventured beyond
Nevada to run a hotel/casino complex in Macau. Their Singapore undertaking is one
of their most audacious yet, especially in these credit-squeezed times. Marina South
is also the site of what's being billed as a new financial centre, though it will comprise
just a few towers to begin with and feels more like a spillover from the existing
banking district than a separate entity. It's easy to reach the area using Marina Bay
MRT or, from 2013 or so, Bayfront MRT, on the new Downtown line.

The centrepiece of the development, on the western, bay-facing side of the area,
is a three-towered hotel topped by a vast roof platform that will not just link the
towers but also house a so-called **Sky Park** that could literally be one of the hottest
stretches of greenery in town, when the cruel tropical sun beats down. The casino
will be situated between the towers and the bay, along with the **ArtScience
Museum** – "devoted to the exploration of art and science and the connections
between them" – and yet more entertainment, conference and shopping facilities,
as if Singapore wasn't already drowning in these. Potentially the most interesting
feature is the glass-and-steel **footbridge** encased in a DNA-like double-helix
design; it will start near the museum and run for almost 300 metres to end up close
to the Singapore Flyer across Marina Bay.

Chinatown and the Central Business District

The two square kilometres of **Chinatown** once constituted the focal point of Chinese life and culture in Singapore. Nowadays, the area is on its last traditional legs, scarred by demolition and dwarfed by the skyscrapers of the financial **Central Business District**, where the island's city slickers oversee the machinations of one of Asia's most dynamic money markets. Even so, a wander through the surviving nineteenth-century streets still unearths musty and atmospheric temples, traditional craft shops, clan associations and old-style coffee shops and restaurants. Provision stores crammed with birds' nests, dried cuttlefish, ginger, chillies, mushrooms and salted fish do a brisk trade, and you might hear the rattle of a game of mahjong being played. Chinatown is bounded by New Bridge Road to the west, Neil and Maxwell roads to the south and Cecil Street to the east, while to the north, the Singapore River snakes west and inland passing the last few surviving godowns from Singapore's original trade boom.

Chinatown

The area now known as **CHINATOWN** was earmarked for settlement by the Chinese community by Sir Stamford Raffles himself, who decided in June 1819 that the ethnic communities should live separately. As increasing numbers of **immigrants** poured into Singapore, Chinatown became just that – a Chinese town, where new arrivals from the mainland, mostly from the Canton and Fujian provinces, would have been pleased to find temples, shops and, most importantly, clan associations (*kongsi*), which helped them to find food, lodgings and work, mainly as small traders and coolies. The prevalent architectural form was the **shophouse**, a shuttered building with a moulded facade fronting living rooms upstairs and a shop on the ground floor. The three-day Verandah Riots of 1888

Songbirds

One of the most enduringly popular of Singaporean hobbies is the keeping and training of **songbirds**. Every Sunday morning (around 9am), enthusiasts and their birds congregate at the small square on the corner of Tiong Bahru and Seng Poh roads, west of Chinatown. Songbird competitions are commonplace in Singapore, but this gathering is an informal affair with bird owners coming to show off their pets and admire those of fellow collectors. The **exquisite cages** that house the birds are hung from a frame with birds grouped according to their breed, lest they pick up the distinctive songs of other breeds. The various breeds of bird you'll see include the delicate green mata puteh, or "white eye bird"; the jambul, with its showy black crest and red eye patches; and the sharma, with beautiful long tail feathers.

Housing estates around the city now house some of the bigger songbird gatherings. One venue of note is at Block 430 Avenue 3 in Clementi (Clementi MRT; 9am).

erupted when colonial administrators ordered Chinatown's merchants to clear their five-foot ways of stalls and produce to enable pedestrians to pass by.

By the mid-twentieth century, the area southwest of the Singapore River was rich with the imported cultural heritage of China, but with independence came ambition. The government regarded the tumbledown slums of Chinatown as an eyesore and embarked upon a catastrophic **redevelopment** campaign that saw whole roads bulldozed to make way for new shopping centres, and street traders relocated into organized complexes. Only in the last decade has public opinion finally convinced the Singaporean authorities to restore rather than redevelop Chinatown. There are some renovated buildings that remain faithful to the original designs, but character is often sacrificed in the process. Unfortunately, spiralling rents have driven out all but a few families and traditional businesses like medicine shops, bakers and makers of *popiah* skin (the soft wrapping used to make spring rolls), leaving the area open for full exploitation by bistros, advertising agencies and souvenir shops. If you want to get a taste of the old ways of Chinatown, you'll need to spurn its central streets and head into the surrounding housing blocks.

Along Telok Ayer Street

Skirting the southern end of Chinatown is **Telok Ayer Street**, whose Malay name – meaning "Watery Bay" – recalls a time when the street would have run along the shoreline of the Straits of Singapore. Nowadays, thanks to land reclamation, it's no closer to a beach than is Beach Road, but alongside the shops and offices there are still a number of temples and mosques that have survived from the time when immigrants and sailors stepping ashore wanted to thank the gods for their safe passage.

At the southern end of the street resides the square **Chinese Methodist Church**, built in 1889, whose design – portholes and windows adorned with white crosses and capped by a Chinese pagoda-style roof – is a pleasing blend of East and West. The Muslim faith holds sway a short walk up the street, where the simple lines of the sky-blue **Al-Abrar Mosque** mark the spot where Chulia worshippers from the coast of southern India first set up a thatched *kuchu palli* ("small mosque" in Tamil), in 1827.

Thian Hock Keng Temple

Further up, the enormous **Thian Hock Keng Temple** (Temple of Heavenly Happiness; daily 7.30am–5.30pm) is a hugely impressive Hokkien building. Built

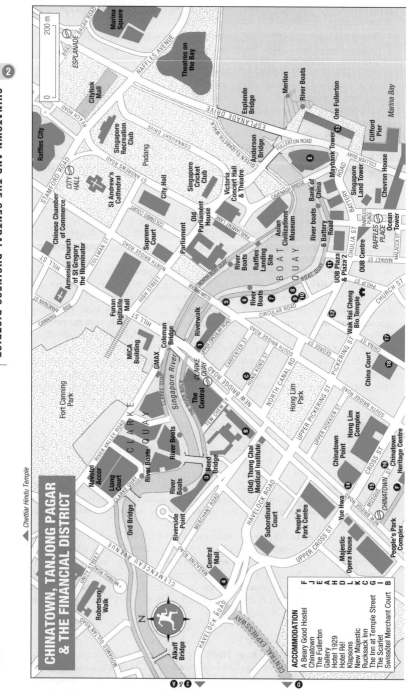

CHINATOWN, TANJONG PAGAR & THE FINANCIAL DISTRICT

▲ Chettiar Hindu Temple

200 m

Marina Bay

ACCOMMODATION
A Beary Good Hostel   F
Chinatown   J
The Fullerton   E
Gallery   A
Hotel 1929   H
Hotel Rél   D
Klapsons   L
New Majestic   K
Rucksack Inn   C
The Inn at Temple Street G
The Scarlet   I
Swissôtel Merchant Court B

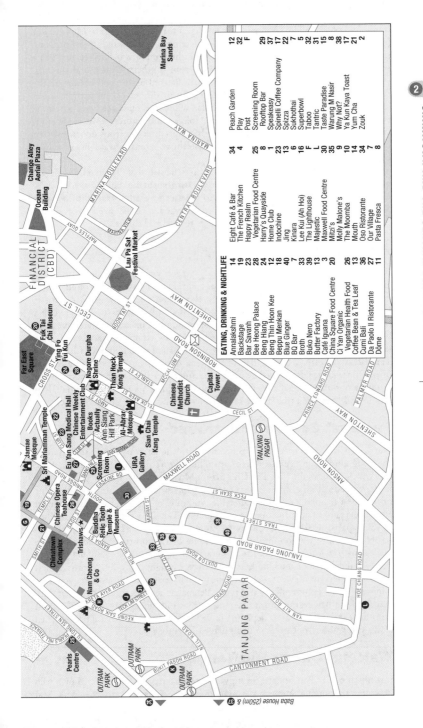

EATING, DRINKING & NIGHTLIFE

Annalakshmi	14
Backstage	19
Bar Savanh	23
Bee Heong Palace	28
Beng Hiang	24
Beng Thin Hoon Kee	12
Beppu Menkan	18
Blue Ginger	40
BQ Bar	7
Broth	33
Buko Nero	39
Butter Factory	13
Café Iguana	3
China Square Food Centre	20
Ci Yan Organic	
Vegetarian Health Food	26
Coffee Bean & Tea Leaf	13
Cumi Bali	36
Da Paolo Il Ristorante	27
Dôme	11
Eight Café & Bar	34
The French Kitchen	4
Happy Realm	
Vegetarian Food Centre	25
Harry's Quayside	8
Home Club	1
Indochine	23
Jing	13
Kinara	6
Lee Kui (Ah Hoi)	16
The Lighthouse	F
Majestic	L
Maxwell Food Centre	30
Mitzi's	35
Molly Malone's	9
The Moomba	10
Mouth	14
Oso Ristorante	34
Our Village	7
Pasta Fresca	8
Peach Garden	12
Play	32
Post	F
Screening Room	29
Rooftop Bar	37
Speakeasy	17
Spizza	22
Spinelli Coffee Company	7
Sukhothai	5
Superbowl	32
Taboo	31
Tantric	15
Taste Paradise	38
Warung M Nasir	8
Why Not?	17
Ya Kun Kaya Toast	21
Yum Cha	2
Zouk	

on the site of a small joss house where immigrants made offerings to Ma Chu Por (or Tian Hou), the queen of heaven, the temple was started in 1839 using materials imported from China. By the time the temple was finished in 1842 a statue of the goddess had been shipped in from southern China, and this still stands in the centre of the temple's main hall, flanked by the god of war on the right and the protector of life on the left. From the street, the temple looks spectacular: dragons stalk its broad roofs, while the entrance to the temple compound bristles with ceramic flowers, foliage and figures. Two stone lions stand guard at the entrance, and door gods, painted on the front doors, prevent evil spirits from entering. Look out for the huge ovens, always lit, in which offerings to gods and ancestors are burnt.

It's a testament to Singapore's multicultural nature that Thian Hock Keng's next-door neighbour should be the **Nagore Durgha shrine**, built in the 1820s by Chulias from southern India as a shrine to the ascetic, Shahul Hamid of Nagore. **Telok Ayer Green**, a tranquil, paved garden dotted with life-sized metal statues depicting the area's earliest settlers, separates temple and shrine.

Amoy Street

A block west of Telok Ayer Street is **Amoy Street**, which – together with China and Telok Ayer streets – was designated as a Hokkien enclave in the colony's early days. Long terraces of shophouses flank the street, all featuring characteristic **five-foot ways**, or covered walkways, so called simply because they jut five feet out from the house. A few of the shophouses are in a ramshackle state, but most have been marvellously renovated and bought up by companies in need of some fancy office space. It's worth walking down to mustard-coloured **Sian Chai Kang Temple**, at 66 Amoy Street. Below the fiery dragons on its roof, it's a musty, open-fronted place dominated by huge urns, full to the brim with ash from untold numbers of burned incense sticks. Guarding the temple are two carved stone lions whose fancy red neck ribbons are said to attract good fortune and prosperity.

Far East Square and around

North of Cross Street, Amoy Street strikes into the heart of **Far East Square**, a shopping-cum-dining centre which taps Chinatown's heritage for its inspiration, and which includes the **Fuk Tak Ch'i Street Museum** (daily 10am–10pm; free) as its party piece. It's the surest sign yet of the gentrification of Chinatown that one of its oldest temples has had to suffer the ignominy of being turned into a tourist attraction – and a fairly dull one at that. The **Fuk Tak Ch'i Temple** was established by Singapore's Hakka and Cantonese communities in 1824. The temple has scrubbed up nicely – too nicely, in fact: none of the musty ambience that once made it such an interesting and atmospheric place has survived its $200,000 renovation. A model junk of the kind that would have brought across Singapore's earliest Chinese settlers sits on what used to be the temple's main altar. Elsewhere, you'll see odds and sods – opium pillows and pipes, Peranakan jewellery, an instrument once used by food hawkers to drum up trade – from old Singapore, though the most arresting exhibit is a diorama depicting how Telok Ayer would have appeared when it was still a waterfront street in the nineteenth century.

Wak Hai Cheng Bio Temple

Just north of Far East Square, an ugly concrete courtyard, crisscrossed by a web of ropes supporting numerous spiralled incense sticks, fronts the **Wak Hai**

Cheng Bio Temple (daily 6am–6pm) on Philip Street. Its name means "Temple of the Calm Sea", which made it a logical choice for early worshippers who had arrived safely in Singapore; an effigy of Tian Hou, the queen of heaven and protector of seafarers, is housed in the temple's right-hand chamber. This temple, too, has an incredibly ornate roof, crammed with tiny models of Chinese village scenes.

China Street and Club Street

Far East Square has subsumed **China Street** and its offshoots, meaning another slice of residential Chinatown has been lost forever. To get a flavour of the old ways that survived in these streets until the turn of the millennium you'll have to push on across South Bridge Road into the **Hong Lim Complex**, a modern housing estate where old men in white T-shirts and striped pyjama trousers sit chewing the cud in walkways lined with medical halls, chop makers, and stores selling birds' nests, pork floss, dried mushrooms and gold jewellery.

At the southern end of China Street is steep **Club Street**, once noted for its temple-carving shops, though these too have now fallen to the demolition ball and been replaced by swish apartment blocks, swanky bars and restaurants and boutique shops. An impromptu **flea market** still takes place on the far side of the car park opposite, where traders squat on their haunches surrounded by catalogues, old coins, sleeveless records and phonecards.

Even the **clan associations** and **guilds** that gave Club Street its name are fast disappearing, though there are still a few to be seen, higher up the hill. These are easy to spot; black-and-white photos of old members cover the walls, and behind the screens that almost invariably span the doorway, old men sit and chat. From upstairs, the clacking sound of mahjong tiles reaches the street. Most notable of all is the **Chinese Weekly Entertainment Club** at no. 76 – flanked by roaring lion heads, it's an imposing, 1891-built mansion that was established by a Peranakan millionaire.

Along South Bridge Road

South Bridge Road, stretching all the way from the Elgin Bridge to Tanjong Pagar, is Chinatown's backbone. During the Japanese occupation roadblocks were set up at the point where South Bridge meets Cross Street, and Singaporeans were vetted at an interrogation post for signs of anti-Japanese feeling in the infamous Sook Ching campaign (see p.86). Those whose answers failed to satisfy the guards and their hooded local informants either ended up as POWs or were never seen again. Today, South Bridge Road is fast becoming antiques-central, as more and more of the numerous dingy shops that line it are spruced up and turned into Asian arts curiosity shops.

Eu Yan Sang Medical Hall

The beautifully renovated **Eu Yan Sang Medical Hall** (Mon–Sat 8.30am–6pm), at 267–271 South Bridge Road, offers a great introduction to traditional Chinese medicines. First opened in 1910, the shop is now partially geared to the tourist trade. Besides the usual herbs and roots favoured by the Chinese are various dubious remedies derived from exotic and endangered species. Blood circulation problems and external injuries are eased with centipedes and insects crushed into a "rubbing liquor", the ground-up gall bladders of snakes or bears apparently work wonders on pimples, monkey's gallstones aid asthmatics, and deer penis is supposed to provide a lift to any sexual problem. Antlers, sea horses, scorpions and

▲ Eu Yan Sang Medical Hall

turtle shells also feature regularly in Chinese prescriptions, though the greatest cure-all of Oriental medicine is said to be **ginseng**, a clever little root that will combat anything from weakness of the heart to acne and jet lag.

At the back of the hall is the small but engaging **Birds Nest Gallery** which casts light on the history, harvesting and processing of this most famous of Chinese delicacies. Birds' nests emerged as a prized supplement among China's royal and noble classes during the Ming Dynasty, and today they are still valued for their high glycoprotein, calcium, iron and vitamin B1 content, and for their efficacy in boosting the immune system and curing bronchial ailments. Produced by swiftlets in the limestone and coastal caves of Southeast Asia, birds' nests are a mixture of saliva, moss and grass. It's the painstaking process of picking out this moss and grass by hand that makes the product so expensive – that, and the slow and precarious business of initial harvesting. A screen presentation in English shows nest harvesters or "spidermen" scaling bamboo poles as long as 25 metres in the caves of Borneo, with only the torches attached to the poles to guide them.

Sri Mariamman Hindu Temple and the Jamae Mosque

Opposite the Eu Yan Sang Medical Hall on South Bridge Road, the compound of the recently renovated **Sri Mariamman Hindu Temple** bursts with primary-coloured, wild-looking statues of deities and animals. There's always some ritual or other being attended to by one of the temple's priests, drafted in from the subcontinent and dressed in simple loincloths. A wood-and-atap hut was erected on this site in 1827, on land belonging to Naraina Pillay – a government clerk who arrived in Singapore on the same ship as Stamford Raffles. The present temple was completed in 1843 and boasts a superb *gopuram* over the front entrance. Once inside the temple, look up at the roof and you'll see splendidly vivid friezes depicting a host of Hindu deities, including the three manifestations of the supreme being: Brahma the Creator (with three of his four heads showing), Vishnu the Preserver, and Shiva the Destroyer (holding one of his sons). The main sanctum, facing you as you walk inside, is devoted to Goddess Mariamman, who's worshipped for her power to cure diseases. Smaller sanctums dotted about the open walkway which runs round the temple honour a host of other deities. In the one dedicated to Goddess Periachi Amman, a sculpture portrays her with a queen lying on her lap, whose evil child she has ripped from her womb. Odd, then, that the Periachi Amman should be the protector of children, to whom one-month-old babies are brought. Sri Aravan, with his bushy moustache and big ears, is far less intimidating. His sanctum is at the back on the right-hand side of the complex.

To the left of the main sanctum there's a patch of sand which, once a year during the festival of **Thimithi** (see p.152), is covered in red-hot coals, across which male Hindus run to prove the strength of their faith. The participants, who line up all the way along South Bridge Road waiting their turn, are supposedly protected from the heat of the coals by the power of prayer, though the ambulance parked round the back of the temple suggests that some aren't praying quite hard enough.

Hanging a left out of the temple quickly brings you to the twin octagonal minarets of the **Jamae Mosque**, at 218 South Bridge Road. Established by southern Indian Muslims in 1826, the mosque has barely changed since its completion four years later.

The URA Gallery

A skip around the **URA Gallery** (Mon–Sat 9am–5pm; free; ☎63218321) at the URA Centre, set back from South Bridge Road at 45 Maxwell Road, offers a fascinating insight into the grand designs of Singapore's Urban Redevelopment Authority. Town planning may not sound the most inspiring premise for a gallery; but, then again, no other nation plans with such extravagant ambition as Singapore, whose land architects continue to remould their island like a ball of putty, erasing roads here and reclaiming land there. You need only consider the distance between downtown Beach Road and the shoreline it used to abut to appreciate the extent of change that Singapore has undergone up to now.

Interactive exhibits, touch-screen terminals and scale models trace Singapore's progress from sleepy backwater to modern metropolis and chart ongoing efforts to reshape and redefine specific regions of the island. The URA has rightly been criticized in the past for its disregard for Singapore's architectural heritage, so it is heartening to see displays making such reassuring noises about the future of the venerable shophouses and colonial villas that remain in such districts as Balestier Road, Tanjong Katong and Joo Chiat. But the gallery's emphasis is more upon the future than the past. A vast model of the downtown area of Singapore – which highlights districts currently under development and offers new arrivals to the island the chance to get their bearings – is best scrutinized through one of the telescopes set up on the floor above. Elsewhere on the upper floor, there is the chance to control a Skycam high above the city, try your hand at a little municipal planning and learn more about Singapore's state-of-the-art MRT system.

Tanjong Pagar

The district of **Tanjong Pagar** at the southern tip of South Bridge Road, between Neil and Keong Saik roads, has changed beyond recognition in recent years. Once a veritable sewer of brothels and opium dens, it was earmarked as a conservation area, following which more than two hundred shophouses were painstakingly restored, painted in sickly pastel hues and converted into bars, restaurants and shops. The emergence of other entertainment hubs such as Clarke Quay, Dempsey and CHIJMES has seen the area's star wane, though there are plans – as the URA Gallery will attest – to reinvent it.

Taking Chinese tea

If you're in need of a quick, thirst-quenching drink, avoid **Chinese teahouses**: the art of tea-making is heavily bound up with **ritual**, and unhurried preparation time is crucial to the production of a pleasing brew. What's more, when you do get a cup, it's barely more than a mouthful and then the whole process kicks off again.

Tea-drinking in China traces its origins back thousands of years. Legend has it that the first cuppa was drunk by Emperor Shen Nong, who was pleasantly surprised by the aroma produced by some dried tea leaves falling into the water he was boiling. He was even more pleased when he tasted the brew. By the eighth century, the art form was so complex that Chinese scholar Lu Yu produced a three-volume tome on the processes involved.

Teashops normally have conventional tables and chairs but the authentic experience involves kneeling at a much lower traditional table. The basic procedure is as follows: the server places a towel in front of himself and his guest, with the folded edge facing the guest, and stuffs leaves into the pot with a bamboo scoop. Water, boiled over a flame, has to reach an optimum temperature, depending on which type of tea is being made; experts can tell its heat by the size of the bubbles rising, which are described, rather confusingly, as "sand eyes", "prawn eyes" and "fish eyes". Once the pot has been warmed inside and out, the first pot of tea is made, transferred into the pouring jar and then poured back over the pot – the thinking being that over a period of time, the porous clay of the pot becomes infused with the fragrance of the tea. Once a second pot is ready, a draught is poured into the sniffing cup, from which the aroma of the brew is savoured. Only now is it time actually to drink the tea and, if you want a second cup, the whole procedure starts again.

While touring Tanjong Pagar, it's worth making time for a stop at one of the traditional **teahouses** along Neil Road. At *Tea Chapter*, no. 9a–11a (daily 11am–11pm), you can learn in detail about the intricacies of the Chinese tea ceremony and the various leaves' health benefits (see box above).

Baba House

Further down Neil Road towards Outram Park MRT is **Baba House** (℡ 62275731, 🄴 babahouse@nus.edu.sg; tours by appointment Tues & Thurs; $10), a restored Peranakan house that was built in the late nineteenth century for the wealthy family of shipping tycoon, Wee Bin. The house was opened by the National University of Singapore as the city's first heritage house in 2008, after lying empty since the 1970s. Its exterior is one of the loveliest in Singapore, with its vivid indigo colour and a pair of phoenix birds, intertwined with red peony flowers made from painted porcelain chips, above its entrance. At either side of the doorway are blocked up archways, which once would have allowed passage between the houses before the space between the houses and the road was increased.

The interior is impressively ornate, with intricately carved wooden furniture, gold painted buttresses, and mosaic tiling depicting auspicious Chinese symbols at the base of the walls. The **front hall** has two mirrors facing one other, a practice employed to confuse ugly evil spirits entering the house whom, upon seeing their own ghastly reflection, would flee the house in fear. The hall is dominated by an impressive family altar with its guardian deity Guan Gong, a Chinese emperor who lived almost two thousand years ago and later became a deity worshipped for his power to bestow sons upon a family. The following room is the **ancestral hall** where family photographs and officially commissioned portraits (believed to possess the powers of the person they represented and only displayed posthumously), line the walls. The **ancestral altar** at the far end of the hall is said to hold tablets representing the souls of deceased family members, while its exterior is delicately carved with depictions of the 24 paragons of filial piety. Look closely to see a young woman breastfeeding what is said to be her malnourished mother-in-law – a rather extreme example of just how far an individual could be expected to go in order to demonstrate loyalty and respect to their family.

Sago Street to Mosque Street

Today, the tight knot of streets west of South Bridge Road between Sago Street and Mosque Street is tour-bus Chinatown, heaving with tourists in search of tacky Chinese mementos. But in days gone by these streets formed Chinatown's nucleus, their shophouses harbouring opium dens and brothels, their streets teeming with trishaw drivers, peddlers and food hawkers. From the upper windows of tumble-down shophouses, wizened old men would stare out from behind wooden gates, flanked by songbird cages and laundry poles hung with washing.

Until as recently as the 1950s, **Sago Street** was home to several death houses – rudimentary hospices where skeletal citizens saw out their final hours on rattan camp beds. These houses were finally deemed indecent and have all now gone, replaced by restaurants, bakeries, medicine halls and shops stacked to the rafters with Chinese vases, teapots and jade. Sago, Smith, Temple and Pagoda streets only really recapture their youth around the time of Chinese New Year, when they're crammed to bursting with stalls selling festive branches of blossom, oranges, sausages and waxed chickens – which look as if they have melted to reveal a handful of bones inside.

Despite the hordes of tourists in the area, and the shops selling Singapore Airlines uniforms, presentation chopstick sets and silk hats with false pigtails, there are occasional glimpses of Chinatown's **old trades** and industries, such as Nam's Supplies at 22 Smith Street, which offers shirts, Rolex watches, Nokia mobile phones, money, laptops and passports – all made out of paper – which the Chinese burn to ensure their ancestors don't want for creature comforts in the next life. They even have "Otherworld Bank" credit cards, "Hell Airlines" air tickets and "Hell City" cigarettes. Nam Cheong and Co, off nearby Kreta Ayer Street, takes this industry to its logical conclusion, producing huge paper houses and near life-sized paper safes, servants and Mercedes for the self-respecting ghost about town; the shop is at 01-04 Block 334 Keong Saik Road, between Chinatown Complex and New Bridge Road.

The Chinatown Complex

The hideous concrete exterior of the **Chinatown Complex**, at the end of Sago Street, belies the charm of the teeming market it houses. Walk up the front steps, past the garlic, fruit and nut hawkers, and once you're inside, the market's many twists and turns reveal stalls selling silk, kimonos, rattan, leather, jade, tea, Buddhist paraphernalia and clothes. There are no fixed prices, so you'll need to haggle. Deep in the market's belly is shop 01-K3, selling Buddhist amulets; while the Capitol Plastics stall (01-16) specializes in **mahjong sets**. There's a food centre on the second floor, and the wet market within the complex gets pretty packed early in the morning, when locals come to buy fresh fish or meat. Here, abacuses are still used to tally bills and sugar canes lean like spears against the wall.

Buddha Tooth Relic Temple and Museum

Opposite the Chinatown Complex stands the monolithic **Buddha Tooth Relic Temple and Museum** (daily 7am–7pm; free; ☏62200220) one of the most lavish

▲ Buddhas lining the walls at the Buddha Tooth Relic Temple

temples in Singapore. The imposing structure has a lacquered finish in majestic shades of blood red and emerald green and comprises many tiers, each flourished with a dramatically upturned corner. These architectural references hark back to a style popular during the Tang Dynasty era, a period in Chinese history when Buddhism flourished.

The first hall is relatively small and features a multi-armed statue of Bodhisattva Avalokitesvara seated upon a lotus leaf throne and surrounded by the flickering flames of candles in brightly coloured glass jars. Here worshippers take it in turns to remove their shoes and kneel on small red cushions in reverence. The temple's most impressive aspect is the **One Hundred Dragons Hall**, situated directly behind the first hall. Its huge, high-ceilinged space is dominated by a gigantic seated Maitreya (the future Buddha), carved from 1000-year-old juniper timber from Taiwan. It's difficult not to be awestruck by the majesty of the beautiful statue, set against a backdrop of miniature Buddha-lined walls and the sound of chanting. The magnificent spectacle of the hall can also be absorbed from the viewing balcony on the mezzanine level, a particularly good point from which to watch the saffron robed monks conducting religious ceremonies.

The **teahouse** and **bookshop** on level 2 are the ideal spots for a breather before moving up to level 3, where you'll find the **Nagapuspa Buddhist Cultural Museum** (daily 8am–6pm; free). The collection of more than three hundred Buddhist artefacts and works of art from around Asia is definitely worth seeing. Finally, on level 4 is the **Sacred Buddha Tooth Relic Chamber** (daily 8am–6pm; free) where the golden relic stupa is the centre of focus in the resplendent room. Disappointingly, though, the tooth can only be viewed from the public viewing area, although a TV screen shows close-ups of the surprisingly crystal-like relic. A further flight of stairs leads up to a tranquil roof garden.

The Chinatown Heritage Centre

Many of Chinatown's links with its cultural and mercantile history have been erased, but at least the excellent **Chinatown Heritage Centre** (daily 9am–6.30pm;

$10/$6), a few streets north of the Buddha Tooth Relic Temple at 48 Pagoda Street, offers a window on the district's past. If you go to just one museum in Singapore, this should be it. Housed in three superbly restored shophouses, the centre is an invaluable social document, where the history, culture, pastimes and employments of Singapore's Chinese settlers spring vividly to life. The museum is crammed to bursting with displays, artefacts and information boards; but its masterstroke is to give voice to former local residents, whose first-hand accounts of Chinatown life, projected onto walls at every turn, form a unique oral history of the Chinese in Singapore.

A model junk, like those on which early immigrants ("singkehs") came in search of work, sets the scene at the start of the tour. Accounts on the wall tell the story of their perilous journeys across the South China Sea. Once ashore at Bullock Cart Water (the name they gave the area that would become Chinatown), settlers quickly formed clan associations, or less savoury secret societies, and looked for employment. As you move through the centre's narrow shophouse corridors, these associations and societies, and every other facet of Chinatown life, work and leisure, are made flesh. All the while, you progress to a soundtrack of crashing gongs and cymbals, age-old songs of mourning and Fifties' crooners on scratchy 78s.

The genius of the centre lies in its detail, from the mock-up of the shabby flour-ishes of a prostitute's boudoir, and the marble table of a traditional coffee shop, to the pictures and footage of thin and haunted addicts seeking escape from the pain of their backbreaking work through opium, their "devastating master". Look out for an example of an original hawker stall – a charcoal burner and a collection of ingredients yoked over the shoulders and carried from street to street, and a million miles away from the air-conditioned luxury of today's incarnations. The tour climaxes with a superb re-creation of the unbearable living quarters that settlers endured in the shophouses of Chinatown. Landlords were known to shoehorn as many as forty tenants into a single floor; their cramped cubicles, cooking and bathing facilities are reproduced in all their grisly squalor. The absence of the cooling effect of any air conditioning goes some way towards conveying the stifling heat that residents daily suffered.

Back on the ground floor is a tailor's shop, the mercantile element of the shophouse. Beside that, a traditional *kopitiam*, featuring old metal signs advertising Horlicks, Brylcreem, and huge biscuit boxes on the counter, is a good place to grab a coffee and reflect on what you've seen. There are sometimes walking tours of Chinatown based out of the centre; call ☏63252878 for more details.

New Bridge Road and Eu Tong Sen Street

Chinatown's main shopping drag comprises southbound **New Bridge Road** and northbound **Eu Tong Sen Street**, along which are found a handful of large malls. Try to pop into one of the *bak kwa* barbecue pork vendors around the intersection of Pagoda Street and New Bridge Road – the squares of red, fatty, delicious meat that they cook on wire meshes over fires produce an odour that is pure Chinatown. As you eat your *bak kwa*, check out two striking buildings across the road. Nearest is the flat-fronted **Majestic Opera House**, which no longer hosts performances but still has five images of Chinese opera stars over its doors. Just beside it, the Yue Hwa Chinese Products Emporium occupies the former **Great Southern Hotel**, which was built in 1927 by Eu Tong Sen, the son of Eu Yan Sang. In its fifth-floor nightclub, *Southern Cabaret*, wealthy locals would drink liquor, smoke opium and pay to dance with so-called local "taxi girls".

At the top of Eu Tong Sen Street is **Thong Chai Medical Institute**, which opened its doors in 1892 with the intention of dispensing free medical help regardless of race, colour or creed. Now listed as a national monument, the beautiful southern

Chinese-style building was used as the premises for the medical institute until 1976, when it moved to its current location on Chin Swee Road.

②

The Central Business District

Until an early exercise in land reclamation in the mid-1820s rendered the zone fit for building, the patch of land south of the river where Raffles Place now stands was a swampland. However, within just a few years, Commercial Square (later renamed Raffles Place) was the colony's busiest business address, with the banks, ship's chandlers and warehouses of a burgeoning trading port. The square now forms the nucleus of the **CENTRAL BUSINESS DISTRICT**, the commercial heart of the state and home to many of its banks and financial institutions. Cutting through the district is **Battery Road**, whose name recalls the days when Fort Fullerton (named after Robert Fullerton, first governor of the Straits Settlements) and its attendant battery of guns used to stand on the site of the Fullerton Building.

Raffles Place and the south riverbank

Raffles Place was Singapore's central shopping area until Orchard Road super-seded it in the late 1960s. Two department stores, Robinsons and John Little, dominated the area then, but subsequent development turned it into the epicentre of Singapore's financial district, ringed by buildings so tall that pedestrians crossing the square feel like ants in a canyon. The most striking way to experience the giddy heights of the Central Business District is by surfacing from Raffles Place MRT, following the signs for Raffles Place itself out of the station, and looking up to gleaming towers, blue skies and racing clouds. To your left is the soaring metallic triangle of the **OUB Centre** (Overseas Union Bank), and to its right, the rocket-shaped **UOB Plaza 2** (United Overseas Bank); in front of you are the rich brown walls of **6 Battery Road**, and to your right rise sturdy **Singapore Land Tower** and the almost Art Deco **Chevron House**. A smallish statue, entitled *Progress and Advancement*, stands at the northern end of Raffles Place. Erected in 1988, it's a miniature version of what was then the skyline of central Singapore. Inevitably, the very progress and advancement it celebrates has already rendered it out of date – not featured, for instance, is the **UOB Plaza**, a vast monolith of a building beside its twin, the UOB Plaza 2. The three roads that run southwest from Raffles Place – Cecil Street, Robinson Road and Shenton Way – are all chock-a-block with more high-rise banks and financial houses; to the west is Chinatown.

The Barings Bank scandal

Singapore hit the international headlines early in 1995, when the City of London's oldest merchant bank, **Barings**, collapsed as a result of massive unauthorized dealings in derivatives on the Japanese stock market. The culprit, Nick Leeson, was an Englishman dealing out of the bank's offices in the Central Business District of Singapore. Leeson had gambled huge funds in the hope of recouping losses made through ill-judged trading, only calling it a day when the bank's losses were approaching one billion pounds. He was eventually arrested and pleaded guilty to two charges of deceit, receiving a six-and-a-half-year sentence.

Boat Quay

Just north of Raffles Place, and beneath the "elephant's trunk" curve of the Singapore River, the pedestrianized row of shophouses known as **Boat Quay** is filled with bars and restaurants popular with both expats from the financial district looking to let their hair down after work and tourists looking for an easy bar crawl. Derelict until the early 1990s, it's currently one of Singapore's most fashionable hangouts sporting a huge collection of thriving restaurants and bars, and is an excellent spot for an alfresco meal or drink.

Around Raffles Place

Branching off the second floor of the Clifford Centre, on the eastern side of Raffles Place, is **Change Alley Aerial Plaza**. The original Change Alley was a cheap, bustling, street-level bazaar which redevelopment wiped off the face of Singapore; all that remains is a sanitized, modern-day version, housed on a covered footbridge across Collyer Quay. The tailors here have a persuasive line in patter – you'll have to be very determined not to waste half an hour being convinced that you need a new suit. But if you do want to have a suit made, there are better places to make for (see p.158).

Walking through Change Alley Aerial Plaza deposits you at **Clifford Pier**, once the departure point for trips on the Singapore River and to the southern islands, though these days the Marina Bay barrage has eliminated access to the sea from here. Now the Art Deco structure has been refurbished as yet another dining and shopping complex. Just north of Clifford Pier, **One Fullerton** is an entertainment venue constructed on land reclaimed from Marina Bay; its bars, restaurants and nightclub share peerless views out over the bay. Just above One Fullerton, a statue of Singapore's national symbol, the **Merlion**, guards the mouth of the Singapore River. Half-lion, half-fish, and wholly ugly, the creature reflects Singapore's name (*Singapura* means "Lion City" in Sanskrit) and its historical links with the sea.

Across the road stands the elegant **Fullerton Building**, fronted by sturdy pillars. Built in 1928 as the headquarters for the General Post Office – a role it fulfilled until the mid-1990s – this was, remarkably, once one of Singapore's tallest buildings. Old photographs of Singapore depict Japanese soldiers marching past the building after the surrender of the Allied forces during World War II. These days, the building is a luxury hotel (see p.115) and the lighthouse that used to flash up on the roof is a swanky restaurant.

Back at Clifford Pier, it's a short walk south along Raffles Quay to **Lau Pa Sat Festival Market**. Built in 1884 on land reclaimed from the sea, its octagonal cast-iron frame houses Singapore's most tasteful food centre (daily 24hr), which offers a range of Southeast Asian cuisine, as well as laying on free entertainment such as local bands and Chinese opera. After 7pm, the portion of adjacent Boon Tat Street between Robinson Road and Shenton Way is closed to traffic, and traditional satay stalls and other hawker stalls take over the street.

Bras Basah, Little India and the Arab Quarter

ead a little way north of the Colonial District and you arrive at Singapore's most atmospheric old districts: if you have time for little else on your stay, this is where to come. **Little India**, centred on Serangoon Road, has retained far more cultural integrity than Chinatown: here Indian pop music blares from shops, the air is perfumed with incense, spices and jasmine garlands, Hindu women promenade in bright saris, a wealth of restaurants serve up superior curries and there are a couple of busy temples to visit, too. No more than a ten-minute stroll east is the **Arab Quarter**, dominated by the domes of the Sultan Mosque and truly one of the island's most relaxed and appealing little enclaves, with interesting craft shops and plenty of inexpensive eating places to spend an evening in.

Walking to either of these areas from the Colonial District means heading northeast across **Bras Basah Road**. The **Singapore Art Museum** aside, the surrounding area seems an uninteresting jumble of commercial towers at first, but look closer and you'll discover that a fair number of old buildings have survived, including a sprinkling of churches, temples and shophouses.

Bras Basah Road to Rochor Road

The name of **Bras Basah Road** – the main thoroughfare between Orchard Road and Marina Centre – literally means something like "wet rice" in Malay, apparently because once upon a time rice arriving on cargo boats was brought here to be dried by a creek. The zone between Bras Basah Road and **Rochor Road** at the edge of Little India has a transitional sort of feel, sitting as it does between the Colonial District and what were intended to be "ethnic" enclaves to the northeast. In recent times city planners have transformed the area into a nexus for the arts, with many distinguished old properties on and around Waterloo Street being turned over to arts organizations, including the **Singapore Art Museum**. The country's leading institutes in the field have also been lured here, among them the **Nanyang Academy of Fine Arts** (NAFA) on Bencoolen Street; the **Lasalle College of the Arts**, whose futuristic glass buildings under a translucent canopy between McNally Street and Albert Street deserve a visit; and the **School of the Arts**, in a grand building next to the Cathay cinema.

CHIJMES

On Bras Basah Road right next door to the gargantuan Raffles City development is one of Singapore's most aesthetically pleasing eating venues, **CHIJMES** (pronounced "chimes"), a complex of restaurants, bars and shops in the neo-Gothic husk of the former Convent of the Holy Infant Jesus – from which the complex's acronym is partly derived. Its lawns, courtyards, waterfalls, fountains and sunken forecourt give a sense of spatial dynamics that is rare indeed in Singapore, though some locals see it as rather crass that planners allowed this, one of several historic schools in the area, to assume its present role; if the idea of Bras Basah as an arts district had emerged earlier, things might have been very different for CHIJMES. A relic from CHIJMES' convent days survives on its Victoria Street flank, where local families left unwanted babies at the **Gate of Hope** to be taken in by the convent.

Singapore Art Museum

The **Singapore Art Museum** at 71 Bras Basah Road (daily 10am–7pm, Fri till 9pm; $10, free Fri 6–9pm; guided tours Mon 2pm, Tues–Thurs 11am & 2pm, Fri 11am, 2pm & 7pm, Sat & Sun 11am, 2pm & 3.30pm; ☏63323222) has a peerless location in the venerable St Joseph's Institution, Singapore's first Catholic school, whose silvery dome rang to the sounds of school bells until 1987. Though extensions have been necessary, many of the original rooms survive, among them the school chapel. There's also an annexe, **8Q**, housing more art in another former Catholic school round the corner at 8 Queen Street. The museum showcases a certain amount of international work, including occasional visiting exhibitions featuring artists of world renown, but much greater emphasis is placed on a diverse and challenging range of contemporary local art.

Waterloo Street

Head up Waterloo Street from the Art Museum and almost immediately you encounter one of the area's many places of worship, the peach-coloured **Maghain Aboth Synagogue**, looking for all the world like a colonial mansion except for the Stars of David on the facade. The surrounding area was once something of a Jewish enclave – you'll see another building prominently bearing the Star of David midway along nearby Selegie Road – though the Jewish community, largely of Middle Eastern origin, never numbered more than about a thousand. The synagogue, which dates from the 1870s, can be visited, though this must be arranged in advance by calling ☏63372189. Opposite is the blue-and-white **Church of Sts Peter and Paul**, built around the same time and likewise dwarfed by the hypermodern National Library tower a couple of blocks beyond.

A couple of minutes' walk on, at the intersection with Middle Road, is a tiny orange-painted building bearing a striking resemblance to a church, which is no surprise given that it was erected in the 1870s as the Christian Institute. Soon after it became the focal point of Singapore's Methodist missionaries before becoming a Malay-language church, serving the Peranakan community, in 1894. Today it is

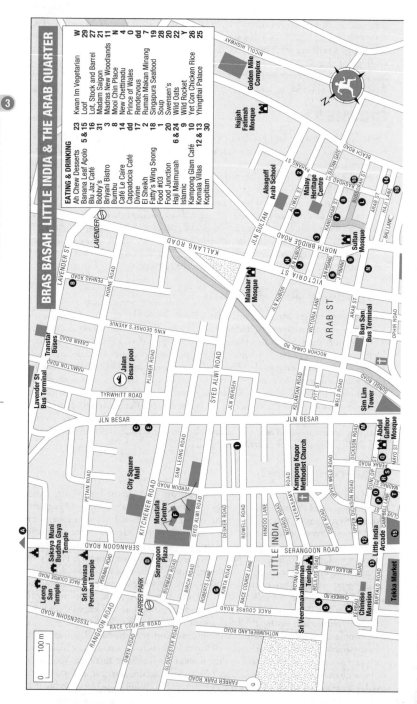

BRAS BASAH, LITTLE INDIA & THE ARAB QUARTER

EATING & DRINKING		Kwan Im Vegetarian	W
Ah Chew Desserts	23	Loof	29
Banana Leaf Apolo	5 & 15	Lot, Stock and Barrel	27
Blu Jaz Café	16	Madam Saigon	21
Bobby's	31	Madras New Woodlands	11
Briyani Bistro	3	Mooi Chin Place	N
Bumbu	8	New Chettinadu	4
Café Le Caire	14	Prince of Wales	0
Cappadocia Café	dd	Rendezvous	dd
Divine	17	Rumah Makan Minang	7
El Sheikh	2	Singapura Seafood	19
Fatty's Wing Seong	18	Soup	28
Food #03	1	Swensen's	20
Food Junction	20	Wild Oats	22
Haji Maimunah	6 & 24	Wild Rocket	Y
Islamic	9	Yet Con Chicken Rice	26
Kampong Glam Café	10	Yhingthai Palace	25
Komala Villas	12 & 13		
Kopitiam	30		

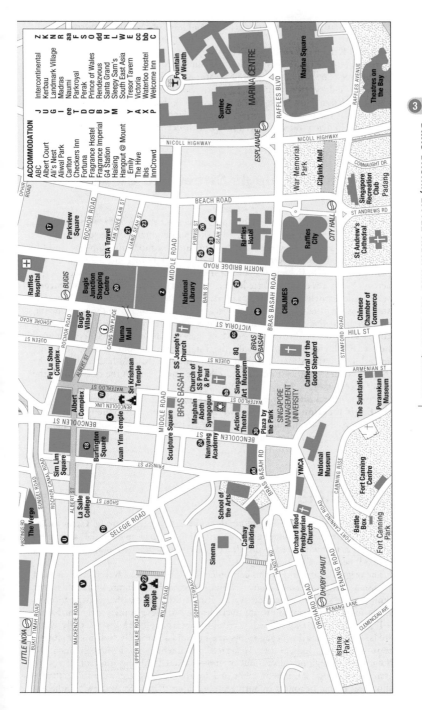

ACCOMMODATION

ABC	Z	Intercontinental	J
Albert Court	K	Kerbau	U
Ali's Nest	N	Landmark Village	G
Aliwal Park	R	Madras	I
Carlton	aa	Naumi	ee
Checkers Inn	F	Parkroyal	T
Fortuna	S	Perak	D
Fragrance Hostel	O	Prince of Wales	Q
Fragrance Imperial	dd	Rendezvous	B
G4 Station	H	Santa Grand	V
Haising	L	Sleepy Sam's	M
Hangout @ Mount	W	South East Asia	Y
Emily	E	Tresor Tavern	A
The Hive	cc	Victoria	X
Ibis	bb	Waterloo Hostel	P
InnCrowd	C	Welcome Inn	

known as **Sculpture Square**, its grounds and interior featuring modernist works by local artists.

The **Sri Krishnan Temple**, across the way, began life in 1870, when it amounted to nothing more than a thatched hut containing a statue of Lord Krishna under a banyan tree. The present-day temple is a fine example of Southeast Asian religious harmony and syncretism in action, with worshippers from the neighbouring Buddhist **Kuan Yim Temple** often to be seen praying outside. This temple, named after the goddess of mercy, is one of Singapore's most popular, and you may well find it positively overflowing with devotees during festivals. As you might anticipate, fortune-tellers, religious artefact shops and other traders operate in a little swarm just outside.

Albert Street, Bugis Street and Bugis Junction

Intersecting Waterloo Street just before it meets Rochor Road is **Albert Street**, which half a century ago was lined with shophouses offering some of Singapore's finest street eating. Now the street is dominated by modern complexes and has been so remodelled it doesn't even appear in its entirety on some maps, though its past is hinted at in the few restaurants trading at ground level. Follow the street across Queen Street to the once legendary **Bugis** (pronounced "boogis") **Street**, which once crawled with rowdy sailors, prostitutes and ladyboys by night. The street was eventually cleared, partly because it was anathema to the government, and partly so that the Bugis MRT station could be built. In its place today is **Bugis Village**, a claustrophobic bunch of market stalls and snack sellers crammed into two alleyways. While hardly the Bugis Street of old, it does recapture something of the bazaar feel some Singapore markets once had, and amid the T-shirt vendors is at least one outlet selling sex aids – about the only link to the street's seedy past.

Across Victoria Street from here, the past survives, in a manner of speaking, at the **Bugis Junction** development, where whole streets of shophouses have been gutted, scrubbed clean and encased under glass roofs as part of a modern shopping mall and hotel, the *Intercontinental*.

Little India

Of all the old districts of Singapore, the most charismatic has to be **Little India**. Though the remaining shophouses are fast being touched up from the same pastel paintbox as that which restored Chinatown to its present cuteness, the results seem to work better in an Indian context.

The original occupants of this convenient downtown niche were Europeans and Eurasians who established country houses here, and for whom a racecourse was built (on the site of modern-day Farrer Park) in the 1840s. Many of the roads in Little India started out as private tracks leading to these houses, and their names – Dunlop, Cuff, Desker, Norris – recall these early colonial settlers. Only when Indian-run **brick kilns** began to operate here did a markedly Indian community start to evolve. Indians have featured prominently in the development of Singapore, though not always out of choice: from 1825 onwards, convicts were transported from the subcontinent and by the 1840s there were more than a thousand Indian prisoners labouring on buildings such as St Andrew's Cathedral and the Istana. Today, migrant Tamil and Bengali men labour to build the island's MRT stations, shopping malls and villas, and on weekends they descend on Little India in their thousands, making the place look like downtown Chennai or Calcutta after a major cricket match.

The district's backbone is **Serangoon Road**, dating from 1822 and hence one of the island's oldest roadways. Its southwestern end is a kaleidoscopic whirl of Indian life, packed with restaurants and shops selling everything from nose studs and ankle bracelets to incense sticks and kumkum powder (used to make the red dot Hindus wear on their foreheads). Here you might even spot a parrot-wielding **fortune-teller** – you tell the man your name, he passes your name onto his feathered partner, and the bird then picks out a card with your fortune on it. To the southeast, stretching as far as Jalan Besar, is a tight knot of roads that's good for exploration. Parallel to Serangoon Road is **Race Course Road**, at whose far end are a couple of noteworthy temples.

Tekka Market

At the southwestern end of Serangoon Road, **Tekka Market** is a must-see, combining many of Little India's commercial elements under one roof. It's best to arrive in the morning when the wet market – as Singaporeans term a traditional market where the floor is periodically cleaned by hosing it down – is at its busiest. More sanitary than it once was thanks to recent renovations, the market is nevertheless hardly sanitized – halal butchers push around trolleys piled high with goats' heads, while at seafood stalls live crabs, their claws tied together, shuffle in buckets. Look out also for a couple of stalls selling nothing but banana leaves, used to serve up delicious curry meals all over Singapore but especially in Little India. The cooked food at the **hawker centre** here is excellent, and though the same can't be said of the mundane outlets upstairs selling Indian fabrics and household items, there are great views over the wet market to be had from here.

▲ Fishmongers at Tekka Market

Buffalo and Kerbau roads

A number of **cattle** and **buffalo yards** opened in the area in the latter half of the nineteenth century, and street names hark back to this trade: side by side are Buffalo Road, on the northern side of Tekka Market, and Kerbau ("buffalo" in Malay, confusingly) Road, along both of which cattle were kept in slaughter pens. Singapore's largest maternity hospital, nearby on Bukit Timah Road, is called Kandang Kerbau ("buffalo pen").

Buffalo Road has a cluster of provisions stores with Ayurvedic medicines, incense sticks, sacks of spices and fresh coconut, ground using primitive machines. **Kerbau Road** is noteworthy for its meticulously renovated shophouses and for being, like Waterloo Street 1km to the south, a designated "arts belt", home to theatre companies and other creative organizations. Curiously, the road has been split into two, with a pedestrianized bit of greenery in the middle. Here, at no. 37, you can't miss the gaudily restored **Chinese mansion**, built by one Tan Teng Niah, a confectionery magnate, in 1900 and now housing several businesses. Look out also for the traditional Indian picture framer's shop at no. 29, packed with images of Hindu deities. A right turn from Kerbau Road takes you onto Race Course Road, where there are more restaurants serving fine north and south Indian food.

Little India Arcade and around

Across from Tekka Market on the other side of Serangoon Road, the restored block of shophouses comprising **Little India Arcade** is a sort of Little India in microcosm: behind its pastel-coloured walls and green shutters you can purchase textiles and tapestries, bangles, religious statuary, Indian sweets, tapes and CDs, and even traditional medicines.

The roads nearby are also worth exploring. Exiting the arcade onto Campbell Lane leaves you opposite the riot of colours of **Jothi flower shop** where staff thread jasmine, roses and marigolds into garlands, or *jothi*, for prayer offerings. The next street along, Dunlop Street, has become something of a backpacker enclave in the past few years, but it remains defined by beautiful **Abdul Gaffoor Mosque**

▲ Abdul Gaffoor Mosque

Deepavali

Never dull, Little India springs even more gloriously to life over the colourful Hindu festival of **Deepavali** (or Diwali), which falls in October or November. Local Hindus mark the festival by lighting oil lamps (*diyas*) or candles in their homes. And no wonder – this is, after all, the Festival of Lights. The festival marks Lord Krishna's slaying of the demon Narakasura, who ruled the kingdom of Pradyoshapuram by terror, torturing his subjects, and kidnapping the women and imprisoning them in his palace. Lord Krishna destroyed the demon, and Hindus across the world have given praise ever since. More universally, the festival celebrates the triumph of light over darkness, and of good over evil.

For Hindus, Deepavali is a period of great excitement, a time to dress up in colourful new clothes, deck their houses out in colourful decorations, prepare festive delicacies, exchange cards and gifts, and pay respects to their elders. On the morning of the festival itself, worshippers bathe themselves in oil, then proceed to the temple to thank the gods for the happiness, knowledge, peace and prosperity they have enjoyed in the year past, and to pray for more of the same in the coming year.

If you visit Little India in the run-up to Deepavali, you may find special **markets** selling decorations, confectionery, garlands and clothes around the Little India Arcade and also in the open area beyond the Angullia Mosque (opposite Syed Alwi Road).

(at no. 41; daily 8.30am–noon & 2.30–4pm), whose green dome and bristling minarets have enjoyed a comprehensive and sympathetic renovation. Set amid gardens of palms and bougainvillea and within cream walls decorated with stars and crescent moons, the mosque features an unusual sundial whose face is ringed by elaborate Arabic script denoting the names of 25 Islamic prophets. The renovated shophouses to the left of the mosque as you enter the grounds have been converted into a madrasah, or Islamic school.

One more street along are Dickson Road and, back towards Serangoon Road, **Upper Dickson Road**, where an unexpectedly swish little shop and café at no. 15 sells pricey *kulfi* (Indian ice cream). Next along is **Cuff Road**, home to a tiny, primitive spice grinder's shop at no. 2, open mainly at weekends. At the eastern end of Cuff Road, the simple white **Kampong Kapor Methodist Church** is just one of many fine but unsung examples of Art Deco that you'll see in downtown Singapore. Dwarfed by nearby tower blocks, it grew out of the Waterloo Street church that is now Sculpture Square (see p.70).

The Sri Veeramakaliamman Temple

The most prominent shrine on Serangoon Road, the **Sri Veeramakaliamman Temple** is opposite Veerasamy Road and features a fanciful *gopuram* that's flanked by lions on the temple walls. Worshippers ring the bells hanging on the temple doors as they enter, in the hope that their prayers may be answered. The *mandapam*, or worship hall, holds an image of the Hindu goddess Kali, to whom the temple is dedicated, depicted holding a club. Flanking her are her sons, Ganesh (left) and Murugan.

The Mustafa Centre and around

Syed Alwi Road, a couple of minutes' walk up Serangoon Road from the temple, is notable for being the hub of the shopping phenomenon that is the **Mustafa Centre** (just "Mustafa" to locals), an agglomeration of department store, money-changer, travel agent, jeweller, fast-food joint and supermarket, much of the place open 24/7. The business started modestly and somehow knew no bounds, growing into the behemoth that occupies two adjacent buildings of its own as well as part of the Serangoon Plaza on the main drag. You'll probably find a visit here much more appealing than Orchard Road, as you rub shoulders with Indian families salivating over confectionery from Delhi, Chinese and Malays seeking pots and pans or luggage, even Africans buying consumer goods that are hard to find back home.

Just before you reach Mustafa are a couple of streets that have long been synonymous in Singapore with vice. It might seem odd to spend any time at all here, but there's something about the openness of goings-on on **Rowell and Desker roads** that's almost radical on this straitlaced island. Between the two roads, running along the backs of the shophouses, is an alleyway whose doorways are illuminated at night. Here gaggles of bored-looking prostitutes sit watching TV, apparently oblivious to the men gathered outsidewho seem more inclined to observe than gawp, as though the whole thing is some kind of street entertainment.

Running along the back of the Mustafa Centre is **Sam Leong Road**, worth a detour for its attractive **Peranakan shophouses**, their facades decorated with depictions of stags, lotuses and egrets.

North of Rangoon and Kitchener roads

Rangoon and Kitchener roads more or less mark the northern boundary of Little India proper, but it's worth venturing beyond to discover a couple of temples and yet more restored **Peranakan shophouses** on **Petain Road**, which are covered with elegant ceramic tiles reminiscent of Portuguese *azulejos*. There's more Peranakan architecture on display on Jalan Besar – turn right at the end of Petain Road.

The Sri Srinivasa Perumal Temple

Back on Serangoon Road, opposite the start of Petain Road, is the **Sri Srinivasa Perumal Temple**, dedicated to Lord Perumal (Vishnu), the Preserver of the Universe. Besides a five-tiered *gopuram*, it features a sculpted elephant, leg caught

▲ Sri Srinivasa Perumal Temple

in a crocodile's mouth, on the wall to the right of the front gate. But the temple's main claim to fame is that it is the starting point for the gruesome melee of activity at Thaipusam (see p.150), when Hindu devotees don huge metal frames (*kavadis*) which are fastened to their flesh with hooks and prongs. The devotees then leave the temple, stopping only while a coconut is smashed at their feet for good luck, and parade all the way to the Chettiar Temple on Tank Road (see p.49).

The Sakaya Muni Buddha Gaya Temple

Just beyond the Sri Srinivasa temple, a small path leads northwest to Race Course Road, where the **Sakaya Muni Buddha Gaya Temple** (or Temple of the Thousand Lights; daily 8am–4.45pm) is a slightly kitsch affair that betrays a strong Thai influence – not surprising, since it was built by a Thai monk. On the left of the temple as you enter is a huge Buddha's footprint, inlaid with mother-of-pearl, and beyond it a 15-metre-high Buddha ringed by the thousand electric lights from which the temple takes its alternative name. Twenty-five scenes from the Buddha's life decorate the pedestal on which he sits. It is possible to walk inside the statue, through a door in its back; inside is a smaller Buddha, this time reclining. The left wall of the temple features a sort of wheel of fortune – to discover your fate, spin it (for a small donation) and take the numbered sheet of paper that corresponds to the number at which the wheel stops.

The Arab Quarter

Before the arrival of Raffles, the area of Singapore west of the Rochor River housed a Malay village known as **Kampong Glam**, possibly after the name of a type of tree that used to grow here, though it is also said that a group of sea gypsies once resident here gave their name to the area. After signing a dubious treaty with the newly installed "Sultan" Hussein Mohammed Shah, Raffles allotted the area to the sultan and designated the land around it as a Muslim settlement. Soon the zone was attracting Malays, Sumatrans and Javanese, as well as traders from what is now eastern Yemen, as the road names in today's **ARAB QUARTER** – Arab Street, Bali Lane and so on – suggest. Today, Singapore's Arab community, descended from those Yemeni traders, is thought to number around fifteen thousand, though, having intermarried with the rest of Singapore society and being resident in no particular area, they are not distinctive by appearance or locale.

Like Little India, the area remains one of the most atmospheric pockets of old Singapore, despite the fact that its Islamic character has been diluted over the years as gentrification has started to take hold. Now it's the schizophrenia of the place that appeals: rubbing shoulders with the **Sultan Mosque**, traditional fabric stores and old-style curry houses are brash Middle Eastern restaurants and a peppering of alternative boutiques and shops selling crafts and curios.

Arab Street, Haji Lane and Bali Lane

While Little India is memorable for its fragrances, it's the vibrant colours of the shops of **Arab Street** and its environs that stick in the memory. Textile stores and outlets selling Persian carpets are the most prominent, but you'll also see leather and jewellery for sale. Most of the shops have been modernized, though one or two (such as Bamadhaj Brothers at no. 97 and Aik Bee at no. 69) still retain their original dark-wood and glass cabinets, and wide wooden benches where the shopkeepers sit. There's also a good range of basketware and rattanwork – fans, hats and walking sticks at Rishi Handicrafts, at no. 58. It's easy to spend a couple of hours weaving in and out of the stores, but don't expect a quiet window-shopping session – some traders are old hands are drawing you into conversation and before you know it, you'll be loaded up with sarongs, baskets and leather bags.

South of Arab Street, **Haji Lane** and tiny **Bali Lane** – which peters out into the wide walkway next to Ophir Road – have both smartened up a fair bit of late. Their shophouses are now home to many a trendy boutique and, on Bali Lane, the excellent *Blu Jaz Café* (see p.136).

Sultan Mosque

Pause at the Baghdad Street end of pedestrianized Bussorah Street for a good view of the golden onion domes of the **Sultan Mosque** or Masjid Sultan (Mon–Sat 9am–4pm outside prayer times, Fri closed 11.30am–2pm), the beating heart of the Muslim faith in Singapore. An earlier mosque stood on this site, finished in 1825 and constructed with the help of a $3000 donation from the East India Company. The present building was completed a century later to a design by colonial architects Swan and MacLaren. Look carefully at the base of the main dome and you'll see a dark band that's actually made of the bottoms of thousands of glass bottles, an incongruity which sets the tone for the rest of the building. Steps at the top of Bussorah Street lead past palm trees into a wide lobby, where a digital display lists prayer times. Beyond and out of bounds to non-Muslims is the main prayer hall, a large, bare chamber fronted by two more digital clocks.

During the Muslim fasting month of Ramadan, neighbouring **Kandahar Street** is awash with stalls from mid-afternoon onwards, selling *biriyani*, *murtabak*, dates and cakes. Relaxed **Bussorah Street** itself has some excellent souvenir and craft outlets.

Istana Kampong Glam and Gedung Kuning

Squatting between Kandahar and Aliwal streets, the colonially styled **Istana Kampong Glam** was built as the royal palace of Sultan Ali Iskandar Shah, son of Sultan Hussein who negotiated with Raffles to hand over Singapore to the British. Until just a few years ago the house was still home to the sultan's descendants, though it had fallen into disrepair. Then the government acquired it and the similar but smaller dark yellow house in the same grounds. The istana is now the over-smart **Malay Heritage Centre** (Mon 1–6pm, Tues–Sun 10am–6pm; $4; T63910450), a mixed bag of history and culture spanning maps, model boats, cannons, ceremonial drums and daggers from around the Malay archipelago. The most engaging exhibits are upstairs, where touch screens cast light on Malay community life in the prewar years, and you can peek inside a mock-up of a village house – a worthy idea, as not a single Malay village survives on the main island of Singapore. The centre also has its own **art workshops** where pottery, batik design and the like are taught by leading local practitioners; you can pop in for a look if they're not busy. As for the yellow house, **Gedung Kuning**, it used to belong to the descendants of a wealthy merchant but is now home to an upmarket Malay restaurant, *Tepak Sireh*.

North of Sultan Mosque

The Arab Quarter's most evocative patch is the stretch of **North Bridge Road** between Arab Street and Jalan Sultan. The shops and restaurants here are geared more towards locals than tourists: Kazura Aromatics, at 705 North Bridge Road, for instance, sells alcohol-free perfumes, while neighbouring shops stock rosaries, prayer mats and the *songkok* hats worn by Muslim males in mosques, and *miswak* sticks – twigs the width of a finger used by some locals to clean their teeth.

Several roads run off the western side of North Bridge Road, including Jalan Kubor (Grave Street) which, across Victoria Street, takes you to an unkempt Muslim **cemetery** where, it is said, Malay royalty are buried. Turn right here up Kallang Road to reach Jalan Sultan and the blue **Malabar Mosque**, built for Muslims from the south Indian state of Kerala. Its traditional styling, with more golden domes, belies its age – the mosque was completed in the early 1960s.

Along Beach Road

At the southern boundary of the Arab Quarter, **Beach Road** still has shops that betray its former proximity to the sea – ships' chandlers and fishing tackle specialists. It's also home to the **Hajjah Fatimah Mosque**, named after a wealthy businesswoman from Malacca who amassed a fortune through her mercantile vessels, and whose family home formerly stood here. After two break-ins and an arson attack on her home, Hajjah Fatimah decided to move elsewhere, then underwrote the construction of a mosque on the site. The minaret, looking strangely like a steeple (perhaps because its architect was European) has a six-degree tilt – locals call it Singapore's Leaning Tower of Pisa. Across from the mosque, the Golden Mile Complex is a major social focus for Singapore's Thai community – bus firms selling tickets to Thailand operate out of here, while inside, outlets sell Thai food and cafés serve Singha beer.

It's worth heading southwest down Beach Road to see the two logic-defying office buildings that together comprise **The Gateway**. Designed by I.M. Pei (who also designed the *Swissôtel* complex, see p.44), they rise magnificently into the air like vast razor blades and appear two-dimensional when viewed from certain angles. When **Parkview Square**, the huge, Gotham-esque building across Beach Road was built, much care was taken to site it dead between the Gateway's sharp points for feng shui considerations.

Orchard Road

I t would be hard to conjure an image more opposed to the reality of modern-day **ORCHARD ROAD** than C.M. Turnbull's description of it during early colonial times as "a country lane lined with bamboo hedges and shrubbery, with trees meeting overhead for its whole length". One hundred years ago, a stroll down Orchard Road would have passed row upon row of nutmeg trees and would have been enjoyed in the company of strolling merchants taking their daily constitutionals, followed at a discreet distance by their trusty manservants. Today, Orchard Road is synonymous with **shopping** – indeed, tourist brochures refer to it as the "Fifth Avenue, the Regent Street, the Champs Elysées, the Via Veneto and the Ginza of Singapore". Huge malls selling everything you can imagine line the road, but don't expect shopping to be relaxing as hordes of dawdling Singaporeans and tourists make browsing difficult. The road runs northwest from Fort Canning Hill and is served by three MRT stations: Orchard, Somerset and Dhoby Ghaut, of which Orchard is the most convenient for shopping expeditions.

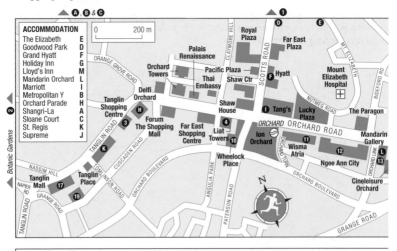

ACCOMMODATION	
The Elizabeth	E
Goodwood Park	D
Grand Hyatt	F
Holiday Inn	G
Lloyd's Inn	M
Mandarin Orchard	L
Marriott	I
Metropolitan Y	B
Orchard Parade	H
Shangri-La	A
Sloane Court	C
St. Regis	K
Supreme	J

EATING, DRINKING & NIGHTLIFE							
Alley Bar	8	Blu	A	Crystal Jade	12	Hacienda	2	Jim Thompson	2
Astor Bar	K	Brix	F	De Sté	15	Halia	2	KPO	14
Bar Stop	20	Café l'Espresso	D	The Dubliner	18	Ice Cold Beer	5	Lao Beijing	7
Bedrock Bar & Grill	16	Chili's Grill & Bar	17	Food Republic	11 & 15	Iggy's	19	Lawry's The
						Ippudo	13	Prime Rib	13

Mindful that several of its older shopping centres were looking a little on the shabby side, the Singapore government recently pumped $40m into redeveloping parts of the stretch. Several new shopping centres, including **ION Orchard** with its huge multi-sensory canvas that dominates the wall above its main entrance, have also been built in recent years. **Orchard Central**, **313@Somerset** and the upmarket **Mandarin Gallery** housed inside the *Mandarin Orchard hotel*, are further additions to what has become an over-saturated shopping scene.

Orchard Road does have one or two other diversions if you get tired of staring at CDs, watches and clothes. Near its eastern extent, the president of Singapore's abode – the **Istana Negara Singapura** – is open to the public a few times a year. And, way up beyond the westernmost point of the road, the **Singapore Botanic Gardens** make for a relaxing stroll in beautiful surroundings. On the whole, though, people really only come to Orchard Road in the daytime to shop and at night for a whole host of bars (see p.154 & p.142 for details).

Dhoby Ghaut to Emerald Hill

In the **Dhoby Ghaut** area, at the eastern tip of Orchard Road, Indian *dhobies*, or laundrymen, used to wash clothes in the Stamford Canal, which once ran along Orchard and Stamford roads. Three minutes' walk west along Orchard Road from Dhoby Ghaut MRT takes you past Plaza Singapura, beyond which stern-looking soldiers guard the gate of the **Istana Negara Singapura**. Built in 1869, the istana, with its ornate cornices, elegant louvred shutters and high mansard roof, was originally the official residence of Singapore's British governors, though on independence it became the residence of the president of Singapore – currently S.R. Nathan, whose portrait you'll see in banks, post offices and shops across the state. The shuttered palace is only open to visitors five times a year, on Chinese New Year, Deepavali, Hari Raya Puasa, Labour Day and National Day ($1); on

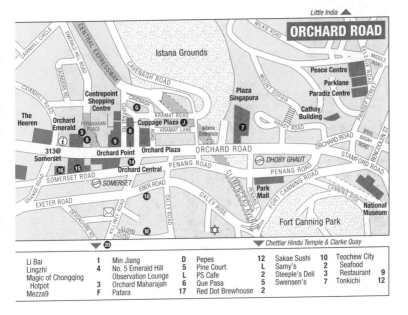

Li Bai	1	Min Jiang	D	Pepes	12	Sakae Sushi	10	Teochew City	
Lingzhi	4	No. 5 Emerald Hill	5	Pine Court	L	Samy's	2	Seafood	
Magic of Chongqing		Observation Lounge	L	PS Cafe	2	Steeple's Deli	3	Restaurant	9
Hotpot	3	Orchard Maharajah	6	Que Pasa	5	Swensen's	7	Tonkichi	12
Mezza9	F	Patara	17	Red Dot Brewhouse	2				

these days the president goes walkabout as thousands of Singaporeans flock to picnic on the well-landscaped lawns, and local brass bands belt out jaunty tunes. The changing of the guard ceremony at the istana takes place at 6pm on the first Sunday of the month.

The **Tan Yeok Nee Mansion**, across Orchard Road from the Istana Negara Singapura at 207 Clemenceau Avenue, is now home to the Chicago Graduate School of Business. Built in traditional South Chinese style for a wealthy Teochew

▲ Emerald Hill

pepper and gambier (a resin used in tanning) merchant, and featuring ornate roofs and massive granite pillars, the mid-1880s mansion served as headquarters to the Singapore Salvation Army from 1940 until 1991.

Further west, in the **Emerald Hill** area, most of Cuppage Road has been pedestrianized, making it a great place to sit out and have a beer or a meal. **Cuppage Terrace**, halfway along Cuppage Road is an unusually (for Orchard Road) old row of shophouses, where a successful restaurant and bar scene has developed. A number of even more architecturally notable houses have also survived the developers' bulldozers in Emerald Hill Road, parallel to Cuppage Road. Emerald Hill was granted to Englishman William Cuppage in 1845 and for some years afterwards was the site of a large nutmeg plantation. After Cuppage's death in 1872, the land was subdivided and sold off, much of it bought by members of the **Peranakan** community, which evolved in Malaya as a result of the intermarriage between early Chinese settlers and Malay women. A walk up Emerald Hill Road takes you past a number of exquisitely crafted houses dating from this period, built in a decorative architectural style known as Chinese Baroque, typified by brightly coloured ceramic tiles, carved swing doors, shuttered windows and pastel-shaded walls with fine plaster mouldings.

West to the Botanic Gardens and Dempsey

West of Emerald Hill Road, the shopping centres of Orchard Road come thick and fast. A couple of minutes north of Orchard Road along Scotts Road, the impressive **Goodwood Park Hotel** started life in 1900 as the *Teutonia Club* for German expats. With the start of war across Europe in 1914, the club was commandeered by the British Custodian of Enemy Property, and it didn't open again until 1918, after which it served for several years as a function hall. In 1929, it became a hotel, though by 1942 the *Goodwood* – like *Raffles* – was lodging Japanese officers. Fittingly, after the war the hotel was chosen as one of the venues for a war crimes court.

After a few hours' shopping you'll be glad of the open space afforded by the **Singapore Botanic Gardens** (daily 5am–midnight), a ten-minute walk beyond the western end of Orchard Road on Cluny Road. Founded in 1859, it was here, in 1877, that the Brazilian seeds from which grew the great **rubber plantations** of Malaysia were first nurtured. No one had taken much notice of them by the time Henry Ridley was named director of the Botanic Gardens the following year, but he recognized their financial potential and spent the next twenty years of his life persuading Malayan plantation-owners to convert to this new crop, an occupation which earned him the nickname "Mad" Ridley. The fifty-odd hectares of land feature a mini-jungle rose garden, topiary, fernery, palm valley and lakes that are home to turtles and swans. At dawn and dusk, joggers and students of t'ai chi haunt the lawns and paths of the gardens, while at the weekend, newlyweds bundle down from church for their photos to be taken – a ritual recalled in Lee Tzu Pheng's poem *Bridal Party at the Botanics*, whose bride's "two hundred dollar face/is melting in the sun", while beside her is her groom, "black-stuffed, oil-slicked, fainting/in his finery, by the shrubbery".

The serene and rather gorgeous **National Orchid Garden** (daily 8.30am–7pm; $5, children under 12 free) holds one thousand species and two thousand hybrids. A particular highlight is the **Celebrity Orchid Garden**, a section that contains hybrid orchids named after celebrities like Margaret Thatcher, Jackie Chan and Lady Diana. In the shop you can buy unusual orchid jewellery, made by plating real flowers with gold – pieces start from around $35. Other highlights include the **Jacob Ballas Children's Garden** (Tues–Sun 8am–7pm) which includes a café, water fountains to splash around in, and various interactive educational devices such as one on photosynthesis and a mini-garden that showcases the different uses of plants. Look out for the elegant sculptures dotted around the grounds, including the bronze *Girl on a Bicycle* and *Girl on a Swing* by British artist Sydney Harpley, as well as the beautifully tranquil Swan Lake which has a magnificent *Flight of Swans* sculpture in the middle of it, depicting swans gliding gracefully over its surface.

You can pick up a free **map** of the grounds at the ranger's office, a little to the right of the main gate; free guided tours are offered by the park's volunteers at weekends – enquire at the Visitor Services Desks.

The area of **Dempsey Hill**, located off Holland Road at the southern end of the Botanic Gardens, was formerly home to a British army barracks. The blocks have now been converted into an array of popular upmarket bars and restaurants, and the lush surrounding greenery and charming outdoor areas make this one of the more pleasant places to spend an evening, and well worth the taxi ride from Orchard Road.

5

Northern Singapore

While land reclamation has radically altered the east coast and industriali-
zation the west, the **northern** expanses of the island up to the Straits of
Johor still retain pockets of the **rainforest** and mangrove swamp that
blanketed Singapore until the British arrival in 1819. These are inter-
spersed today with sprawling, maze-like **new towns** such as Toa Payoh, Bishan
and Ang Mo Kio, built in the 1970s. The name of the last, meaning "red-haired
devil's bridge", refers to the nineteenth-century British surveyor, John Turnbull
Thomson, under whose supervision the transport network of Singapore began to
penetrate the interior of the island. Man-eating tigers roamed these parts well into
the twentieth century, and it was here that Allied forces confronted the invading
Japanese army in 1942, a period of Singaporean history movingly recalled by the
Kranji War Memorial on Woodlands Road and the new **Memories at Old Ford
Factory** gallery in Bukit Timah. Still visible at the far northern sweep of the island
are the remnants of Singapore's agricultural past; you'll see prawn and poultry
farms, orchards and vegetable gardens when travelling in these parts. Dominating
the central northern region are two nature reserves, divided by the main road route
to Malaysia, the Bukit Timah Expressway. West of the expressway is **Bukit Timah
Nature Reserve**, an accessible slice of primary rainforest, while to the east, the
four reservoirs of the Central Catchment Area are one of Singapore's main sources
of water. In recent years the National Parks Board has made huge steps towards
achieving its vision of creating a "City in a Garden"(as opposed to a garden in a
city). Part of this has been the establishment of a Park Connector Network (PCN)
to link all the parks, nature sites and housing estates in Singapore. The park
connectors (a series of paths between the parks), vary in length, and so far cover
100km – by 2015 the city hopes to have constructed a further 200km, in a bid to
form a "green matrix" across the whole island and encourage people to get out
into nature.

North of Bukit Timah, the principal tourist attractions are the excellent
Singapore Zoo and the adjacent **Night Safari**, sited on a finger of land pointing
into the Seletar Reservoir. To the east are two of Singapore's most eye-catching
Buddhist temples – **Lian Shan Shuang Lin Temple** and **Phor Kark See Temple**
– as well as tiny Tai Gin Road, where the sometime residence of Chinese nationalist
leader Dr **Sun Yat Sen** and Singapore's **Burmese Temple** are found.

Travel between northern Singapore's attractions is decidedly tricky unless you are
driving, or in a cab, so don't expect to take in everything in a day. However, Lian Shan
Shuang Lin Temple, Sun Yat Sen Villa and the Burmese Temple all nestle around the
outskirts of Toa Payoh new town and could be incorporated into a single expedition,
as could the zoo, Mandai Orchid Gardens and the Kranji War cemetery and memorial.
The Kong Meng San Phor Kark See temple complex really requires a separate
journey, or can be tacked onto the end of a visit to MacRitchie Reservoir Park.

NORTHERN SINGAPORE

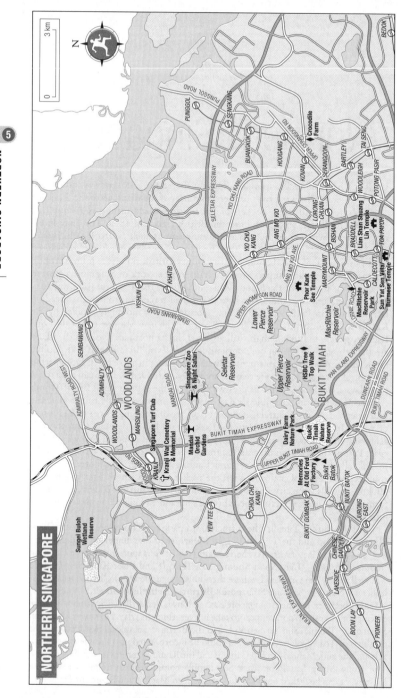

N

0   3 km

Sungei Buloh Wetland Reserve

Singapore Turf Club

Kranji War Cemetery & Memorial

Mandai Orchid Gardens

Singapore Zoo & Night Safari

WOODLANDS

WOODLANDS

MARSILING

ADMIRALTY

SEMBAWANG

YISHUN

KHATIB

ADMIRALTY ROAD WEST

SEMBAWANG ROAD

MANDAI ROAD

KRANJI ROAD

BUKIT TIMAH EXPRESSWAY

UPPER BUKIT TIMAH ROAD

Memories At Old Ford Factory

Bukit Batok

BUKIT GOMBAK

BUKIT BATOK

CHOA CHU KANG

YEW TEE

Seletar Reservoir

Lower Pierce Reservoir

Upper Pierce Reservoir

HSBC Tree Top Walk

BUKIT TIMAH

Dairy Farm Nature Park

Bukit Timah Nature Reserve

MacRitchie Reservoir

MacRitchie Reservoir Park

CORNE ROAD

Sun Yat Sen Villa

Burmese Temple

CALDECOTT

Phor Kark See Temple

UPPER THOMPSON ROAD

ANG MO KIO AVE

YIO CHU KANG

MARYMOUNT

ANG MO KIO

BISHAN

LORONG CHUAN

BRADDELL

Lian Shan Shuang Lin Temple

TOA PAYOH

WOODLEIGH

POTONG PASIR

BARTLEY

TAI SENG

SERANGOON

KOVAN

HOUGANG

BUANGKOK

SENGKANG

PUNGGOL

Crocodile Farm

PUNGGOL ROAD

UPPER SERANGOON RD

YIO CHU KANG ROAD

SELETAR EXPRESSWAY

PAN ISLAND EXPRESSWAY

DUNEARN ROAD

BUKIT TIMAH ROAD

KRANJI EXPRESSWAY

CHINESE GARDEN

JURONG EAST

LAKESIDE

BOON LAY

PIONEER

BEDOK

Bukit Timah Nature Reserve and around

Bukit Timah Road runs northwest from the junction of Selegie and Serangoon roads, to the faceless town of **Bukit Timah**, 8km further on. Bukit Timah boasts Singapore's last remaining pocket of primary rainforest, which now comprises **Bukit Timah Nature Reserve** (daily 6am–7pm; free; ☎1800/4685736). Visiting this area of Singapore in the mid-eighteenth century, natural historian Alfred Russel Wallace found Bukit Timah's vegetation "most luxuriant...in about two months I obtained no less than 700 species of beetles...in all my subsequent travels in the East I rarely if ever met with so productive a spot". Wallace reported "tiger pits, carefully covered with sticks and leaves and so well concealed, that in several cases I had a narrow escape from falling into them...Formerly a sharp stake was stuck erect in the bottom," he continued, "but after an unfortunate traveller had been killed by falling into one, its use was forbidden."

Today the reserve, established in 1883 by Nathaniel Cantley, who was superintendent of the Botanic Gardens, yields no such hazards and is a refuge for the dwindling numbers of species still extant in Singapore – only 25 types of mammal now inhabit the island. Creatures you're most likely to see in Bukit Timah are long-tailed macaques, butterflies and other insects, and birds like the dark-necked tailorbird, which builds its nest by sewing leaves together. Scorpions, snakes, flying lemurs and pangolins (anteaters, whose name is derived from the Malay word peng-goling, meaning "roller", a reference to the animal's habit of rolling into a ball when threatened) still roam here too.

You'd be well advised to begin your trip at the informative **visitor centre** (daily 8.30am–6pm), full of displays, specimens and photos relating to the reserve's flora and fauna. Several paths from the centre twist and turn through the forest around and to the top of **Bukit Timah Hill**, which, at a paltry 163m, is actually Singapore's highest hill. These paths are all well signposted, colour-coded and dotted with rest points, and they're clearly mapped on the free leaflet handed out to all visitors. Bike tracks have also been added, but it's rather rough terrain and probably for mountain bike enthusiasts only. Bus #171 passes along Somerset and

▲ Macaque in Bukit Timah Native Reserve

Scotts roads en route to Bukit Timah Reserve; a second option is to take bus #170 from the Ban San Terminal on Queen Street. Both buses drop you beside a row of shops on Upper Bukit Timah Road, where you can pick up light snacks and bottled water to take into the reserve. The best times to visit are the cool of early morning and midweek, when there are fewer visitors.

Dairy Farm Nature Park

Skirting the Bukit Timah nature reserve, and linked by a park connector trail, is the **Dairy Farm Nature Park** (daily 6am–7pm; free). Established in colonial times as the world's first tropical dairy farm, it is now a relatively large and tranquil nature park, the highlight of which is a former quarry that has been transformed into a gorgeous wetland with a viewing platform. Bring binoculars and you are likely to catch sight of the white-bellied eagle or even the endangered little grebe which has begun to nest here. For those interested in finding out about naturalist Alfred Russel Wallace and his work in Singapore, there's also the informative **Wallace Education Centre** which recounts his invaluable contribution to Darwin's theory of evolution.

Memories at Old Ford Factory and Bukit Batok

Across Upper Bukit Timah Road from the reserve, another forested hill, **Bukit Batok**, is where British and Australian POWs were forced to erect a fifteen-metre-high wooden shrine, the Syonan Tyureito, for their Japanese captors in 1945. Only the steps at its base remain, and the hill is now topped by a communications transmitter. Legend has it that termites, which the prisoners secretly introduced to the structure, destroyed the shrine itself. Gone, too, is the wooden cross erected by the POWs to honour their dead. The hill is located at the end of Lorong Sesuai, a left turn opposite Bukit Timah fire station, 500m further up the road from the entrance to Bukit Timah reserve. Lorong Sesuai was laid by the same prisoners who built the shrine.

The surrender that consigned them to such labours took place 400m further up Upper Bukit Timah Road, at the Art Deco Old Ford car factory; a gallery, **Memories at Old Ford Factory** (Mon–Sat 9am–5.30pm, Sun noon–5.30pm; $3), tells the story of that surrender, and of the dark years of Japanese occupation from 1942 to 1945. The exhibition uses period newspapers, first-hand audio accounts and relics such as Morse coders, anti-tank guns, signal lamps and grenades to fascinating effect. Details of life as a POW are kept to a minimum (this facet of Singaporean history is well covered at Changi Prison Museum, see p.94); instead, it's the civilian experience of Japanese occupation that comes to life.

When the factory opened in October 1941, it was the first car assembly plant in Southeast Asia. During the Malayan campaign, its assembly equipment was used by the RAF to assemble fighter planes. But by February 1942, Japanese forces had advanced into Singapore, and on February 15, Lt Gen Percival, head of the Allied forces in Singapore, surrendered to Japan's General Yamashita in the Ford Motor Company Board Room. While Percival was taken to Changi prison as a POW (he would fly to Tokyo Bay three years later to witness the Japanese surrender), the Japanese commanders gathered for a ritual ceremony of thanks, ate their Emperor's gifts of dried cuttlefish and chestnuts and drank a silent *sake* toast.

Then it was down to business. Stung by overseas Chinese efforts to raise funds for China's defence against Japan, Japanese troops launched Sook Ching, a brutal purge of anti-Japanese Chinese in Singapore. Kempeitai (military police) officers established screening centres, to which Chinese men had to report. Even the most tenuous of evidence – tattoos, a Chinese education, wearing glasses or having the soft hands of the educated – could result in individuals being loaded onto lorries and taken to massacre grounds around the island. The Japanese estimated the number of dead around five thousand; Singapore's Chinese Chamber of Commerce thought it was eight times that many.

Concurrently, the occupying army began a mass "Japanization" process. Locals were urged to learn Japanese and celebrate imperial birthdays; the press was controlled by the Japanese Propaganda Department; and Japanese cultural shows were held at Victoria Theatre and memorial hall. The new currency introduced by the Japanese came to be known as "banana money", as the $10 note featured a banana plant. The gallery ends with images of General Seishiro, commander in chief of Japanese 7th Area Army, surrendering to Admiral Lord Louis Mountbatten, Supreme Allied Commander of Southeast Asia, on September 12, 1945. At the ceremony, Allied troops raised the same Union Jack that had been handed over at the Ford Factory three years earlier.

Oil palm, tapioca, sweet potato, papaya and other food crops grown during the occupation have been planted in the **wartime garden** outside the factory, but the garden's location among the air-conditioning units behind the building is puzzling.

MacRitchie Reservoir Park

East of Bukit Timah, the shoreline and environs of MacRitchie Reservoir Park play host to the **MacRitchie Trails** (daily 6.30am–7.30pm; free), a network of six colour-coded tracks (3–11km) and boardwalks that allow you to experience Singapore's lowland tropical dipterocarp forest. Bisecting lush vegetation and skirting the reservoir's glassy waters, the trails offer the chance to see macaques, monitor lizards, terrapins, squirrels, eagles and kingfishers in the wild. If you happen to be in town on the second Sunday of the month, you can join the free nature appreciation walk that starts from the head of the Prunus Trail at 9.30am or 10.30am (☎65545127 to pre-book at least three days before the walk).

One of the longer trails, MacRitchie Nature Trail, leads to the **HSBC TreeTop Walk** (Tues–Fri 9am–5pm, Sat & Sun 8.30am–5pm; free), a freestanding, 25-metre-high, 250-metre-long suspension bridge that gives you a monkey's-eye view of the forest canopy. As long as there are no noisy school parties bustling across, you've got a pretty good chance of spotting some colourful fauna and birdlife. There's also the opportunity to enjoy a spot of kayaking at the reservoir's Paddle Lodge (Tues–Sun 9.30am–4pm; ☎63446337).

The MacRitchie Trails all start at MacRitchie Reservoir Park, where there are restrooms, a café and information boards. To reach the park, take bus #132, #166 or #167 from downtown, and alight at Thomson Road, or take the MRT to Braddell, then a cab for the remaining portion. If you don't fancy the 4km hike to the TreeTop Walk, stay on any of the buses listed previously at the turning to the Singapore Island Country Club, on Upper Thomson Road.

Tai Gin Road: Sun Yat Sen Villa and the Burmese Temple

Between Jalan Toa Payoh to the north, and Balestier Road to the south, is **Sun Yat Sen Villa** (Tues–Sun 9am–5pm; $4; ☎62567377) on Tai Gin Road (off Ah Hood Road), reached by bus #139 from outside Dhoby Ghaut MRT station. Built to house the mistress of a wealthy Chinese businessman, this attractive Palladian-style bungalow changed hands in 1905, when one Teo Eng Hock bought it for his mother. Chinese nationalist leader (China's answer to Che Guevara) Dr Sun Yat Sen paid the first of several visits to Singapore the following year, and was invited by Teo to stay at Tai Gin Road, where he quickly established a Singapore branch of the Tong Meng Hui – a society dedicated to replacing the Manchu dynasty in China with a modern republic. It is now a museum with six galleries, whose displays, artefacts and visuals variously focus upon the villa's history, the life of Dr Sun, and the historical context to the Chinese revolution in which he played such a substantial part. There's enough to engage the mind for a while, but in all honesty this is best left to visitors with an active interest in Chinese history.

Next door to the Sun Yat Sen Villa is the **Sasanaramsi Burmese Buddhist Temple** (daily 6.30am–9pm; ☎62511717), which is worth a cursory look after a visit to the Villa, if only to marvel at the sheer tastelessness of the large, white marble statue of the Buddha bedecked with flashing neon lights.

Phor Kark See Temple

The largest temple complex in Singapore – and one of the largest in Southeast Asia – lies north of MacRitchie Reservoir right in the middle of the island and is worth tacking onto the end of your day if you're in the area. **Phor Kark See Temple** (known in full as the Kong Meng San Phor Kark See Monastery; daily 6am–9.30pm, main office and temples 8.30am–4.30pm), at 88 Bright Hill Road, spreads over nineteen acres and combines temples, pagodas, pavilions, a Buddhist library and a vast crematorium. The sheer magnitude and exuberant decor have lent the site an almost film-set-like quality, so much so that it has been used several times as a backdrop to Chinese kung fu movies.

It is not a tasteful complex, with its multi-tiered roofs that bristle with ceramic dragons, phoenixes, birds and human figures, and statues of deities of varying heights scattered around – including a nine-metre-high marble statue of Kuan Yin, Goddess of Mercy, and a soaring pagoda capped by a golden *chedi* (reliquary tower) – all of which seem to test the accepted boundaries of scale, harmony and balance to their very limits and would cause a classicist to recoil in horror. Below the Thai-style crematorium is a huge pond housing thousands of turtles, surrounded by an ugly metal grating that is presumably there to prevent worshippers from putting new turtles into the pond, a practice supposed to bring good luck. To **reach the complex** take bus #130 up Victoria Street, alighting at the far end of Sin Ming Drive or hop on the #52 outside the MacRitchie Gardens.

Lian Shan Shuang Lin Temple

The name of the **Lian Shan Shuang Lin Temple** (daily 7am–5pm), at 184e Jalan Toa Payoh in the Toa Payoh new town, means "Twin Groves of the Lotus Mountain" – a reference to the Buddha's birth in a grove of trees and his death under a Bodhi tree. Set behind a half-moon pool, it is accessed by the **Hall of Celestial Kings**, where statues of the Four Kings of Heaven stand guard to repel evil, symbolized by the demons under their feet. The kings flank Maitreya Bodhisattva, the **Laughing Buddha**, believed to grant good luck if you rub his stomach. Beyond, a courtyard dotted with bonsai plants leads to the main Mahavira Hall, where a sakyamuni Buddha in lotus position takes centre stage. To **get here**, take the MRT to Toa Payoh station, from where the temple is a ten-minute walk.

Singapore Zoo and Night Safari

Singapore Zoo (daily 8.30am–6pm; $18/$12, $32/$20 with Night Safari, $45/$28 with Night Safari and Bird Park; ☎62693411), on Mandai Lake Road, is spread over a promontory jutting into peaceful Seletar Reservoir. The gardens attract 1.6 million visitors a year – a fact perhaps explained by their status as one of the world's few open zoos, where moats are preferred to cages. Spacious exhibits manage to approximate the natural habitats of the animals, and though leopards, pumas and jaguars still have to be kept behind bars, this is a thoughtful, humane environment, described as "one of the really beautiful zoos" by no less an authority than conservationist Sir Peter Scott.

There are some 2500 animals here, representing more than 315 species (sixteen percent of which are endangered), so it's best to allow a whole day for your visit. A **tram** ($5/3 for three stops) circles the grounds on a one-way circuit, while a **boat** skirts half the park perimeter ($5/3) in a leisurely fashion, but otherwise be prepared for a lot of footwork. Highlights include polar bears, which you view underwater from a gallery, and getting up close and personal with orang-utans which are housed on a moat-surrounded island where they are free to lope about. Also worth checking out are the white tigers (believed to be extinct in the wild), especially at feeding time when great hunks of meat are thrown across the moat for the majestic creatures to catch in their mouths; and the delightfully comical Proboscis monkeys who resemble a creation from Jim Henson's Creature Shop.

No exhibit lets you get closer to the resident animals than the awesome **Fragile Forest** biodome, a magical area where you can walk amid ring-tailed lemurs, tree kangaroos, sloths and fruit bats. Various **animal** and **feeding shows** run throughout the day from 9.15am until 5pm, featuring sea lions, elephants, polar bears and other exotic creatures. There are also elephant ($8) and pony ($6 child-only) rides and, in the **Rainforest Kidzworld**, an excellent water park (bring swimming gear and sunblock) and demonstrations on how to groom a horse. In the mornings, it's even possible to share breakfast with orang-utans, elephants and snakes (daily 9–10.30am; $29/$19 plus tax; see p.122).

The **Night Safari** (daily 7.30pm–midnight; $22/$15, $32/$20 with zoo, $45/$28 with zoo and Bird Park) houses a thousand animals representing more than a hundred species – elephants, rhinos, giraffes and leopards, hyenas and otters – who play out their nocturnal routines under a forest of standard lamps. Three walking trails covering five zones will take you through the haunts of the leopards, giant flying squirrels and the incredibly cute fishing cats. However, only five of the safari's eight zones are walkable – to see the rest you'll need to take a 45-minute tram ride ($10/$6), and tolerate the rather grating commentary of the guides. There's also a rather cheesy but entertaining "Creatures of the Night" show (7.30pm, 8.30pm & 9.30pm) featuring binturongs, otters, raccoons, owl and wolves.

A meal at one of the restaurants at the entrance – the standout option is *Ulu Ulu* which serves up excellent examples of Singapore's culinary highlights – will help pass the time between the zoo closing and the Night Safari opening.

To **get to** the zoo and the Night Safari, take bus #171 to Mandai Road, then #927, or go to Ang Mo Kio MRT and follow the signs to the bus interchange where you should take bus #138.

Mandai Orchid Gardens

It's only a ten-minute walk from Singapore Zoo down Mandai Lake Road to the **Mandai Orchid Gardens** (daily 8am–7pm; $3.50; ☎ 62691036) or you can take the #138 bus from the zoo, which stops right outside. The orchids here are culti-vated on a gentle slope, tended by old ladies in wide-brimmed hats. But it's not exceptional and there's no information, so unless you are a keen horticulturist, the place is of limited interest.

Woodlands: Kranji War Cemetery and around

Five kilometres north of the zoo is the bustling town of **Woodlands**, from where a **causeway** spans the Straits of Johor linking Singapore to Johor Bahru in Malaysia. At peak hours (6.30–9.30am & 5.50–7.30pm) and at weekends, the roads leading to the causeway seethe with cars and trucks – all full of petrol, after a law passed in the early 1990s banned Singaporeans from driving out of the country on an empty tank. Previously, people crossed into Malaysia, filled up with cut-price fuel and then headed home; now, signs line the roads approaching the causeway requesting that "Singapore cars please top up to tank" – or risk a $500 fine.

Bus #170 from Ban San Terminal on Queen Street heads towards Woodlands on its way to Johor Bahru, passing the **Kranji War Cemetery and Memorial** (daily 7am–6pm) on Woodlands Road, where only the sound of birds and insects breaks the silence in the immaculately kept grounds. (You can also get here by alighting at Kranji MRT station, from where it's a five-hundred-metre walk.) The cemetery is the resting place of the many Allied troops who died in the defence of Singapore. As you enter, row upon row of graves slope up the landscaped hill in front of you, some identified only as "known unto God". The graves are bare: flowers are banned as still water encourages mosquitoes to breed. A simple stone cross stands over the cemetery and above is the **memorial**, around which are recorded all the names of more than twenty thousand soldiers (from Britain, Canada, Sri Lanka, India, Malaysia, the Netherlands, New Zealand and Singapore) who died in this region during World War II. Two unassuming **tombs** stand on the wide lawns below the cemetery, belonging to Yusof Bin Ishak and Dr Benjamin Henry Sheares, independent Singapore's first two presidents.

Sungei Buloh Wetland Reserve

The 130-hectare swathe of **Sungei Buloh Wetland Reserve** (Mon–Sat 7.30am–7pm, Sun 7am–7pm; free except Sat & Sun $1/50c; ☎67941401), 4km northwest of Kranji cemetery on the north coast of Singapore, is the island's only protected wetland nature park. Beyond its visitor centre, café and video theatre, walking routes thread through an expanse of mangrove, mud flats, orchards and grassland, home to kingfishers, herons, sandpipers, kites and sea eagles and, in the waters, mudskippers, needlefish and archerfish – which squirt water into the air to knock insects into devouring range. The reserve's five-hundred-metre-long mangrove boardwalk offers an easy means of getting a sense of the shoreline environment. You'll take your stroll to the accompaniment of cicadas and birdsong. En route, you'll spot tortoises, crabs and mudskippers among the reaching fingers of the mangrove swamp. From here you can graduate to walks ranging from three to seven kilometres into the guts of the reserve. Visit between September and March and you're likely to catch sight of migratory birds from as far as Siberia roosting and feeding (223 species have been recorded). If you come on a Saturday you can join a free guided tour (9.30am & 3.30pm); at other times you'll need to pre-book if you want a tour ($60 per group).

To get to Sungei Buloh, take the MRT to Kranji MRT station, then transfer to bus #925, which stops at Kranji Reservoir car park from Monday to Saturday (you then need to walk a further fifteen to twenty minutes to reach the entrance) and at the reserve's entrance on Sundays.

6

Eastern Singapore

Around thirty years ago, eastern Singapore was largely rural, dotted with Malay kampung villages that perched on stilts over the shoreline, harbouring the odd weekend retreat owned by Europeans or monied locals. Massive land reclamation and development programmes have altered the region beyond recognition, wiping out all traces of the kampungs and throwing up huge housing projects in their place. Today, former seafront suburbs like Bedok are separated from the Straits of Singapore by a broad crescent of man-made land, much of which constitutes the **East Coast Park**, a fifteen-kilometre strip with leisure and watersports facilities, imported sand beaches and seafood restaurants. Despite the massive upheavals that have ruptured the communities of the east coast, parts of it, including the suburbs of Geylang and Katong, have managed to retain a strong Malay identity.

Dominating the eastern tip of the island is Changi Airport, and beyond that **Changi Village**, where the Japanese interned Allied troops and civilians during World War II – a period of history commemorated at the thought-provoking **Changi Museum**. From Changi Point, it's possible to take a boat to **Pulau Ubin**, a small rustic island that has echoes of pre-development Singapore.

▲ Playing frisbee at the East Coast Park

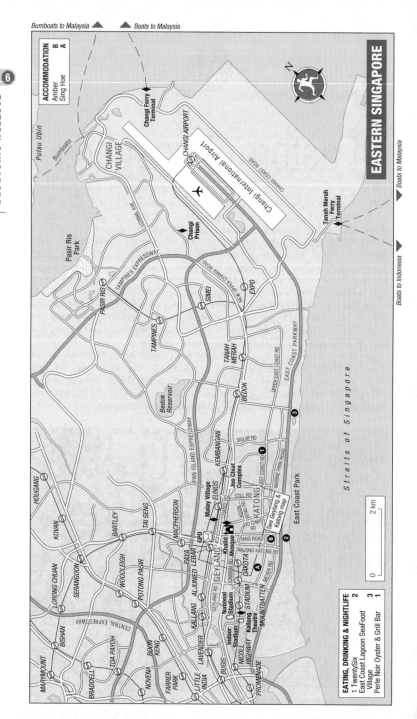

Bumboats to Malaysia

Boats to Malaysia

ACCOMMODATION
Amber   B
Sing Hoe   A

EASTERN SINGAPORE

N

Pulau Ubin

Bumboats

Changi Ferry Terminal

CHANGI VILLAGE

CHANGI AIRPORT

Changi International Airport

CHANGI COAST ROAD

Pasir Ris Park

Tanah Merah Ferry Terminal

Changi Prison

Boats to Malaysia

Boats to Indonesia

Straits of Singapore

PASIR RIS

TAMPINES EXPRESSWAY

LORONG AVE

TAMPINES

SIMEI

NEW UPPER CHANGI ROAD

EXPO

TANAH MERAH

BEDOK

UPPER EAST COAST RD

EAST COAST PARKWAY

Bedok Reservoir

PAN ISLAND EXPRESSWAY

KEMBANGAN

SIGLAP RD

MARINE PARK ROAD

EAST COAST RD

Joo Chiat Complex

STILL RD

JOO CHIAT RD

KATONG

See Geylang & Katong map

East Coast Park

EUNOS

Malay Village

PAYA

MACPHERSON

TAI SENG

HOUGANG

KOVAN

BARTLEY

SERANGOON

LORONG CHUAN

WOODLEIGH

POTONG PASIR

ALJUNIED

GEYLANG

Khalid Mosque

GPO

HAIG ROAD

TANJONG KATONG

DUNMAN RD

DAKOTA

MOUNTBATTEN

National Stadium

Indoor Stadium

Kallang Theatre

Kallang STADIUM

NICOLL HIGHWAY

KALLANG

LAVENDER

GEYLANG RD

BUGIS

PROMENADE

LITTLE INDIA

FARRER PARK

NOVENA

BOON KENG

TOA PAYOH

BISHAN

MARYMOUNT

BRADDELL

CENTRAL EXPRESSWAY

0   2 km

EATING, DRINKING & NIGHTLIFE
1 TwentySix   2
East Coast Lagoon SeaFood
Village   3
Perle Noir Oyster & Grill Bar   1

Geylang and Katong

Malay culture has held sway in and around the adjoining suburbs of **Geylang** and **Katong** since the mid-nineteenth century, when Malays and Indonesians first arrived to work in the local *copra* (coconut husk) processing factory and later on its *serai* (lemon grass) farms. Many of its shophouses, restaurants and food centres are Malay-influenced – less so the thriving trade in prostitution that carries on here, unchecked by the local authorities. Geylang Road runs east from the Kallang River; off the road are 42 lorongs, or lanes, down which clusters of brothels are easily recognized by their fairy lights. At its far eastern end, Geylang Road meets **Joo Chiat Road**, which – after the restrictions of downtown Singapore – has a refreshingly laidback and somewhat shambolic air.

The Malay Village

Before striking off down Joo Chiat Road, cross Changi Road, to the north, where, on a side street called Geylang Serai, a **hawker centre** and wet market of the same name provides an authentic Malay atmosphere, from the clove cigarettes to the line of sarong sellers beyond the food stalls. The doomed **Malay Village** (daily 10am–9pm; $5/$3 for attractions, otherwise free) is located on the other side of Geylang Serai, and a short walk from Paya Lebar MRT. Opened in 1990, and conceived as a celebration of the cuisine, music, dance, arts and crafts of the Malays, the village has conspicuously failed either to woo tourists or to rent out its replica wooden kampung-style shops to locals. Its "attractions" include the humdrum **Kampung Museum**, the dismal **Kampung Days** exhibition and the rather half-hearted **Cultural Demonstration Corner**. Unsurprisingly, the government is now planning to turn it into a more profitable shopping mall (albeit one with a Malay heritage exhibition at its centre).

Joo Chiat Road and East Coast Road

As you walk south down Joo Chiat Road from Geylang Road, you'll have to negotiate the piles of merchandise that spill out of shophouses and onto the pavement – but before you do, be sure to visit the **Joo Chiat Complex** at the northern end of the road, where textile merchants drape their wares on any available floor and wall space, transforming the drab interior. More market than shopping centre, it's a prime destination for anyone interested in buying silk, batik, rugs, muslin or the traditional *baju kurung* worn by Malay women. Stalls around the perimeter of the complex sell dates, honey, Malay CDs and *jamu* (Malay medicine).

With its ochre-tiled roof and green walls, low-key **Khalid Mosque**, a stone's throw from Joo Chiat Complex, belies the eye-catching architecture on view elsewhere on or around Joo Chiat Road. Joo Chiat itself has some beautifully restored shophouses – like Chiang Pow Joss Paper Trading at no. 252, where funerary paraphernalia is made beneath elaborate facades of flowers and dragons – but none as magnificent as the immaculate **Peranakan shophouses** on Koon Seng Road (on the left about halfway down Joo Chiat Road), where painstaking work has restored multicoloured facades, French windows, eaves and mouldings.

Back on Joo Chiat, several shops are worthy of a detour. Kway Guan Huat at no. 95 makes *popiah* skin; while mackerel *otah* is produced at no. 267. At 282 is JiamGe, an informal but excellent reflexology centre where the therapists will knead your aching feet and flagging body back into action ($30/hr).

Hang a right when Joo Chiat hits East Coast Road and at no. 113 you'll find **Rumah Bebe**, a delightful Peranakan shop that sells beaded shoes and handbags, costume jewellery, porcelain tiffin carriers and the traditional garb – *kebaya* and *sarong* – of Nonya women. A few doors down at 109 East Coast

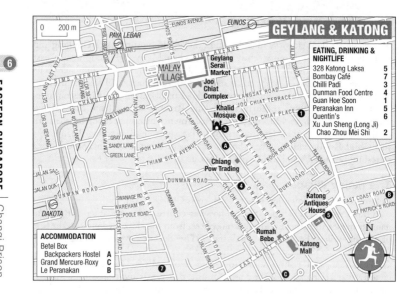

EATING, DRINKING & NIGHTLIFE

328 Katong Laksa	5
Bombay Café	7
Chilli Padi	3
Dunman Food Centre	4
Guan Hoe Soon	1
Peranakan Inn	5
Quentin's	6
Xu Jun Sheng (Long Ji)	
Chao Zhou Mei Shi	2

ACCOMMODATION

Betel Box	
Backpackers Hostel	A
Grand Mercure·Roxy	C
Le Peranakan	B

Road is **Kim Choo**, selling even more Peranakan fare. From here it's just a couple of minutes' walk east to the **Katong Antiques House** at 208 East Coast Road where owner Peter Wee has amassed a treasure trove of Peranakan artefacts, from wedding costumes to furniture. You'll need to call ahead (☎63458544) to book an appointment. Head west from Rumah Bebe, to the junction with Ceylon Road, and you'll find a clutch of venerable food stalls selling peerless Katong *laksa*.

Changi Prison

Infamous **Changi Prison** was the site of a World War II POW camp in which Japanese jailers subjected Allied prisoners to the harshest of treatment. The prison itself is still in use (drug offenders are periodically executed here), and its terrible past is marked in the hugely moving **Changi Museum** (daily 9.30am–5pm; free; ☎62142451), just up the road.

The museum's power lies more in the many cruelties it portrays, than in the miscellanies it has amassed. Sketches, photographs and information boards plot the Japanese occupation of Singapore and the fate of the soldiers and civilians subsequently incarcerated in camps around the Changi area. Most movingly of all, though, is the board of remembrance, where children, wives and compatriots have pinned messages for the dead.

Novelist James Clavell was a young British artillery officer in Singapore at the time of the Japanese invasion; later, he drew on his own experience of the "obscene forbidding prison" at Changi in writing *King Rat*, never forgetting that in the cells of the prison camp, "…the stench was nauseating. Stench from rotten bodies. Stench from a generation of confined human bodies." You can get the merest sense of what Clavell means by entering the Changi Cell, a dark, stuffy alleyway that approximates the cramped confinement suffered by POWs, and in which the voices of former POWs recall enduring the "howling, crying, shouting" of fellow inmates being tortured in the middle of the night.

Clavell's recollections are borne out by the selection of photos by **George Aspinall**, in a cabinet at the entrance to the museum. Aspinall, then a young Australian trooper, recorded the appalling living conditions and illnesses suffered by POWs in Malaya and Thailand during the occupation using a folding Kodak 2 camera, later developing his shots with a stock of processing materials which he found while working on a labour gang in Singapore's docks.

The museum's **gallery** section showcases the work of various prison artists, among them W.R.M. Haxworth, who produced more than four hundred paintings and sketches during his internment. Haxworth's tongue-in-cheek sketches of daily Changi life reveal the dry sense of humour and stiff upper lips that sustained internees in the face of adversity. One, entitled "Changi Comforts", depicts a variety of rickety stools, some fruit and a battered biscuit tin. Another sketch, in which a character holds up two shirts, one white and one black, is entitled "White and Changi white". Elsewhere, there are full-scale reproductions of the murals of Stanley Warren, who used camouflage paint, crushed snooker chalk and aircraft paints smuggled in by fellow POWs to paint bible scenes on a Changi chapel wall.

Outside in a courtyard is a replica of a simple wooden chapel, typical of those erected in Singapore's wartime camps; the brass cross on its altar was crafted from spent ammunition casings, while its walls carry more poignant messages of remembrance penned by visiting former POWs and relatives.

Journey's end is at the **museum shop**, where a video screen plays footage of the Japanese attack and the living conditions in Changi. On a lighter note, among the war-related books stocked in the shop is *The Happiness Box*, the first copy of which was written, illustrated and bound by POWs in Changi in 1942 as a Christmas present for children in the prison. The Japanese became suspicious of the POWs' motives when they noticed one of the book's central characters was called Winston, but it was buried in the prison grounds before it could be confiscated, and only recovered after the war had ended.

To **get to** the museum, take bus #2 from Chinatown or Victoria Street; alternatively, you could take the MRT to Tanah Merah station, and pick up the #2 there.

Changi Village

There's little to bring you out to sleepy **CHANGI VILLAGE**, ten minutes further on from the prison on bus #2, save to catch a boat from **Changi Point**, behind the bus terminal, for Pulau Ubin (see p.46) or for the coast of Johor in Malaysia (see p.25). The left-hand jetty is for Ubin, the right-hand one for bumboats to Johor, and just beyond the jetty is the picturesque Changi Coastal Walk, which hugs the coastline for 2km.

A stroll over the footbridge to the right of the two jetties takes you to **Changi Beach**, the execution site of many thousands of Singaporean civilians by Japanese soldiers during World War II. As a beach it wins few prizes – apart from its casuarinas and palms. Its most pleasant aspect is its view; to your left as you look out to sea is Pulau Ubin, while slightly to the right is the island of Tekong (a military zone), behind which you can see a hill on mainland Malaysia. In the water you'll find boats galore, from bumboats to supertankers. The beach is now at the beginning of the Eastern Coastal Park Connector Network, (a 42km route that forms part of the Connector Network programme, see p.83), a series of paths suitable for walking or cycling that links to other beaches along the east coast, such as the fifteen-kilometre-long East Coast Park (8km away).

Changi Village Road, the village's main drag, has a growing number of decent restaurants and a few bars, or try the hawker centre near the bus terminal.

Pulau Ubin

PULAU UBIN, 2km offshore, gives visitors a pretty good idea of what Singapore would have been like fifty years ago. A lazy backwater tucked into the Straits of Johor, it's a great place to come if you're tired of shops, high-rises and traffic. It's almost worth coming for the ten-minute boat trip alone, made in an old, oil-stained bumboat ($2.50 each way) that chugs noisily across Serangoon Harbour. Boats depart from Changi Point Ferry Terminal throughout the day from 6am onwards, leaving whenever they are full. The last boat back to Changi leaves as late as 9.30pm, if there's demand, but you should plan to be at the jetty by 8.30pm at the latest just in case.

Boats dock at the pier in **Ubin Village**, where palm trees slope and Malay stilt houses teeter over a sludgy mangrove beach that's stippled with the remains of collapsed, rotting jetties. Bear left from the jetty, and you'll soon hit the village square – but before that, swing by the **information kiosk** (daily 8.30am–5pm; ☏65424108, ⓦwww.nparks.gov.sg) to the right of the jetty for an island map. Just to the right of the kiosk, a short, circular **sensory trail**, put together by schoolchildren volunteers, takes in herbs, spices and orchids.

The main road into the village is lined with scores of battered old mopeds, while locals sit around, watching the day take its course, and roosters run free in the dirt and dogs bask under the hot sun. The best, and most enjoyable, way to explore the dirt tracks of Ubin is by bicycle; meandering along underneath foliage-filtered sunlight is wholly restorative after a few days in the hectic city. A cluster of **bike rental shops** operates along the jetty road next to the village's main square, charging $2–10 for a day's rental, depending upon the bike and the season. It's best to stock up on refreshments before you head off to explore the island. For **food**, there are a couple of decent restaurants dotted around the square; *Season Live Seafood* offers gorgeous sea views and delicious fresh crab or try the kampung chicken at the *Sin Lam Huat*.

A labyrinth of tracks veins Ubin, but it's only a small island (just 7km by 2km) and all roads are well signposted, so you won't get lost. As you go, look out for the monitor lizards, long-tailed macaques, lizards, butterflies, kites, oriental pied hornbills and eagles that inhabit Ubin, and listen for the distinctive rattle-buzz of cicadas.

The **hall** on the left flank of the square next to the bike rental shops is used periodically for Chinese opera, ceremonial occasions and other Ubin functions. Opposite it is a tiny, fiery-red Chinese temple. Bear left past the hall until you come to a basketball court, where a left turn takes you to the west of the island and a right turn to the east.

If you take the left turn west, after about five minutes you'll come to an impressively deep and beautiful turquoise water-filled **quarry**, from which granite was taken to build the causeway linking Singapore to Johor Bahru – Ubin is the Malay word for granite. Don't swim in this or any other Ubin quarry, however tempting it might be: the government has erected signs warning of hefty fines for doing so. A right turn after the first bridge you cross brings you to a peaceful lean-to **Chinese temple** fronted by wind chimes, a shrine holding three colourful figurines of tigers and a pool of carp, and shielded from the surrounding mangrove by a pretty lily-pad pond.

Biking **east** from the basketball court takes you past the prawn and fish farms, rubber trees and raised kampung houses of the centre and eastern side of Ubin. **Noordin Beach**, at the top of the island, offers an unprepossessing but smart enough patch of sand, though its views across the Johor Straits to southern Malaysia have been spoilt by the ugly metal fence erected in the water to keep out illegal immigrants. Further east, towards **Kampong Melayu**, are some beautifully maintained and brightly painted examples of kampung-style stilt houses. Beyond the village, **Tanjong Chek Jawa**, the far eastern tip of the island constitutes Ubin's most pristine patch of mangrove. Covering one hundred hectares, it comprises sandy and rocky beach, seagrass lagoon, coral rubble, mangroves and coastal forest. The visitors' centre (daily 8.30am–6pm) is situated at the entrance to Tanjong Chek Jawa inside a Tudor-style house, but there's not much information of interest. You may be able to catch a glimpse of the rare Malayan False Vampire bats in the old water tower beside the house. The area boasts a picturesque viewing jetty that stretches out to sea and a wooden boardwalk that offers an enjoyable stroll though both the mangroves and the coastline. If you're feeling adventurous, you can also scale the 20m-high viewing tower for panoramic views out to sea. Visitors can wander around these walking trails on their own, or book a guided walk via the island's information kiosk (see opposite).

Western Singapore

illy and exceptionally green, the western part of the island is home to the country's premier university, the National University of Singapore at Kent Ridge. This lies at the start of a nine-kilometre coastal ridge which has various names en route but has now been collectively labelled the **Southern Ridges**, stretching all the way southeast to **Mount Faber** near Tanjong Pagar downtown. Several minor attractions nestle along the route, the best of which is the World War II museum **Reflections at Bukit Chandu**, but a major part of the ridges' appeal is the chance to do a couple of hours' walk from one lush hill to another using a network of fancy interconnecting bridges. Further west is the industrial new town of **Jurong**, not the dull mixture of factories and state housing you might expect. True to form, Singapore's planners have woven several sights and leisure facilities into the fabric of the town, the pick of them being the **Jurong Bird Park**. In between these areas and downtown is the suburb of **Holland Village**, with a whole string of restaurants and bars popular with foreigners.

The Southern Ridges and Pasir Panjang

Along the southwest coast of Singapore is **Pasir Panjang**, a district whose name means "long sands" in Malay, though any significant beach has long gone – as have the sleepy villages that used to dominate what is becoming an increasingly urbanized area. It's home to one worthy sight, the droll Buddhist theme park that is **Haw Par Villa**, which makes a reasonable starting point for an exploration of the **Southern Ridges** just inland. The chief attractions here are the wartime museum **Reflections at Bukit Chandu** and the views from **Mount Faber**. The latter looms above the massive **VivoCity** mall at the southern tip of Singapore, where you can assuage the appetite and thirst you will inevitably work up on the ridges (which is why it makes sense to end, rather than start, a ridges walk here). Conveniently beneath the mall is HarbourFront MRT, while the MRT's Circle line makes it easy to travel through Pasir Panjang.

If you do walk the Southern Ridges, bear in mind that the creation of the trail and its bridges required a certain amount of land clearance: until the trees regrow, you should be especially assiduous about **sun protection**.

Haw Par Villa

As an entertaining exercise in bad taste, **Haw Par Villa** (daily 9am–7pm; free) at 262 Pasir Panjang Road has few equals. It describes itself as a "historical theme

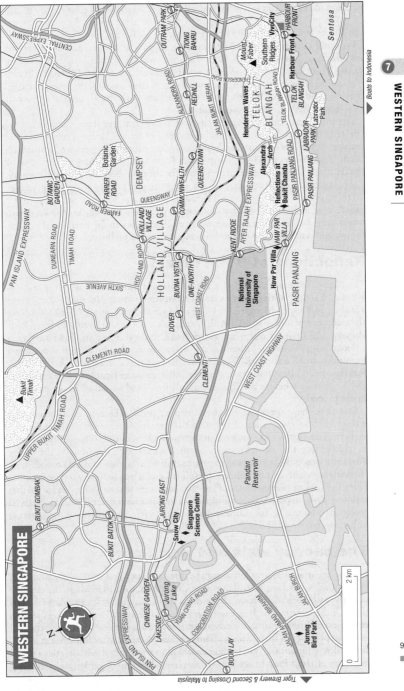

▶ Boats to Indonesia

WESTERN SINGAPORE

N

2 km

0

▲ Tiger Brewery & Second Crossing to Malaysia

park founded on Chinese legends and values", for which read a gaudy, gory parade of grotesque statues. An MRT station of the same name is next door, and the site can also be reached on bus #51 from Chinatown MRT.

Previously known as Tiger Balm Gardens, the park was once a zoo owned by the Aw brothers, Boon Haw and Boon Par, who made a fortune early last century selling Tiger Balm – a cure-all unguent created by their father. When the British introduced licensing governing the ownership of large animals, the brothers closed their zoo and replaced it with statuary; subsequently the park acquired its current title, a mishmash of the brothers' names.

The statues in question feature characters and creatures from Chinese legend and religion, as well as a fantastical menagerie of snakes, dragons, elephants and crabs with women's heads. The best – and most gruesome – series of statues lies in the **Ten Courts of Hell** exhibit (daily 9am–5pm; $2), whose explanation of the Buddhist belief in reincarnation is not for the faint-hearted. Accessed through the open mouth of a huge dragon, the statues depict sinners undergoing a range of tortures meted out by leering demons: prostitutes are drowned in pools of blood, drug addicts tied to a red-hot copper pillar and loan sharks thrown onto a hill of knives. Finally the dead are wiped of all memory in the Pavilion of Forgetfulness and sent back to earth to have another stab at godliness.

Reflections at Bukit Chandu

The Malay Regiment's defence of Pasir Panjang during World War II is remembered at the tiny **Reflections at Bukit Chandu** museum (Tues–Sun 9am–5pm; $2/$1 or $4/$3 with Memories at Old Ford Factory, see p.86; T63752510). Near the midpoint of the Southern Ridges trail, it's a ten-minute walk up from Pasir Panjang MRT: head north up Pepys Road until you see the lone surviving colonial house at no. 31k, built as officers' accommodation though it became a munitions store during the war. It was here that 'C' company of the Malay Regiment's 2nd Battalion made a brave stand against the Japanese on February 13, 1942 – two days before the British capitulation – and sustained heavy casualties in the process.

There's nothing special about the museum's small collection of artefacts, and indeed you can glean a lot of the salient information by perusing the museum's website. The displays do, however, get across the human toll of the conflict as well as highlighting British ambivalence about working with the Malays: the Malay Regiment was only begun as an experiment in what is now Malaysia to see "how the Malays would react to military discipline", and it was only when they began to prove themselves that members of the regiment were sent to Singapore for further training. This supposed slighting of the Malay community is still cited in Malaysia today as one reason for maintaining its controversial positive discrimination policies in favour of Malays.

The canopy walk and Hort Park

Leaving the museum, bear left along the ridge for your first taste of the Southern Ridges trail – and a wonderful introduction it is too, for this is where the elevated **canopy walk** begins. Soaring above the actual trail, the walkway takes you east through the treetops, with signage pointing out common Singapore trees such as cinnamon and tembusu, and views north across rolling grassy landscapes, the odd mansion poking out from within clumps of mature trees. After just a few minutes, the walkway rejoins the trail leading downhill to some mundane nurseries and the west gate of **Hort Park** (daily 6am–10pm; free). A hybrid of garden and gardening resource centre, it's sadly dull, and you'll probably want to exit promptly to Alexandra Road via the east gate.

Alexandra Arch to Mount Faber

The Alexandra Road end of Hort Park is very close to one of the huge, purpose-built footbridges on the Southern Ridges trail, the white **Alexandra Arch**, meant to resemble a leaf but looking more like the Singapore River's Elgin Bridge on steroids. It's not a bad point to begin a Southern Ridges walk, and can be reached on bus #166 from HarbourFront MRT or #51 from Chinatown MRT.

On the east side of Alexandra Arch, a long, elevated metal walkway zigzags off into the distance; it's called the **forest walk** though it passes through nothing denser than mature woodland on its kilometre-long journey east. The walkway zigzags even more severely as it rises steeply to the top of **Telok Blangah Hill** (you can save a bit of time by using a flight of steps that begins before the last few bends), whose park offers views of the usual public housing tower blocks to the north and east, and of Mount Faber and Sentosa to the southeast.

Proceed downhill and east, following signage for **Henderson Waves**, and after 700m or so you come to a vast footbridge of wooden slats over metal. Way up in the air over wide Henderson Road, the bridge has high undulating parapets – Henderson Waves indeed – featuring built-in shelters against the sun or rain.

On the far side, the bridge deposits you on the road to the top of leafy **Mount Faber**, named in 1845 after government engineer Captain Charles Edward Faber. In bygone years this was a favourite recreation spot for its superb views over downtown, but these days you'll have to look out for breaks in the dense foliage (the odd gap does offer vistas over Bukit Merah new town to Chinatown and the Financial District), or head to the **Jewel Box**, a complex of pricey bars and restaurants at the very apex of the summit. The Jewel Box is also the departure point for the **Jewel Ride** – state-of-the-art eight-seater **cable cars**, each glittering with lights on the outside, to the HarbourFront Centre and on to Sentosa island. At the time of writing the system was about to reopen after a major overhaul; for times and prices, call ☎63779688 or visit ⓦwww .mountfaber.com.sg.

To descend from Mount Faber, follow signs for the **Marang Trail**, which eventually leads down a flight of steps on the south side of the hill to VivoCity. If you do want to try the hike up from VivoCity, note that it only takes ten minutes but is steep in places.

VivoCity and the HarbourFront Centre

The most interesting thing at the foot of Mount Faber is the **VivoCity** mall, with a curious fretted white facade that looks like it was cut out of a set of giant false teeth, and housing three good food courts (in particular *Food Republic* on level 3), a slew of restaurants, a cinema and other amenities. The red-brick box of a building with the huge chimney east (on the left if you're descending the hill) of the mall, and connected to it by an elevated walkway, is **St James Power Station**, a bevy of clubs and bars housed in, surprise surprise, a converted power plant. In the other direction on Telok Blangah Road is the **HarbourFront Centre**, a glorified ferry terminal from where boats set off for Indonesia's Riau archipelago, as well as being the departure point for cable cars heading to Mount Faber and Sentosa Island.

Jurong and Tuas

The new town of **Jurong** was created out of swampy terrain in the 1960s, amid great scepticism about its chances of success. Today it and neighbouring **Tuas** boast a diverse portfolio of industries, including pharmaceuticals and oil refining – in which Singapore is a world leader despite having nary a drop of black gold of its own – and Jurong's centre is being remodelled with new leisure facilities in mind. As far as sights are concerned, Jurong's **Bird Park** is presently the only must-see, though the **Singapore Science Centre** is ahead of the curve as far as science museums go, and is not to be missed if you've got kids to entertain. More pertinent to grown-ups are tours of the **Tiger Brewery**, though note that these have to be booked in advance.

Jurong Bird Park

The **Jurong Bird Park** (daily 8.30am–6pm; S$18/$12, or $32/$20 with zoo or Night Safari, or $45/$28 with zoo and Night Safari; ☎66617830) on Jalan Ahmad Ibrahim is home to one of the world's biggest bird collections, with more than six hundred species. You'll need at least a couple of hours to have a good look around the grounds, which are large enough that the management saw fit to install a circular Panorail (S$5/$3), like an airport transit train, with commentary describing the main attractions.

One of the big draws, just inside the entrance, is the **Penguin Expedition** (feeding times 10.30am & 3.30pm), a glass enclosure with a pool where the water level is at head height, affording great views of the birds diving and swimming. Another highlight is the **Southeast Asian Birds** section, where'll you see fairy bluebirds and other small but delightful birds feasting on papaya slices, with a simulated thunderstorm at midday. Close by, the **Lory Loft** is a giant aviary under netting, its foliage meant to simulate the Australian bush. Its denizens are dozens of multicoloured lories and lorikeets, which have no qualms about perching at the viewing balcony or perhaps even on your arm, hoping for a bit of food (you can

▲ Jurong Bird Park

buy suitable feed here for $2). At the far end of the park is the **African Waterfall Aviary**, another large space under netting and long the pride of the park, with a tract of "rainforest" that includes a thirty-metre-high waterfall. The aviary's design not only allows visitors to enter on foot but also lets the Panorail chug in without providing an escape route for the 1500 winged inhabitants – including carmine bee-eaters and South African crowned cranes.

For something a bit different, head to **World of Darkness**, a fascinating owl showcase that swaps day for night using specially designed lighting. There are also a variety of **bird shows** throughout the day, the best of which involve birds of prey such as vultures and brahminy kites being fed; check the park's website for details of the current programme.

To reach the park, take either bus #194 or #251 from Boon Lay MRT station (10min). Heading back, note that you can pick up the #194 from the stop where you arrived, while for the #251 you should cross to the other side of the road.

Singapore Science Centre

Interactivity is the watchword at the **Singapore Science Centre** (Tues–Sun 10am–6pm; $6/$3; ☎64252500), on the eastern edge of the parkland around the artificial Jurong Lake. Here a range of galleries hold hundreds of hands-on displays designed to inject interest into even the most impenetrable scientific principles. The majority of the visitors are seemingly hyper schoolchildren, who sweep around in deafening waves trying out anything and everything. Exhibitions focusing on genetics, space science, marine ecology and other disciplines allow you to experience sight through an insect's eyes, write in Braille and see a thermal heat reflection of yourself.

At the northern end of the site is the **Omni-Theatre** (Tues–Sun 10am–8pm; $10/$5, joint ticket with Science Centre $12.80/$6.40), showing hourly IMAX movies about the natural world and housing an **observatory** which the public can access (Fri 7.50–10pm; free). If you're here with kids in tow, you might want to extend your visit to check out the winter-themed **Snow City** next to the Omni-Theatre, featuring tobogganing and opportunities to explore an igloo or build snowmen (Tues–Sun 9.45am–5.15pm; $16/$14 joint ticket with the Science Centre including 1hr at Snow City with warm clothing/boots provided).

Bus #335 comes here from Jurong East MRT, or it's just a ten-minute walk from the station. Alternatively, there's bus #66 all the way from Little India.

Tiger Brewery

Tiger Beer has been brewed in Singapore since 1931, when its home was the Malayan Breweries on Alexandra Road, where it was developed with help from Heineken. A few years later, the establishment of Archipelago Brewery by German giants Beck's seemed to set the scene for a Singaporean beer war, especially as Tiger's newer rival, Anchor, was priced slightly lower. But Archipelago was bought out by Malayan Breweries in 1941, and since then the organization has gone from strength to strength. In 1990 it moved into its present plant at 459 Jalan Ahmad Ibrahim in Tuas and changed its name to Asia Pacific Breweries, though lots of people still use the name Tiger Brewery.

A **tour** of the brewery (Mon–Fri 10.30am, 2pm, 4pm & 6.30pm; $10.70; book on ☎68603005, ⊛www.apb.com.sg/exp-breweryTour.html) lets you see the space-age brewing, canning and bottling halls, and finally partake in some free quaffing in the company's own bar. The brewery is a twenty-minute ride west from Boon Lay MRT on bus #182.

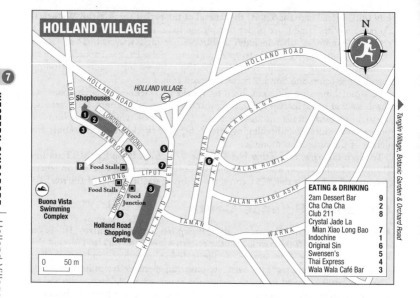

Holland Village

Decades ago, **Holland Village** was home to some of the British troops based in Singapore and now it's still packed with foreigners, with many an expat helping to pack out its restaurants and bars. At the heart of this residential suburb is the **Holland Village Shopping Centre**, a good place to find stores selling antiques and novel home furnishings. The relevant listings chapters cover these places in more detail. The MRT's Circle line connects HarbourFront and points on the Southern Ridges with Holland Village, while it's also straightforward to get here from Orchard Road or the Botanic Gardens on bus #7 or #77.

Sentosa and the southern isles

SENTOSA AND THE SOUTHERN ISLES | Sentosa

Though only just off the south coast of the main island of Singapore and linked to it by a bridge, **Sentosa** still has something of an out-of-town feel to it, and locals treat it as a kind of resort for full-day trips or weekend breaks. Don't expect a quiet, unspoilt desert isle, though – this is effectively one giant theme park, as epitomized by the newly launched Universal Studios, and the three beaches that do exist are decidedly ordinary. That said, if you have kids in tow you'll find plenty to keep them entertained for hours. Other, much smaller, islands lie further south within Singapore's territorial waters, including **St John's** and **Kusu**. They're easy enough to reach by ferry, and while not blighted by development, they are hardly unspoilt either, having become somewhat manicured in true Singapore style.

Sentosa

Given the rampant development over the past thirty years that has transformed **Sentosa** (℡1-800/7368672, Ⓦwww.sentosa.com.sg) into the most developed of Singapore's southern islands (with the possible exception of one or two that are home to petrochemical installations), it's ironic that its name means "tranquil" in Malay. Sentosa has come a long way since colonial times, when it had the charming name Pulau Blakang Mati, or the "Island of Death Behind", and was home to a British military base. Contrived but enjoyable in parts, the Sentosa of today is promoted for its rides, passable beaches, hotels and massive new integrated resort on the northern shore. Besides the mandatory casino and much-hyped Universal Studios theme park, *Resorts World Sentosa* has four new hotels, almost doubling the amount of accommodation on the island – with two more hotels, a Marine Life Park claimed to be "the world's largest oceanarium" plus a high-tech maritime museum still to come, though when these would be completed was uncertain at the time of writing. If you decide to go to Sentosa, it's best to come on a weekday (and not during the school holidays either; see p.34) unless you don't mind the place being overrun.

105

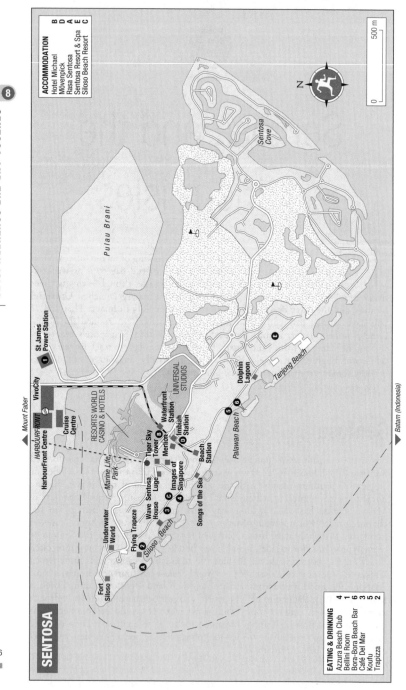

SENTOSA

▲ *Mount Faber*

Pulau Brani

Sentosa Cove

St James Power Station ❶

VivoCity

HARBOURFRONT
HarbourFront Centre

Cruise
Centre

RESORTS WORLD
CASINO & HOTELS

UNIVERSAL
STUDIOS

Waterfront
Station ❽

Tiger Sky
Tower
Merlion

Imbiah
Station ❹

Beach
Station

Dolphin
Lagoon

Tanjong Beach

*Marine Life
Park*

Underwater
World

Flying Trapeze

Wave Sentosa
House Luge ❸

Images of
Singapore ❹

Songs of the Sea

Fort
Siloso

Siloso Beach

Palawan Beach ❺ ❻

Ⓐ Ⓒ Ⓑ Ⓓ Ⓔ

N

0   500 m

▼ *Batam (Indonesia)*

ACCOMMODATION
Hotel Michael   B
Mövenpick   D
Rasa Sentosa   A
Sentosa Resort & Spa   E
Siloso Beach Resort   C

EATING & DRINKING
Azzura Beach Club   4
Bellini Room   1
Bora-Bora Beach Bar   6
Café Del Mar   3
Koufu   5
Trapizza   2

Travel practicalities

There are multiple options for reaching the island, the most spectacular of which is by **cable car** from either Mount Faber or the HarbourFront Centre on Telok Blangah Road (see p.101). The closest you can get by MRT or ordinary bus is the HarbourFront Centre, from where the #RWS8 bus (daily 6am–11.30pm; $2) heads to *Resorts World*, and orange Sentosa buses (daily 7am–11pm, midnight at weekends; $2) set off for Beach Station on the southern shore of the island, and you can get off anywhere en route. Beach Station is also served by the convenient **Sentosa Express** (daily 7am–midnight; $3), a light rail system with its northern terminus on level 3 of the VivoCity mall (see p.101). Trains call at Waterfront station on Sentosa's northern shore for the casino resort, then at the central Imbiah Station close to the Merlion replica, and finally at Beach Station. You can also simply **walk** across to Sentosa from VivoCity using a covered boardwalk ($2) or get a **taxi** to the island, though trips incur a surcharge of between $2 and $6 per vehicle depending on the time of the trip. For late owls, there are weekend **night buses**, with route numbers prefixed NR, between downtown and *Resorts World* (every 20–30min; Fri & Sat 11.30pm–4.30am; $3.50 fare plus $2 to set foot on the island).

Sentosa Express tickets can be used for unlimited travel on the island and to head back (on the return leg you can use either the train or the orange bus as long as you arrived on one or the other). Once back at HarbourFront, however, you will need to buy another ticket if you want to use public transport to return to Sentosa that day.

The island also has three colour-coded internal buses that run on loop routes, plus a so-called beach tram running the length of the southern beaches; both are free to use and are explained on the comprehensive map which you're given if you arrive by public transport. Renting a **bike** (from $8 per hour) isn't a bad idea; there are a couple of rental outfits behind the beaches, though note that you must return the bike to the outlet where you got it.

The main attractions

Spreading out either side of Waterfront station, the **Resorts World** development (℡ 65778888, ⓦ www.rwsentosa.com) is as expensive as it is visually plastic, looking at best like something out of a Silicon Valley corporate headquarters. Its saving grace is the **Universal Studios** theme park (daily 10am–7pm; $66/$48, plus a $6/$4 surcharge at weekends), where the ersatz quality becomes rather entertaining as fairy-tale castles and American cityscapes rear bizarrely into view in the sultry heat. The park is divided into seven themed zones, encompassing everything from ancient Egypt – the least convincing of the lot – to DreamWorks' animated hit *Madagascar*. Standard tickets offer unlimited rides, but there's more to do than get flung around on cutting-edge roller coasters: there are also shows and museum-type exhibits exploring the world of film production, plus a recreation of Hollywood's Pantages theatre where you can watch musical spectaculars.

At the western corner of the island, **Underwater World** (daily 9am–9pm; $23/$15) is a high-tech aquarium where a moving walkway in a hundred-metre tunnel takes you through two large tanks of sharks, huge stingrays and immense shoals of gaily coloured fish. A touch pool by the entrance allows you to pick up starfish and sea cucumbers – the latter rather like socks filled with wet sand. It's also possible to dive with the sharks and dugongs (from $90) or swim with the dolphins ($150), and if you prefer to get close up to marine creatures while staying dry, have a go on their user-controlled video camera system, the Ocean Invader. Another highlight is the **dolphin lagoon**, where the marine acrobatics of Indo-Pacific humpback dolphins are best viewed during a "Meet the Dolphins" session (daily 11.30am, 2.30pm & 5.45pm).

Nearby is **Fort Siloso** (daily 10am–6pm; $8/$5; free tours Sat & Sun 11am & 4pm), one of the island's earliest attractions. The fort – actually a cluster of buildings and gun emplacements above a series of tunnels bored into the island – guarded Singapore's western approaches from the 1880s until 1956, but its obsolescence was shown up when the Japanese marched down into Singapore from Malaysia. Today, the recorded voice of Battery Sergeant Major Cooper talks you through a mock-up of a nineteenth-century barracks, complete with living quarters, guard room, laundry and assault course. Be sure to check out the Surrender Chambers, where life-sized figures re-enact the British and Japanese surrenders of 1942 and 1945, respectively. After that you can explore the complex's hefty gun emplacements and tunnels.

Other attractions

At Imbiah station you're greeted by the 37-metre-tall **Merlion**, somehow even uglier than the original at the mouth of the Singapore River. It's possible to walk up through it to viewing decks (daily 10am–8pm; $8) for vistas of the mainland skyline. There are more views nearby at the **Tiger Sky Tower** (daily 9am–9pm; $12/$8), basically a ring-shaped glass cabin which glides up a very tall pole and then back down again. But the star attraction in this cluster is **Images of Singapore** (daily 9am–7pm; $10/$7), using life-sized dioramas to present Singapore's history and heritage from the fourteenth century through to 1945. Iconic images from Singapore's past – Raffles forging a treaty with the island's Malay rulers, rubber-tappers at the Botanic Gardens, coolies at the Singapore River – spring to life, and actors dressed as labourers and villagers are on hand to provide further insight.

From the Merlion, it's a short downhill stroll along the **Merlion Walk**, with abstract mosaics supposedly inspired by Gaudí, to Beach station. One ride nearby on the right is worth considering, the **Luge and Skyride** (daily 10am–9.30pm). The Skyride ($7), akin to a ski lift, takes you up a leafy slope, after which you ride your luge ($12) – like a small unmotorized go-kart – and coast down either of two curving tracks back to the starting point. (If you prefer to do the luge only, use the entry point near the Tiger Sky Tower.)

For something more active, there's **Megazip** (Mon–Fri 2–7pm, Sat & Sun 11am–7pm), near Imbiah station. The main attraction here is a flying-fox setup where you slide down to the bottom of the hill suspended from a steel cable ($29), though there's also a mini-bungee jump ($12) and an obstacle course that's all ropes and netting ($39). Near Beach station, a kiosk rents **Segway** electric scooters for a "fun ride" (on a private circuit; $12) or a half-hour guided beach tour ($38).

If your Sentosa visit extends into the evening, you might well want to catch **Songs of the Sea** (daily 7.40pm & 8.40pm; 25min; $10), a lavish sound-and-light show whose canvas is not ancient monuments but screens of water; seating for the show is right at the seafront just off Beach station.

Beaches

The best that can be said about Sentosa's three beaches, created with vast quantities of imported yellowish sand, is that they're decent enough, with bluey-green water, the odd lagoon and facilities for renting canoes, surfboards and aqua bikes. For tranquility, however, you'd probably do better at Changi Beach (see p.95), because at Sentosa you have to deal not only with crowds but also – Singapore being one of the world's busiest ports – a constant parade of container ships and other vessels.

Siloso Beach, which extends 1500m northwest of Beach station, is the busiest of the three, with well-established resorts and facilities. It's also home to the

▲ Si loso Beach Volleyball

Azzura Beach Club (daily 9am–7pm; ☎62708003) which offers kayaking ($8–12 for 1hr) and other activities, and has a pool and jacuzzi you can use if you're dining there. Nearby is **WaveHouse** (daily 10am till late; ☎63773133), which does for surfing what Universal Studios does for ancient Egypt, creating a semblance of breakers using torrents of water along two contoured plastic slopes (first hour $30 or $40 depending on "ride", $5 more at weekends).

Palawan Beach, just southeast of Beach station, features a suspension bridge leading out to an islet billed as the "Southernmost Point of Continental Asia" – though signs concede that this is so only by virtue of three manmade links, namely the suspension bridge itself, the bridge from HarbourFront to Sentosa, and the Causeway to Malaysia. Beyond Palawan is **Tanjong Beach**, which tends to be slightly quieter than the other two as it starts a full kilometre from Beach station.

Eating, drinking and nightlife

While there are food outlets all over the casino resort, the most atmospheric places to eat are down by the beach. On Siloso Beach, *Trapizza* (daily 11am–10.30pm, food noon–9.30pm; ☎63762662) stands out for its excellent pizzas and pasta dishes, at reasonable prices, as does the *Azzura Beach Club*, with a restaurant serving tapas and other Western and local fare (daily 9am–late), plus funky **beach parties** (Sat & Sun sunset till 3am). Just a little further on, opposite the *Siloso Beach Resort*, is *Café del Mar* (daily 11am–1am, later at weekends; Ⓦwww.cafedelmar.com.sg), an offshoot of the Ibiza original, with a poolside bar, Mediterranean-influenced cuisine, diverse sounds ranging from reggae to electronica, and its own beach parties on the last Saturday of the month (from 5pm; no cover charge). For simple, inexpensive meals, there's the *Koufu* food court on Palawan Beach, with indoor and outdoor tables. Here, you'll also find the cheery *Bora-Bora Beach Bar* (daily 10.30am–9pm, 10pm at weekends; ☎62780838, Ⓦwww.boraborasentosa.com), which has a huge menu featuring everything from seafood platters to banana-and-Kahlua freezes, though they stop serving food at 7.30pm.

Kusu and St John's islands

St John's or **Kusu** islands, 6km south of Singapore, offer some respite from the hubbub of the city state, with decent beaches. The more interesting of the two is Kusu, also known as **Turtle Island**. Singaporean legend tells of a Chinese and a Malay sailor who were saved from drowning by a turtle that transformed itself into an island; today the island is home to a major temple, complete with turtle statues. Once a year during the ninth lunar month (usually in October or November), tens of thousands of Singaporean pilgrims descend upon the **Chinese temple** and **Malay shrine** a few minutes' walk from the jetty on Kusu, to pray for prosperity. Both islands are connected to the mainland by a **ferry** (Mon–Fri two daily, with more frequent sailings at weekends; $15/$12 return ticket with island admission; schedules from ⓣ65349339 or Ⓦwww.islandcruise.com.sg) from the Marina South Pier. Bus #402 travels the 1500m to the pier from Marina Bay MRT station, though it only runs twice an hour.

Listings

Listings

9 Accommodation 113

10 Eating 121

11 Nightlife 140

12 Entertainment and the arts..................................... 146

13 Festivals... 150

14 Shopping 153

15 Sports... 159

16 Kids' Singapore.. 163

Accommodation

Accommodation in Singapore needn't take too big a bite out of your holiday budget. Good deals abound if your expectations aren't too lofty or – at the budget end of the scale – if you don't mind sharing.

The island has plenty of modern, mid-range **hotels** where a room for two with air-conditioning, private bathroom and TV will set you back around $90–150 a night. From there, prices rise steadily, and at the top end Singapore has some extraordinarily opulent hotels, ranging from the colonial splendour of *Raffles* (see p.114) to the awesome spectacle of *Swissôtel The Stamford* (see p.114) – one of the world's tallest hotels. There are also quite a few so-called **boutique hotels**, particularly in Chinatown, which can range from affordable, with a smattering of antique furniture, to ultra-sleek establishments where every room looks like a Manhattan penthouse, with prices to match. At the other end of the scale are Singapore's **hostels** and **guesthouses**, the distinction between which can be blurry: both offer dorms for $20–30 a night and simple private rooms for $50–80, with shared facilities. A few are spartan affairs, but these days most offer air-conditioning, free wi-fi, a comfy communal lounge and a simple self-service breakfast, included in the rate.

One quirk to be aware of is that published tariffs for accommodation are often somewhat meaningless: many of the simpler hotels have **promotional deals** almost year-round that can slash ten to twenty percent off their official rates, while all the more upmarket hotels continually adjust the price of rooms based on demand. The rates quoted in the reviews here represent what you can reasonably hope to be offered most of the year, and include **GST** and the **service charge** (see p.31) where they apply; it's worth reading the fine print on any deals you come across to check if these surcharges have been taken into account.

Reservations are a good idea, and not just for peace of mind: many of the best rates are available only if you book online. In general, however, you shouldn't encounter too many difficulties in finding a room unless your visit coincides with the Formula 1 race in late September, when prices also rocket.

The majority of mid-range and upmarket hotels in Singapore make no charge for **children** under 12 if they are occupying existing spare beds in rooms. However, having an extra bed put in the room usually incurs a surcharge of $30–50 a night, possibly more in upmarket hotels; cots are almost invariably provided free.

The Colonial District and Marina Centre

Between the north bank of the Singapore River and Bras Basah Road (including the area around Fort Canning Park) are a handful of mid-range and pricey hotels, though none owes anything to the area's colonial heritage. East of here, several ultra-swanky hotels are crammed onto the rather soulless triangle of reclaimed land called Marina Centre, forming the northern jaw of Marina Bay. See the map on p.39.

Novotel Clarke Quay 177A River Valley Rd
☏ 63383333, ⓦ www.novotel.com. This dull
tower block might seem like just another
bland business-oriented hotel, but the wood-
panelled lobby and tasteful contemporary
furnishings make clear this is all about giving
the boutique hotels a run for their money.
Comes with the usual four-star amenities,
including pool and jacuzzi. From $320.

Peninsula Excelsior 5 Coleman St ☏ 63372200,
ⓦ www.ytchotels.com.sg. Really two hotels
merged together – as hinted at by the
presence of two swimming pools at either
end, one of which abuts the current lobby –
and nicely modernized, unlike the 1970s
shopping arcades below. Decent value:
rooms start at $220.

Raffles 1 Beach Rd ☏ 63371886, ⓦ www.raffles
hotel.com. Though the modern extension is
a mixed bag, *Raffles* remains refreshingly
low-rise and still has colonial-era charm in
spades, especially evident in the opulent
lobby and the courtyards fringed by frangipani trees and palms. Amenities include a
dozen restaurants and bars, a rooftop pool
and a spa. You'll need deep pockets to
stay, of course: rates for suites – as all
rooms here are – start at around $900.

Ritz-Carlton Millenia 7 Raffles Ave ☏ 63378888,
ⓦ www.ritz-carlton.com. Arguably king of the
pricey hotels in Marina Centre, with magnificent views across to the financial district
even from the bathrooms, where butlers will
fill your bath for you. From $450.

Robertson Quay Hotel 15 Merbau Rd
☏ 67353333, ⓦ www.robertsonquayhotel.com
.sg. Cylindrical riverside hotel, whose
compact but inviting rooms yield great views
of the river and city skyline. There's a cute
circular pool with slide and waterfall on the
third-floor terrace. From $153.

Swissôtel The Stamford 2 Stamford Rd
☏ 63388585, ⓦ www.singapore-stamford
.swissotel.com. Upper-floor rooms – and the
restaurants and bars on the 70th to 72nd
floors – aren't for those with vertigo,
though the views are as splendid as you'd
expect from one of the tallest hotels in the
world. Facilities include a pool, spa and
tennis courts, though the biggest plus is
having City Hall MRT beneath the building.
From $420.

YMCA International House 1 Orchard Rd
☏ 63366000, ⓦ www.ymcaih.com.sg. Nominally
on Orchard Rd but really on the edge of the
Colonial District, this is essentially a rather
staid hotel with its own café and comfortable if slightly institutional rooms, all with
a/c, fridge and modern bathroom. More
exciting are the rooftop pool and the buffet
breakfast, included in the rate. From $140.

YWCA Fort Canning Lodge 6 Fort Canning Rd
☏ 63384222, ⓦ nof.ywca.org.sg. In the same
vein as the YMCA, offering decent
mid-range rooms – and not to women only
as you might assume. Amenities include a
café, pool and tennis courts, and the rate –
from $130 a night – includes breakfast.

Chinatown and the Central Business District

The range of budget and mid-range accommodation in **Chinatown** has grown in
inverse proportion to that of Bencoolen Street's. Whatever your budget, you're
sure to find an address to suit you in this most charismatic of enclaves, which has
a mass of upmarket and boutique hotels. See the map on pp.54–55.

Hostels and guesthouses

A Beary Good Hostel 66A/B Pagoda St
☏ 62224955, ⓦ www.abearygoodhostel.com.
Colourful, chirpy backpacker place, a stone's
throw from Chinatown MRT, with basic but
airy mixed dorms. Facilities include free wi-fi,
all-day breakfast and lockers. Friendly and
good value. Dorm beds from $20.

Rucksack Inn 33B Hong Kong St ☏ 64385146,
ⓦ www.rucksackinn.com. A short stroll from
Clarke Quay, this hostel has friendly and
informed staff and is spotlessly clean. Dorms

and rooms are basic but have fans or a/c,
and shared shower facilities. The main
lounge area has a TV where you can relax
with a DVD or rock out with a game of Guitar
Hero, and the price includes all-day breakfast
and free wi-fi. Dorm beds $26, double $79.

Hotels

Chinatown 12–16 Teck Lim Rd ☏ 62255166,
ⓦ www.chinatownhotel.com. The re-modelled
facade gives a hint at what this original
shophouse building looked like, while the
rooms have smart en-suites, and although

▲ The Fullerton

lacking in natural light the mahogany furniture gives them old-fashioned charm. From $100.

The Fullerton 1 Fullerton Square ☎67338388, ⓦwww.fullertonhotel.com. An expensive treat, this Colonial-era post office with its statu-esque columns is one of Singapore's most stylish hotels, and the one that most obviously aspires to "grand dame" status. Its rooms are luxuriously and tastefully uphol-stered in cream, with those at the front enjoying floor-to-ceiling windows and balconies. The pool overlooks the river, while the rooftop restaurant *The Lighthouse* (see p.134) is a destination in itself. From $527.

Gallery 1 Nanson Rd, Robertson Quay ☎68498686, ⓦwww.galleryhotel.com.sg. Extravagantly lit with neon stripes at night, and feature some striking postmodern architecture, the *Gallery* is one of Singapore's most exciting hotels. Choose from an arresting array of unique rooms, which include Lichenstein-inspired decor, mono-chromatic geometric prints, sprawling beds on wheels and low beds with Bedouin-style drapery. All rooms include wi-fi. From $183.

Hotel 1929 50 Keong Saik Rd ☎63471929, ⓦwww.hotel1929.com. This old shophouse building looks very 1929 on the outside, but the interior has been renovated to look like a twenty-first century version of the early 1960s; it's very retro chic and all tastefully done. From $187.

Hotel Ré! 175A Chin Swee Rd ☎68278288, ⓦwww.hotelre.com.sg. Vibrant retro-themed boutique hotel at Pearl's Hill, adjacent to Chinatown. With gaudy interiors featuring the silhouette of John Travolta and kitsch furniture that includes bubble chairs from the 1960s it's not to everyone's taste, but it is great fun. Facilities include a Continental restaurant, wine bar, massage centre and a free shuttle bus to the city. From $163.

The Inn at Temple Street 36 Temple St ☎62215333, ⓦwww.theinn.com.sg. One of Chinatown's more atmospheric hotels, sculpted out of a row of shophouses and filled to bursting with furnishings and curios from old Singapore. From $108.

Klapsons 15 Hoe Chiang Rd ☎65219030, ⓦwww.klapsons.com. From $329. Small Italian-designed boutique hotel featuring 17 individual bedrooms. Design quirks include open showers, neon plastic tables, ornate mirrors with freestanding sinks and Molton Brown products, while the suites boast jacuzzis and outdoor decking areas. The lobby is also impressive, with a huge space-dominating silver ball that serves as reception. From $329.

New Majestic 31–37 Bukit Pasoh Rd ☎65114700, ⓦwww.newmajestichotel .com. This boutique hotel in the heart of gentrified Chinatown has become something of an institution thanks to its highly original bedrooms, each designed by a local artist. Choose from one with a bed suspended from the ceiling, a racy David LaChapelle-inspired room with velvet bedspread and flashing neon pink "Girls" sign, and cuter affairs with owl murals and outdoor showers. Its eponymous restaurant serving Cantonese cuisine is also popular. From $282.

The Scarlet 33 Erskine Rd ☎65113333, ⓦwww .thescarlethotel.com. Rather glam boutique hotel with sumptuous, comfortable bedrooms, decorated with opulent red and purple velvet and mahogany furniture. The daybeds at the rooftop bar, *Breeze*, are the perfect place from which to admire Chinatown over a leisurely drink. From $206.

Swissôtel Merchant Court 20 Merchant Rd ☎63372288, ⓦwww.swissotel.com/singapore -merchantcourt. Large hotel overlooking Clarke Quay that's popular with families. The rooms, although unoriginal, are exceedingly comfortable, with welcoming touches such as Peranakan tiles in the bathrooms. Kids will love the swimming pool's waterslide, and there's an excellent buffet restaurant. From $290.

Little India, Arab Street and Lavender Street

Little India is very much the centre for budget accommodation in Singapore, and easily accessible thanks to Little India MRT. There are also quite a few decent budget and mid-range places to stay beyond Little India proper, in the zone extending up to Lavender Street, reachable via Farrer Park or Lavender stations, and with an excellent public swimming pool close by (see p.161). The area around Arab Street also has a few good places to stay and is convenient for Bugis MRT station. All the places reviewed here are marked on the top half of the map on pp.68–69.

Hostels and guesthouses

ABC 3 Jalan Kubor ☎62981611, ⊚www .abcbackpackershostel.com. Mundanely named and mundane by nature, this hostel is at least new, tidy and well placed for Arab St. It also offers disabled facilities, free internet access and use of a kitchen. Dorm beds from $15, double from $50 ($70 if en suite).

Ali's Nest 23 Roberts Lane ☎62912938, ⊚alisnest@yahoo.com.sg. One of the very cheapest places to stay in Singapore, rather spartan but the more appealing for that. Some rooms have a/c; amenities are limited to a kitchen, small sitting area and internet access. Rate includes a self-service breakfast. If you have difficulty finding the old shophouse, look out for the "Shanghai Kotat Trading" sign above. Dorm beds $13, double $30.

Checkers Inn 46–50 Campbell Lane ☎63920693, ⊚www.checkersinn.com.sg. This slick place bills itself as a "boutique backpackers", and for once the hype isn't misplaced: the kitchen looks like something out of a posh furnishings store, while dangling from the ceiling of the swanky lounge are dozens of little toys, spray-painted white. The dorms (mixed or single-sex) are unremarkable but, thought-fully, there are hairdryers in all the bathrooms. No private rooms. $25–30.

Fragrance Hostel 63 Dunlop St ☎62956888, ⊚www.fragrancebackpackers.com.sg. Owned by the budget hotel chain, this competently run but rather sterile establishment offers single-sex and mixed dorms, each with six beds. Facilities include a lounge with TV and internet access. Dorm beds $20.

The Hive 624 Serangoon Rd (corner of Lavender St) ☎63415041, ⊚www.thehivebackpackers .com. A large hostel where every room is named after a flower and the exterior is done out in black and yellow. Bee metaphors aside, the place is well managed, with a/c in all rooms and dorms

and free internet access. Breakfast included. Dorm beds from $20, doubles from $42.

InnCrowd 73 Dunlop St (reception) & 35 Campbell Lane ☎62969169, ⊚www .the-inncrowd.com. Endearing, recently renovated hostel with dorms plus a range of rooms with TV and a/c. Shared showers and toilets are kept spotless, and there's a comfy lounge, cheap beer and free internet access. You get breakfast too, whether you're in a dorm ($20) or one of the rooms ($59).

Prince of Wales 101 Dunlop St ☎62990130, ⊚www.pow.com.sg. Justifiably popular place done out in primary colours, with a/c dorms, a couple of double rooms and a 24hr bar/beer garden. Breakfast and wi-fi access are included in the rate. Dorm beds $18, doubles $60.

Sleepy Sam's 55 Bussorah St ☎92774988, ⊚www.sleepysams.com. A well-kept and surprisingly stylish hostel, superbly placed in the heart of the Arab St area and just down from the Sultan Mosque. Besides mixed and women-only dorms, there's a shared triple room plus a single and a double; amenities include a kitchen, a small café, laundry service and free internet access. Dorm beds $28, doubles $89.

Tresor Tavern 243 Jalan Besar ☎62936005, ⊚www.tresortavern.com. It's dorms and more dorms here, with anything from four to twelve beds. Things can be bit cramped though there is some compensation in the unusually swish decor, with designer lounge sofas and bathrooms fittings, and fancy lighting throughout. Rate includes breakfast and internet access (including wi-fi). Dorm beds from $16.

Welcome Inn 259A Jalan Besar ☎62963259, ⊚welcomeinn.com.sg. The pastel lilac exterior is a muted prelude to bright bed linen and snazzy murals on gaudy interior walls. It's all pretty inviting, featuring a spacious lounge with TV and DVD, plus free internet access (including wi-fi), a kitchen and a free self-service breakfast. The mixed-sex dorm is huge, sleeping twenty, though the women's dorm sleeps a more typical six. There are also single and double rooms. Dorm beds from $20, doubles $78.

Hotels

Aliwal Park 77 Aliwal St ☎62939022, ⓔaliwal@pacific.net.sg. The rooms, equipped with TV and kettle, are small and rather gloomy, but they are en suite and rates are keen. $70.
Fortuna 2 Owen Rd ☎62953577, ⓦwww.fortunahotel.com.sg. Some of the otherwise ordinary rooms in this modern hotel have good views over Serangoon Road, though you might prefer a room on the other side of the building as noise can be a problem. From $110.
Fragrance Imperial 28 Penhas Rd ☎62978888, ⓦwww.fragrancehotel.com. A short walk from Lavender MRT, this is a cut above fellow members of the budget chain, with slick if smallish rooms, a café and rooftop swimming pool. Great promotional deals apply most of the time. From $130 including breakfast.
Haising 37 Jalan Besar ☎62981223, ⓦwww.haising.com.sg. Friendly, secure Chinese-run cheapie offering simple, a/c en-suite rooms with TV, rather boxy but not bad for the price. From $60.
Kerbau 54–62 Kerbau Rd ☎62976668, ⓔkerbauinn@pacific.net.sg. In row of restored shophouses, the *Kerbau* is a compact place with en-suite rooms with a/c and TV, and a good location near Tekka Market and Little India MRT. From $70.

Landmark Village 390 Victoria St (main entrance on Arab St) ☎62972828, ⓦwww.stayvillage.com. Beyond the dated shopping centre downstairs is a modern hotel, recently partly refurbished, with its own pool, gym and restaurants. Frequent promotional rates bring starting prices for doubles down to $190.
Madras 28–32 Madras Rd ☎63927889, ⓦwww.madrassingapore.com. Smallish, slightly tatty rooms with the standard mod cons and the bonus of a DVD player in each. From $99.
Parkroyal 181 Kitchener Rd ☎64283000, ⓦwww.parkroyalhotels.com. The classiest place to stay in the Little India area, with a marbled lobby, spacious and tasteful rooms, a pool and a couple of restaurants. If you're heading here by taxi rather than via the nearby Farrer Park MRT, make sure you mention the address as there's a sister hotel of the same name on Beach Rd. From $220.
Perak 12 Perak Rd ☎62997733, ⓦwww.peraklodge.net. Set within a nicely restored shophouse and somewhat sedate – probably not a bad thing given the hulla-balloo of Little India. The hotel is slightly overpriced but makes partial amends with friendly staff, comfy if unremarkable rooms and a pleasant residents-only rest area. From $150, including breakfast.
Santa Grand Bugis 8 Jalan Kubor ☎62988638, ⓦwww.santa.com.sg. This functional, modern hotel has decent rooms, wi-fi, and a pool, but what really edges it ahead of the competition are the family and deluxe rooms in a nicely restored old house next door. From $145 with breakfast.

Bras Basah Road to Rochor Road

The grid of streets between Bras Basah Road and Rochor Road (and a bit beyond, uphill from Selegie Road) has been rendered a bit sterile by redevelopment, which has also eliminated most of the cheap accommodation that once packed Bencoolen Street. What remains are mostly modern mid-range establishments with the notable exception of *Raffles* which, with its colonial connections, is reviewed on p.114. The area remains a good choice if you can afford it, as it's within walking distance of the Singapore River, Little India, Arab Street and the southern end of Orchard Road. The places covered here appear in the lower half of the map on pp.68–69.

Hostels and guesthouses

G4 Station 11 Mackenzie Rd ☎63345644, ⓦg4station.com. Short on atmosphere but impeccably run. Accommodation comprises dorms of various sizes plus double rooms, all with a/c and plenty of modern fittings (including chunky lockers), and sharing immaculate bathrooms and showers. Free internet access available, plus a Wii for gaming, and they run a café at the back, too.

Rates include breakfast. Dorm beds from $33, rooms $80.

Hangout @ Mount Emily 10A Upper Wilkie Rd ☏64385588, Ⓦwww.hangouthotels .com. Owned by the company behind the historic Cathay cinema at the foot of Mount Emily, the *Hangout* is an impressive cross between a hostel and a designer guesthouse, with a breezy rooftop terrace that's great for chilliing out in the evening. The only drawback is that it's a 10-min walk uphill from Selegie Rd. Best to book online, both because the place is popular and so you can get much lower rates (all of which include a buffet breakfast) than if you simply turn up. Dorm beds from $40, rooms from $100.

Waterloo Hostel Fourth floor, Catholic Centre Building, 55 Waterloo St ☏63366555, Ⓦwww .waterloohostel.com.sg. This Catholic-run hostel is staid and slightly ageing but has comfortable a/c rooms with TV and the option of en-suite facilities, though you'll pay at least twenty percent extra for these. Breakfast is included. From $60.

Hotels

Albert Court 180 Albert St ☏63393939, Ⓦwww .albertcourt.com.sg. This self-styled boutique hotel benefits from preserved shophouse facades and amenities such as gym, jacuzzi and sauna. The superior and deluxe rooms have old-fashioned ceiling fans – which you're unlikely to use as there's a/c – while the pricier executive rooms are ultramodern. From $190.

Carlton 76 Bras Basah Rd ☏63388333, Ⓦwww.carltonhotel.sg. Plastic palm trees in the lobby sound the wrong note, but this multistorey tower of a four-star hotel offers elegant rooms, restaurants, a pool and gym – and great promotional rates most of the time. From $300.

Ibis 170 Bencoolen St ☏65932888, Ⓦwww.ibishotel.com. If you've stayed in other hotels run by this no-frills chain, you'd probably describe them as functional, modern and a little dull – a perfect match for Singapore, then. This vast new establishment is well insulated from traffic noise and has

wi-fi throughout. The 7–Eleven shop right in the lobby feels totally apt. From $140.

Intercontinental 80 Middle Rd ☏63387600, Ⓦwww.intercontinental.com. Like the adjoining Bugis Junction mall, the *Intercontinental* incorporates some of the area's original shophouses, here converted into so-called "shophouse rooms" with supposedly Peranakan decor, though this merely amounts to Oriental-looking vases and paintings of tropical fruit. Still, the hotel is luxurious and has all the amenities you could want, and rates can fall by a quarter at weekends. From $300.

Naumi 41 Seah St ☏64036000, Ⓦwww .naumihotel.com. The slate grey exterior, with what look like vines crawling up the building behind netting, doesn't inspire, but inside is a stunning boutique hotel where every room is kitted out like a luxury apartment and boasts an iPod dock, kitchenette and free wi-fi. There's also a rooftop infinity pool and a bar. Rooms on one floor are for women only. From $350.

Rendezvous 9 Bras Basah Rd ☏63360220, Ⓦwww.rendezvoushotels.com. Unmissable at the start of Bras Basah Rd, this comfortable four-star hotel blends the original shophouses on the corner into a huge modern extension beyond. Amenities include a pool, jacuzzi and some good restaurants, most famously the *Rendezvous* curry house (see p.136). From $240.

South East Asia 190 Waterloo St ☏63382394, Ⓦwww.seahotel.com.sg. Behind the yellow and white 1950s facade is a modern hotel with spotless doubles, some en-suite and all featuring the usual mod cons. Downstairs is a vegetarian restaurant serving Continental and Asian breakfasts, and right next door is the lively Kwan Im temple. Slightly dull but good value, with rooms starting at $100 a night including breakfast.

Victoria 87 Victoria St ☏66220909, Ⓦwww .santagrandhotels.com. This compact hotel is dwarfed by the buildings around, but punches above its weight with modern en-suite rooms equipped with flatscreen TV and fridge. No breakfast though. $120.

Orchard Road

Sumptuous hotels abound on and around **Orchard Road**; you should be prepared to spend at least $90 a night. All the hotels in this section are keyed on the map on pp.78–79.

The Elizabeth **24 Mount Elizabeth** ℡67381188, ⓦwww.theelizabeth.com.sg. Within its toy-town exterior, this boutique hotel has delightful and well-appointed rooms. From $202.

Goodwood Park **22 Scotts Rd** ℡67377411, ⓦwww.goodwoodparkhotel.com. This opulent hotel may remind you of *Raffles* – both were designed by the same architect. The building has a long history (see p.81), and it's still a study in elegance, its arching facades fronting exquisitely appointed rooms. From $184.

Grand Hyatt **10 Scott's Rd** ℡67381234, ⓦwww.singapore.grand.hyatt.com. Comfortable, modern bedrooms with excellent en-suites that have a separate shower and ultra-deep bath, but what makes this hotel special is its excellent restaurants, the highlight of which is *Mezza9* on the top floor. There's also a magnificent spa and a luxurious outdoor pool that has daybeds where waiters will bring you drinks at the touch of a button. From $360.

Holiday Inn Orchard City Centre **11 Cavenagh Rd** ℡67338333, ⓦwww.holidayinn.com/sin-orchard. Guests of this plusher-than-average and recently refurbished *Holiday Inn* are next-door neighbours of Singapore's president for the duration of their stay – the palace is just across the road. From $265.

Lloyd's Inn **2 Lloyd Rd** ℡67377309, ⓦwww.lloydinn.com. Motel-style building boasting attractive rooms and a fine location, just five minutes from Orchard Road. From $90.

Mandarin Orchard **333 Orchard Rd** ℡67374411, ⓦwww.meritus-hotels.com. Luxurious behemoth of a hotel annexed to a swanky shopping centre. Rooms have huge beds and are decorated in a mixture of warm and neutral shades with Asian-inspired artwork. Also features a top-notch array of restaurants, an outdoor pool and a gym. From $540.

Marriott **320 Orchard Rd** ℡67355800, ⓦwww.marriotthotels.com. A superior five-star hotel housed in a thirty-storey building with a unique green pagoda-style roof. The sumptuous, spacious rooms are decorated

in warm colours and soft fabrics. Also features a gorgeous outdoor pool, excellent spa and gym. From $390.

Metropolitan Y **60 Stevens Rd** ℡68398333, ⓦwww.ymca.sg. Perfectly adequate rooms with a/c, en-suite, TV and minibar, some suitable for travellers in wheelchairs. From $117.

Orchard Parade Hotel **1 Tanglin Rd** ℡67371133, ⓦwww.orchardparade.com.sg. Located minutes from the bustle of Orchard Road yet affording views of lush greenery, this welcoming hotel offers comfortable bedrooms all of which have a pretty balcony and overlook the lovely Spanish-style outdoor pool. Excellent value for money. From $200.

St Regis **29 Tanglin Rd** ℡65066888, ⓦwww.stregis.com. A superlatively opulent hotel off Orchard Road. Bedrooms are lavishly decorated with silk chandeliers and French marble bathrooms, and there's a butler to cater to your every whim. The hotel's entrance and pool features sculptures by Colombian artist Botero and an atmospheric bar that knocks up fabulous cocktails within Picasso-lined walls. From $530.

Shangri-La Hotel **22 Orange Grove Rd** ℡67373644, ⓦwww.shangri-la.com. Luxury hotel set in six hectares of landscaped greenery, which give it a resort feel despite being only five minutes from Orchard Road. The luxurious bedrooms really have the wow factor, with their elegant furnishings and stunning views – the best of which are from the Garden Wing, overlooking the free-form pool. From $350.

Sloane Court Hotel **17 Balmoral Rd** ℡62353311, ⓔsloane@singnet.com.sg. As close to a Tudor house as you get in Singapore, the *Sloane Court* is tucked away in a prime residential area, near Newton MRT. Basic yet well-appointed rooms. From $108.

Supreme **15 Kramat Rd** ℡67378333, ⓔsupremeh@starhub.net.sg. A great-value budget hotel well placed at the eastern end of Orchard Road. From $145.

Eastern Singapore: Geylang and Katong

Geylang and **Katong**, along Singapore's southeastern coast, have traditionally both been Malay-dominated areas. If you can't face the bustle of central Singapore this region might appeal – certainly its cool sea breezes and Malay markets are an advantage. MRT and buses connect you quickly with downtown Singapore. All the hotels in this section are keyed on the maps on p.92 or p.94.

Hostels

Betel Box Backpackers Hostel 200 Joo Chiat Rd T 62477340, W www.betelbox.com. Relatively close to both the beach and Paya Lebar MRT, this is one of the best hostels in Singapore. Dorms include a female-only option and are spacious with a/c and lockers. Owner and local expert Tony Tan offers excellent free guided tours of the district. Dorms from $20, basic breakfast included.

Hotels

Amber Hotel 40 Amber Rd T 62622929, W www.amberhotelsingapore.com. Recently renovated, this super-friendly hotel has basic but perfectly adequate rooms and is just a short walk from the coast. From $100.
Grand Mercure Roxy 50 East Coast Rd T 63448000, W www.grandmercureroxy.com.sg.

One of the East Coast's more upmarket options, located midway between the city and Changi Airport. Bedrooms are modern, large and comfortable, if a little Identikit. From $140.

Le Peranakan Hotel 400 East Coast Rd T 66655511, W www.leperanakanhotel .com. An excellent value boutique hotel decorated in dramatic black and red hues, with ornately carved wooden furniture. Bedrooms are both cosy and full of character. From $80.
Sing Hoe Hotel 759 Mountbatten Rd T 64403245, F 63465996. One of the few hotels to be housed in a beautifully restored Straits Chinese colonial house, with attractive reliefs on its external walls. The rooms, however, have seen better days and are rather rough round the edges. From $60.

Sentosa

Staying "offshore" on Sentosa isn't such a bad idea if you have young children. Besides the hotels reviewed here, there are two more that should be worth considering but were not open at the time of writing. One is the *Mövenpick* (W www.moevenpick-hotels.com), which promises some of the most characterful accommodation on Sentosa in a refurbished colonial building. It's meant to be opening its doors in 2011, which is also when the *Rasa Sentosa Resort* (T 62750100, W www.shangri-la.com), long one of the nicest beachside places to stay, should reopen after a major overhaul. See map, p.106.

Hotel Michael T 65778888, W www.rwsentosa .com. The only hotel at *Resorts World* that's memorable, thanks to fittings and decor by the American architect and designer Michael Graves. Look out for packages that include Universal Studios, if you're so inclined. From $330.
Sentosa Resort and Spa 2 Bukit Manis Rd T 62750331, W www.thesentosa.com. A swanky affair in secluded grounds above Tanjong Beach, with a spa featuring outdoor pools and imported mud from New Zealand that's said to be great for your skin. There

are other spa hotels on Sentosa that are fancier and stupidly expensive; here rates start at a sensible $320.
Siloso Beach Resort 51 Imbiah Walk T 67223333, W www.silosobeachresort.com. Midway along Siloso Beach is this large complex whose best feature is the swimming pool, its curvy fringes planted with lush vegetation and featuring a waterfall and slides. If arriving by taxi, tell the driver that reception is not on the beach but at the opposite end of the site. From $220.

10

Eating

Along with shopping, **eating** ranks as a national pastime for Singaporeans, and a mind-boggling number of food outlets on just about every street corner cater for this obsession. However, eating out here is not necessarily about refinements or taking things at a gentle pace: as often as not, you'll find yourself eating off plastic plates in boisterous, unpretentious diners and that food arrives so quickly that you're getting up to leave less than an hour after you arrived. Dining out is a family affair, too, so unless you're going really upmarket, don't be shy of taking the kids with you. If they're not culinary adventurers, there are always burger bars or pizza joints near at hand.

The profusion of establishments serving **Chinese** cuisine reflects local demographics, though there are quite a few places offering **north** and **south Indian** cuisine, too, plus a modest number of restaurants serving **Malay**, **Indonesian** and **Nonya** food – the last of these being a hybrid of Chinese and Malay cooking styles developed by the Peranakan community (see p.47). Of course, there are also quite a few restaurants serving other East Asian cuisines, including **Thai**, **Vietnamese**, **Japanese** and **Korean** food.

Western food is plentiful in Singapore too, though it tends to be pricier than other cuisines and don't be too disappointed if, just as in the West, swanky restaurants turn out to serve rather average food. Quite a few of the more run-of-the-mill restaurants swing both ways by offering both Western and Asian dishes, and there's no shortage of upmarket places serving a fusion of the two, with plenty of specialist Western restaurants as well.

Several Chinese and Indian restaurants and a few hawker stalls serve **vegetarian food**. Tread carefully if ordering elsewhere, as bits of chicken or seafood will appear in a whole host of dishes unless you make it absolutely clear that you don't want them, and some dishes may be flavoured with meat stock, *hae ko* or *belachan*, the last two being pungent pastes made from shrimps. **Halal food** is predictably easy to find – most hawker centres have a row of stalls serving halal Indian or Malay food, there's a halal food court chain (*Banquet*), and some locally run Western-style fast food places offer halal burgers and so forth.

While many restaurants charge as much you would pay for a similar meal in Rome or New York, eating in Singapore need not be expensive. The ubiquitous **hawker centres** and **food courts** are both affordable and the most fun places to eat, with scores of stalls letting you mix and match Asian and some Western food. Wherever you eat, be assured that food outlets meet good standards of hygiene.

Tipping is seldom required: mid-range and upmarket restaurants add a service charge and GST (together adding up to around seventeen percent) to your bill, while hawkers and coffee-shop owners don't expect tips.

Markets and supermarkets

Many hostels and guesthouses have cooking facilities, and if you want to take advantage of them, the most interesting places to buy produce and ingredients are **wet markets** – so called because the floors are perpetually damp, and sometimes actually quite wet, thanks to being hosed down from time to time. If you don't know a mango from a mangosteen, vendors are usually very helpful (see also "*Singapore food*" colour section). Probably the most popular, well-stocked and atmospheric of downtown wet markets is the **Tekka Market** at the start of Serangoon Road, a worthwhile stopover on any trip to Little India (see p.71). In addition, Singapore has plenty of **supermarkets**, some of which are franchises of Western or Japanese chains; all stock imported beers and wines and have a deli counter. For more unusual imports, try Market Place (outlets include: Level B1, Tanglin Mall, 163 Tanglin Rd; Level B1, Paragon, 290 Orchard Rd, near Orchard MRT), which is popular with expats for its specialist Western and Japanese food, including organic produce.

Breakfast

Many visitors baulk at **local cooked breakfasts**, but there are some tasty possibilities if you shelve your preconceptions. The classic Chinese breakfast is congee, a watery rice porridge augmented with chopped spring onion, crispy fried onion and strips of meat. An abiding favourite among Malays is *nasi lemak*, rice cooked in coconut milk and served with *sambal ikan bilis* (tiny crisp-fried anchovies in hot chilli paste), fried peanuts and slices of fried or hard-boiled egg. Otherwise, try investigating one of the scores of Indian and Malay establishments that serve up *roti prata*, a griddle bread with a curry sauce. For **Western breakfasts**, there are any number of fast-food type outlets or Western-style cafés, and a few hawker stalls serve up egg and chips.

Note that coffee and tea served in hawker centres, food courts and roadside coffee shops come not with regular milk but with sweetened condensed milk, and plenty of it.

Breakfast With An Orang Utan Singapore Zoo, 80 Mandai Lake Rd ☎62693411; see map, p.84. A bumper buffet-style spread, shared with whichever orang-utan is on duty; $25. Daily 9–10am.

Coffee Bean & Tea Leaf #01-10, One Fullerton, 1 Fullerton Rd ☎64239294; see map, pp.54–55. Enjoy spectacular riverside views at this branch of Singapore's most reliable coffee and tea chain. Sun–Thurs 7.30am–11pm, Fri & Sat 7.30am–1am.

Dôme Ground floor, UOB Plaza, Boat Quay, see map, pp.54–55. Slick café, part of a global chain, boasting an impressive range of coffees and teas and a superb view over the Singapore River. Muffins, toast and croissants are reasonable, and a selection of international papers is on hand for the full breakfast effect. Mon–Fri 8am–8pm, Sat 8am–3pm.

Halia Singapore Botanic Gardens, 1 Cluny Rd ☎64766711; see map, pp.78–79. The weekend à la carte brunch ($12–24) in this peaceful and enchanting restaurant,

serenaded by the sounds of insects, birds and whispering trees, has to be one of Singapore's most relaxing experiences. Sat & Sun 9am–3pm.

Spinelli Coffee Company #01-02 Far East Square, 45 Pekin St, Chinatown (see map, pp.54–55); ground floor, Peninsula Shopping Centre, Coleman St (see map, p.40). Some say *Spinelli* brews the finest coffee in Singapore – you can make your own mind up at either of these compact outlets. Daily 10am–10pm.

Steeple's Deli #02-25 Tanglin Shopping Centre, 19 Tanglin Rd, off Orchard Rd ☎67370701; see map, pp.78–79. Singapore's original deli, *Steeple's* has been knocking out high-quality home-made sandwiches, soups, cakes and savouries for over two decades now. Mon–Sat 9.30am–6.30pm.

Ya Kun Kaya Toast #01-01 Far East Square, 18 China St, Chinatown (see map, pp.54–55) ☎64383638; Takashimaya, Basement 2 food hall, 391A Orchard Rd ☎67384815; see map, pp.78–79. This Hainanese joint started out as a Chinatown stall in 1944, and still offers a stirring start to the day: piping-hot, strong coffee with *kaya* toast – a slab of butter and a splodge of coconut spread oozing from folded toast. Mon–Fri 7.30am–7pm, Sat & Sun 9am–5pm.

Hawker centres and food courts

Eating inexpensively in Singapore is largely about patronizing hawker stalls. Elsewhere in Southeast Asia these still take the form of simple pushcarts set up by the road, with a few stools to sit at, but regulations long ago banished these from Singapore's streets and into purpose-built **hawker centres**, essentially indoor cooked-food markets with alternating rows of tables and stalls. The oldest hawker centres often feature some of the best food, but their age also means they can be cramped and stuffy, and eating can therefore be a hot and even smoky experience if the fumes from the stalls drift your way.

Some more recent hawker centres are much more spacious affairs with air conditioning, and these are usually referred to as **food courts**; they're mostly found occupying one floor of a shopping mall. Some have become major franchise enterprises, notably the Food Republic, Food Junction and Kopitiam chains, which market themselves as offering stalls selected for the quality of their cooking.

Stalls always have signs in English detailing their specialities. If there's more than one price next to a dish, it indicates there are two or more serving sizes available; indicate your preference by quoting the corresponding price. A hearty meal – say, one rice or noodle dish, a fruit juice and a dessert – will cost you around $8, though if your budget doesn't run that far, you can eat well for half the price. Don't assume that hawker-type places and food courts only serve Chinese, Malay and Indian food – a minority of stalls offer other east Asian cuisines and some specialize in simple Western dishes, from steak to burgers with chips.

Hawker centres and food courts are open throughout the day and into the evening, though individual stalls may focus on the breakfast or late-night crowd and thus be closed at other times. If you avoid the peak periods (12.30–1.30pm & 6–7.30pm, you should have no problems in finding a table. There's no need to sit close to the stall you're ordering from: find a free seat or table and tell the vendor roughly where you are (better still, quote the number on the table if there is one). Food is usually paid for when it reaches your table, though at food courts you may be asked to pay when you order.

China Square Food Centre 51 Telok Ayer St; see map, pp.54–55. Three floors of spick-and-span stalls – mainly Chinese but with Japanese, Korean and Western representation.

Chinatown Complex Blk 335 Smith St, at end of New Bridge Rd; see map, pp.54–55. A huge range of dishes with a Chinese bias.

Dunman Food Centre 271 Onan Rd; see map, p.94. Popular local place that serves top notch, cheap fare.

East Coast Lagoon Food Village 1202 East Coast Parkway; see map, p.92. One of two hawker centres in Singapore by the sea, and the only one with a bar at the centre. Seafood is, unsurprisingly, the speciality here – try the chilli crab.

Food Junction Level 3, Bugis Junction, 200 Victoria St; see map, pp.68–69. Justifiably popular food court with a huge selection of local dishes and decent desserts.

Food Republic Level 4, Wisma Atria, 435 Orchard Rd; Level 5, 313@Somerset, 313 Orchard Rd; see map, pp.78–79; Level 3, VivoCity mall, Telok Blangah Rd (see map, p.99). The most upmarket of Singapore's food court franchises, with slick decor and high-quality stalls.

Kopitiam Plaza by the Park, 51 Bras Basah Rd; see map, pp.68–69. Bright and brash food court, especially popular with late-night revellers. Open 24hr.

Lau Pa Sat Festival Market 18 Raffles Quay; see map, pp.54–55. Dating back to the nineteenth century, this is the oldest and most atmospheric selection of hawker stalls in Singapore – but also a mite pricier than

Noodles (mee) and noodle dishes

Bee hoon/mee fun	Thin rice noodles, like vermicelli.
Hokkien fried mee	Yellow and white noodles fried with pieces of pork, prawn and vegetables.
(Char) kuey teow	*Kuey teow* (*hor fun* in Cantonese) are flat rice noodles, like tagliatelle. *Char* indicates the noodles are stir-fried, usually with prawns, Chinese sausage, egg and greens.
La mian	"Pulled noodles", made by spinning dough skipping-rope-style in the air.
Laksa	Noodles, beansprouts, fishcakes and prawns in a spicy coconut soup.
Mee	Yellow wheat noodles, like spaghetti.
Mee goreng	Spicy Indian/Malay fried noodles.
Mee rebus	Classic Malay dish of boiled *mee*, the Singaporean version being served in a sweet sauce based on yellow-bean paste, garnished with tofu, boiled egg and beansprouts.
Sar hor fun	Flat rice noodles served in a chicken stock soup, to which, prawns fried shallots and beansprouts are added.
Wonton mee	Roast pork, noodles and vegetables in a light soup.

Rice (nasi) dishes

Biriyani	Saffron-flavoured rice served with curries or fried chicken.
Claypot rice	Rice topped with meat (as diverse as chicken and turtle), cooked in an earthenware pot over a fire to create a smoky taste.
Hainanese chicken rice	Steamed or boiled chicken slices on rice cooked in chicken stock, served with chicken broth and chilli and ginger sauce.
Mixed rice	The simplest and most popular choice at food courts, this is a spread of meat, fish and vegetable dishes which you point at to order; a large portion of plain rice comes as standard.
Nasi goreng	Malay- or Indian-style fried rice with diced meat and vegetables.
Nasi kunyit	Yellow rice, cooked with turmeric; a side dish.
Nasi lemak	A Malay classic: fried anchovies, cucumber, peanuts and fried or hard-boiled egg slices served on rice cooked in coconut milk.
Nasi padang	Mixed rice featuring dishes cooked in the style of Padang, the town in Sumatra, Indonesia.
Nasi puteh	Plain cooked rice.

Other specialities

Ayam goreng	Malay-style fried chicken.
Bak kut teh	Literally "pork bone tea", a Chinese broth of pork ribs in soy sauce, herbs and spices.
Chye tow kueh	Also known as "carrot cake", this is a delicious sort of scramble made with white radish, flour and egg; it's available plain ("white") or "dark", the latter cooked with sweet soy sauce.
Congee	Watery rice gruel, either unsalted and eaten with slices of egg and salt fish, or else boiled up with chicken, fish or pork.
Dosai/thosai	South Indian pancake, made from ground rice and sometimes other ingredients, and stuffed with dhal or other fillings.
Fishballs/fishcake	Fish-flavoured dumplings, round or in slivers (the "cake" version), used to add substance to noodle dishes and stews.
Fish-head curry	Another Singapore classic, the head of a red snapper (usually), cooked in a spicy curry sauce with tomatoes and okra.

EATING

⑩

Gado gado	Malay/Indonesian salad of lightly cooked vegetables, boiled egg, sticky-rice cubes and a crunchy peanut sauce.
Ikan bilis	Anchovies, usually deep-fried.
Kai pow	Similar to *char siew pow* (see below), but contains chicken and boiled egg.
Kaya	A coconut and egg curd "jam", great with toast.
Keropok	Originally a kind of fish or prawn dumpling, but used in Singapore to mean crackers made of the dumpling mixture, sliced thinly and fried.
Murtabak	A much more substantial take on *roti prata*, stuffed with onion, egg and chicken or mutton.
Otak-otak	Fish mashed with coconut milk and chilli paste and steamed in a banana leaf; a Nonya dish.
Popiah	Spring rolls, steamed rather than fried, and filled with egg, vegetables and a sweet sauce; sometimes known as *lumpia*.
Pow	Cantonese steamed bun; the most popular variety is *char siew pow*, filled with sweet roast pork.
Rendang	Dry, slow-cooked curry of beef, chicken or mutton.
Rojak	A salad of greens, beansprouts, pineapple and cucumber in a peanut-and-prawn paste sauce, similar to *gado gado*. There's also a totally different Indian version, comprising a selection of fritters (as ever, order by pointing) served with sweet spicy dips.
Roti john	French bread spread with egg, chopped onion and spicy chilli sauce (sometimes meat too), then shallow-fried.
Roti prata	Paratha-style Indian griddle bread served with a thin meat or fish curry sauce or dhal – a standard breakfast or snack.
Satay	Marinated pieces of meat, skewered on small sticks and cooked over charcoal; served with peanut sauce.
Sop kambing	Spicy Malay/Indian mutton soup.
Steamboat	Chinese fondue: raw vegetables, meat or fish dunked into a steaming broth until cooked.

Desserts

Bubor cha cha	Sweetened coconut milk with pieces of sweet potato, yam and tapioca balls.
Cheng tng	Surprisingly refreshing Chinese sweet stew of unusual dried fruits and fungi, served hot or iced.
Cendol	Coconut milk, palm sugar syrup and pea-flour noodles poured over shaved ice.
Ice kachang	Slushy ice with beans, cubes of jelly, sweetcorn, rose syrup and evaporated milk.
Pisang goreng	Fried banana fritters.

Drinks

Bandung	Pink drink made with rose-flavoured syrup and a little milk.
Chinchow	Looks like cola gone flat but is actually a sweet drink made from a kind of seaweed, with bits of agar jelly floating around inside.
Kopi	Coffee, normally served with sweetened condensed milk.
-o	Suffix meaning "black" – so say *kopi-o* for black coffee.
Lassi	Sweet or sour Indian yoghurt drink.
tarik	Meaning "pulled" (*tarik*), it refers to pouring tea or coffee between two cups to produce a frothy drink.
Teh	Tea, usually with condensed milk.

10

EATING

the norm. At lunchtime the place is full to bursting with suits from the city; at night the clubbers take over. Open 24hr.

🏃 **Maxwell Food Centre Junction of South Bridge Rd and Maxwell Rd; see map, pp.54–55.** Old-style hawker centre, a stone's throw from the centre of Chinatown. Get there early if you want the Tian Tian Hainanese Chicken Rice at stall ten.

Newton Circus Hawker Centre Corner of Clemenceau Ave North and Bukit Timah Rd, near Newton MRT. A venerable open-air place with a good range of food, in particular seafood, though you can end up paying through the nose for this; prices are on the high side anyway, as the place is very much on the tourist trail. Only really gets going in the late afternoon and stays open till the small hours.

Tekka Market Start of Serangoon Rd; see map, pp.68–69. Terrific and hence often packed, the stalls adjoining the market area here are especially worthwhile for Malay and Indian food.

Restaurants and coffee shops

While there are numerous Western-style cafés as well as familiar international coffee chains, these aren't to be confused with what locals call **coffee shops** or *kopitiams* (Hokkien Chinese for "coffee shop"), which are street-corner restaurants charging about the same as in a hawker centre. Usually open throughout the day, they serve a range of noodle and rice dishes, with the cooking sometimes done in kiosks in the main eating area rather than behind the scenes. Coffee shops are worth seeking out in areas where shophouses still exist as they offer a glimpse of a major slice of traditional eating that's been in decline with the inexorable rise of the shopping mall; Little India, Arab Street and North Bridge Road offer reasonable prospects in this regard.

On the whole, proper **restaurants** are the places you go if you want a bit of comfort and the chance to savour more specialist local food or fine international cuisine. Note that for local food, restaurants aren't necessarily better than food courts or *kopitiams* – they just charge quite a bit extra for posh surroundings and (often indifferent) service. Given the cost of fine dining, consider taking advantage of the two- or three-course **set lunches** which are good value at many restaurants, and, for a blowout, look out for **buffet** and Sunday **brunch** offers.

Chinese, Malay and, to a lesser extent, Indian restaurant meals tend to be shared affairs, where everyone tucks in to a common set of dishes with their own portion of rice as an accompaniment, so it's customary to **order collectively** in these situations. Unless you're in a Muslim restaurant, you'll be able to wash down your meal with a glass of cold **beer**, and smarter restaurants will have a selection of wines and spirits too.

Typical restaurant **hours** are noon to 2pm and 6pm to 10.30pm daily. You should **book** ahead for more upmarket places, particularly on Friday and Saturday night and Sunday lunchtimes, when they are at their busiest. It's worth scanning the glossary on pp.124–125 to familiarize yourself with the most common dishes and terms, and while **English menus** are always available at proper restaurants, note that many of the staff will be migrant workers and may not be able to handle anything but routine English queries.

Chinese

Singapore's Chinese community is largely drawn from three southeastern Chinese provinces, namely Fujian (Hokkien in dialect), Guangdong (Canton) and Hainan Island, and so there are restaurants serving the cuisine of all three. **Cantonese** food is, as you might expect, dominant, reflecting that cuisine's pre-eminence in

Chinese cooking. You'll also come across food from further afield in China, specifically northern **Beijing** (or Peking) and western **Szechuan** cuisines. Whatever the region, it's undoubtedly the real thing, which means it won't always sound particularly appealing to foreigners: the Chinese eat all parts of an animal, from its lips to its entrails, and it's important to retain a sense of adventure when exploring menus.

Beijing

Beijing was traditionally the seat of China's Imperial households, and the sumptuous presentation of its cuisine reflects its opulent past. Meat dominates, typically flavoured with garlic and spring onions, though the dish for which Beijing is most famous is roast duck, served in three courses: the skin is eaten in a pancake filled with spring onion and radish, and smeared with plum sauce.

Lao Beijing #03-01 Plaza Singapura, 68 Orchard Rd ☎67387207; see map, pp.78–79. Charming teahouse-style restaurant. If the braised pork trotters don't appeal, try the more mainstream dishes like sweet-and-sour fish and *popiah*; the steamboat with lamb slices is exceptional. $32–52 for a tasting menu of six courses. Daily 11.30am–3pm & 6–10pm.

Pine Court Restaurant 35th floor, Mandarin Orchard Singapore Hotel, 333 Orchard Rd ☎68316262; see map, pp.78–79. Three elegant pine trees dominate this beautiful restaurant, where the speciality is whole Peking duck ($90) – enough for three hungry people. Reservations advised. Mon–Fri noon–3pm & 6.30–10.30pm, Sat & Sun 11.30am–3pm & 6.30–10.30pm.

Cantonese

Cantonese cuisine is noted for its delicacy of flavour and memorable sauces; dishes are stir-fried, steamed or roasted, and often taken with black bean, lemon, oyster or soy sauce. Fish and seafood weigh in heavily on a Cantonese menu, either fried or steamed, and other specialities include pigeon, roast meats and frogs' legs. **Dim sum** is also a classic Cantonese meal: literally translated as "to touch the heart", it's a blanket term for an array of dumplings, cakes and titbits steamed in bamboo baskets. Though you do occasionally see it on lunch menus, traditionally dim sum is eaten by the Chinese for breakfast, with one basket (of three or four pieces) costing as little as $3.

Fatty's Wing Seong #01-31 Burlington Square, 175 Bencoolen St ☎63381087; see map, pp.68–69. In bygone days when it was run by an avuncular chubby cook, *Fatty's* was an institution on the now-vanished foodie paradise that was Albert St. Today this restaurant maintains the original's *zi char* approach, where Chinese food is cooked to order without frills. Around $20 a head. Daily noon–2.30pm & 5.15–10.15pm.

Table manners

Local dishes are generally eaten with **fork and spoon** – never a knife as the food is usually sliced up enough that one is unnecessary – and it's the spoon you eat off, with the fork playing the supporting role of helping to pick up and move morsels of food, plus rice, onto the spoon. Of course you have the option of using **chopsticks** with Chinese food, but don't make the mistake of trying to consume rice off a plate with them, as that's where the spoon comes into play. Chopsticks go together with a rice bowl, which you hold right to your mouth so you can snaffle the rice using the chopsticks as a shovel. More familiarly, they also serve as tongs: one chopstick is laid between thumb and forefinger, and supported by your fourth and little fingers, while the second chopstick is held between thumb, forefinger and second finger, and manipulated to form a pincer. Indian and Malay food is traditionally eaten using the **right hand** as a scoop and the right thumb to flick food into your mouth, and there are always sinks near the tables for washing before and after the meal.

▲ Dim sum in bamboo steamers

Jing One Fullerton, 1 Fullerton Rd ☏62240088; see map, pp.54–55. Waterside restaurant serving up exquisite modern Cantonese food. Try their signature wasabi prawns ($29), followed by the cream of avocado ice cream served in a coconut. In addition to à la carte, they also offer a weekday buffet ($42) and set menu (from $38.50). Daily 11.45am–2.30pm & 6.30–10.30pm.

Li Bai Sheraton Towers Hotel, 39 Scotts Rd ☏68395623; see map, pp.78–79. Named after a poet of the Tang dynasty, this is a suitably sophisticated place in the bowels of the *Towers*, where your best bet is the five-course luncheon, weighing in at $55; alternatively, you can opt for lighter dim sum. Daily noon–2.30pm & 6.30–10.30pm.

Majestic New Majestic, 31–37 Bukit Pasoh Rd ☏65114718; see map, pp.54–55. The green padded walls, futuristic chairs and modern art work reflect the Cantonese/fusion dishes on offer at this popular hotel restaurant. The soft-shell crab with creamy milk and lime sauce is innovative and excellent, as is the succulent grilled rack of lamb in Chinese honey with pan-fried carrot cake. $95 for a meal for two. Daily 11.45am–2.30pm & 6.30pm–10.30pm.

Mitzi's 62–64 Tanjong Pagar Rd ☏62220929; see map, pp.54–55. This cracking place serves up old-school Cantonese meals.

Try the excellent braised pork ribs. Great value – two can eat for $30. Daily 11.30am–3pm & 5.30–10pm.

Mouth #02-01 Chinatown Point, 133 New Bridge Rd ☏65344233; see map, pp.54–55. Beside a popular dim sum menu, this jam-packed restaurant offers authentic Cantonese cuisine, including Peking dumplings and marmite pork ribs at around $25–30 a head. Mon–Fri 11.30am–11pm, Sat & Sun 10am–11pm (dim sum 11.00am–5.30pm).

Peach Garden #33-01 OCBC Centre, 65 Chulia St ☏65357833; see map, pp.54–55. Upmarket restaurant offering great views of the city from the heart of the business district. The deep fried silverbait with spices and sea perch with plum sauce get rave reviews among local foodies. Set menu for two $42 per person. Daily 11.30am–2.30pm & 6.30–10pm.

Soup 39 Seah St ☏63339388; see map, pp.68–69. So-called *samsui* women once sailed from China's Guangdong province in droves, incredibly, to work on Singapore building sites. This fine little restaurant celebrates the cuisine of these redoubtable women, most famously their ginger chicken; similar to the steamed chicken in Hainanese chicken rice, it comes with a gingery dip and iceberg-lettuce leaves to roll it up in. Reckon on $20 per person. Daily 11.30am–10.30pm.

Taste Paradise 48/49 Mosque St ☏62262959; see map, pp.54–55. This steadily expanding upmarket chain has created a loyal following for its pan-seared foie gras with wasabi mayonnaise prawns and slices of duck, though its Peking duck is also a winner. $80–90 per person. Daily 11.30am–2.30pm & 5.30pm–10.30pm.

Yum Cha #02-01, 20 Trengganu St ☏63721717; see map, pp.54–55. Big, buzzing dim sum joint, above the bustle of Trengganu Street, with marble tables and pictures of dumplings and teapots on the walls. Great fun. Entry is via Temple Street. $12–30 per dish. Mon–Fri 11am–10.30pm, Sat & Sun 9am–10.30pm.

Hainanese

Hainanese cuisine is synonymous in Singapore with chicken rice, a simple but tasty platter featuring, predictably enough, slices of chicken laid on rice that has been cooked in chicken stock, with a chilli and ginger dip. Historically, though, the Hainanese were chefs to the British and kept their colonial employers happy with a range of hybrid dishes, mainly simple meat and chicken preparations, which you'll also find on restaurant menus.

Mooi Chin Place #03-12A Landmark Village Hotel, 390 Victoria St ☏6392600; see map, pp.68–69. Mutton soup and pork chop are cooked to perfection at this venerable restaurant, while whole pomfret sambal is a top speciality ($40). Daily 11am–10pm.

Yet Con Chicken Rice Restaurant 25 Purvis St ☏63376819; see map, pp.68–69. Cheap and cheerful old-time restaurant known not just for chicken rice but also for its roast pork with pickled cabbage and radish. Around $15 for two people. Daily 11am–9.30pm.

Hokkien

The **Hokkien** chef relies heavily upon sauces and broths to cook his meat and (primarily) seafood. Without doubt, the cuisine's most popular dish in Singapore is Hokkien *mee*, though despite the name it doesn't consist of just *mee* – yellow noodles – but also features round white noodles, the combination being fried with prawns and pork for flavour.

Bee Heong Palace 134 Telok Ayer St ☏62229074; see map, pp.54–55. Customers are pumped through at a rate of knots at this bustling joint, but the beggar chicken and dried chilli prawn are recommended, or ask the friendly staff for advice. Cheap. Mon–Sun 11.30am–3pm & 6–10.30pm (excl Wed).

Beng Hiang 115 Amoy St ☏62216695; see map, pp.54–55. Well-cooked food at good-value prices – you can eat heartily for under $15. Daily 11.30am–2.30pm & 6–9.30pm.

Beng Thin Hoon Kee #05-02 OCBC Centre, 65 Chulia St ☏65332818; see map, pp.54–55. Hidden inside the OCBC car park, this minty green restaurant is very popular at lunchtime with city slickers from the nearby business district. Big portions make it a good and filling introduction to Hokkien cuisine. $50–60 per person. Daily 11.30am–3pm & 6–10pm.

Szechuan and Hunanese

Szechuan (or Sichuan) food is hot and spicy, with chilli, pepper, garlic and ginger conspiring to piquant effect in classic dishes such as camphor-and-tea-smoked duck and chicken with dried chilli. The food of neighbouring Hunan province is similarly fiery; popular dishes include Hunanese honey-glazed ham and minced pigeon steamed in a bamboo tube.

Magic of Chongqing Hotpot 4th floor, Tanglin Shopping Centre, 19 Tanglin Rd ☏67348135; see map, pp.78–79. This homely DIY restaurant has local pundits raving over its zesty Szechuan hotpots: choose a stock, drop in ingredients, and fish them out when cooked. Two can dine well for $60–80. Daily noon–3pm & 6–11pm.

Min Jiang Goodwood Park Hotel, 22 Scotts Rd ☏67377411; see map, pp.78–79. The decor's red tones match the fieriness of the food on offer – the hot and sour soup is really challenging, or try the simpler steamed fish in black bean sauce. A meal for two costs around $70. Reservations recommended. Daily noon–2pm & 6.30–10pm.

Teochew

Chaozhou (Teochew in dialect) is a city in Fujian province where steaming is the most commonly used form of cooking, producing light but flavourful dishes such as fish steamed with sour plums. Other Teochew classics are braised goose, steamed crayfish and, at hawker stalls, *mee pok* – a spicy dish of flat noodles with round fishball dumplings.

Lee Kui (Ah Hoi) 8–10 Mosque St ☏62223654; see map, pp.54–55. Occupying three units of shophouses and imbued with faded grandeur, this restaurant is almost unique in a city obsessed with novelty. The (rather pricey at $70) cold crab, which is first steamed then frozen, gets the crowds flocking, and the oyster omelette and braised duck wings are also superb. Daily 11am–2.30pm & 5pm–10pm. Closed alternate Tuesdays.

Teochew City Seafood Restaurant #05-16 Centrepoint, 176 Orchard Rd ☏67333338; see map, pp.78–79. Standard Teochew restaurant whose karaoke facilities are, mercifully, confined to two private rooms. Try the steamed and then chilled cold crabs as an appetizer. From $75 for a set menu. Mon–Fri 10.30am–3pm & 6.30–10pm, Sat & Sun 10.30am–3.30pm & 6–10pm.

Xu Jun Sheng (Long Ji) Chao Zhou Mei Shi 59 Joo Chiat Pl; see map, p.130. This stall housed within a prewar coffee shop serves up Teochew classics like pork knuckles in a thick sauce, fried sweet potato leaves and sumptuous *oh nee* – a dessert made from creamed yam. Great value at $4–35 per dish. Mon, Tues & Thurs–Sat 11.30am–8.30pm.

Other speciality Chinese restaurants

Crystal Jade La Mian Xiao Long Bao 241 Holland Ave ☎64630968 (see map, p.104); and other locations. Very popular chain specializing in Shanghai and Beijing cuisine. The name is a bit of a mouthful, but encapsulates their signature dishes – *xiao long bao*, incredibly succulent pork dumplings, and *la mian*, literally "pulled noodles", the strands of dough being stretched and worked by hand (the version cooked with wood-ear fungus is particularly good). Not great for vegetarians, though veggie versions of a few dishes can be made to order. Daily 11.30am–3pm & 6.30–11pm.

Singapura Seafood #01-31 Selegie House, Blk 9, Selegie Rd ☎63363255; see map, pp.68–69. The seafood isn't bad, but it's the Foochow dishes – from the capital of Fujian province in China – that really hit the spot. At lunchtime they do a good-value set meal for $50, enough to feed two or three, which includes their signature honey pork ribs, prawn rolls and Foochow fried noodles, done with bits of seafood and a dark savoury sauce. Daily 11am–2.30pm & 6–10.30pm.

Superbowl 80 Boat Quay ☎65386066; see map, pp.54–55. An affordable range of 47 congees, served at marble-topped tables recalling a

1950s coffee shop. Mon–Sat 11.30am–3pm & 6–11pm, Sun 12am–3pm & 6pm–10pm.

Vegetarian Chinese

Chinese vegetarian cuisine reflects the importance of Buddhism in traditional culture and is worth sampling, though be aware that mock meats made of soya or textured vegetable protein feature prominently, which may not appeal to everyone.

Ci Yan Organic Vegetarian Health Food 8–10 Smith St ☎62259026; see map, pp.54–55. This humble place in the heart of Chinatown has a small blackboard menu of specials each day, including organic brown rice, noodles and porridge. It also boasts no MSG. Less than $10 a dish. Daily noon–11pm.

Happy Realm Vegetarian Food Centre #03-16 Pearl's Centre, 100 Eu Tong Sen St ☎62226141; see map, pp.54–55. "The way to good health and a sound mind", boasts the restaurant's card; tasty and reasonably priced vegetarian dishes. $5–10 a dish. Daily 11am–8.30pm.

Kwan Im Vegetarian South East Asia Hotel, 190 Waterloo St ☎63382394; see map, pp.68–69. This place may be bland to look at compared to the Kwan Im temple next door, but does serve a great range of classic Chinese food made with the usual mock meats. Most dishes are under $15. Daily 8am–8.30pm.

Lingzhi 05/01 Liat Towers, 541 Orchard Rd ☎67343788; see map, pp.78–79. A real treat, where skewers of vegetables served with satay sauce are the highlight of an imaginative menu; there's also a takeaway counter. Daily 11am–3pm & 6–9.30pm.

Indian and Nepali

As befits a country whose Indian community is largely Tamil, most Indian restaurants in Singapore serve south Indian food, though some feature a small range of northern dishes and the pricier places tend to specialize in northern dishes. **South Indian** food, easily sampled at dozens of outlets in Little India, is generally both spicier and lighter than its northern counterpart. Its staple is either rice or the dosai (pancake), a classic version of which is the masala dosai, stuffed with onions, vegetables and chutney. Many south Indian coffee shops serve daun pisang ("banana-leaf") meals, where rice is placed on a banana-leaf "plate" with small, replenishable heaps of vegetable curries alongside, and more substantial meat, chicken and seafood curries available too. For richer curries, tandoori dishes and nan bread, you'll need to seek out northern Indian restaurants, which tend to be outside Little India.

Annalakshmi B1/02 Chinatown point, 133 New Bridge Rd ☏63399993; see map, pp.54–55. Terrific north and south Indian vegetarian snacks, with a fantastic buffet offering (Fri– Sun lunch & dinner) and à la carte meals every other day. All profits go to Kala Mandhir, an Indian cultural association and many of the staff are volunteers from the Hindu community, so your waiter might just be a doctor or a lawyer. All staff work on the adage that "the guest is god" – and you can choose what you pay. Daily 11.00am–3pm & 6–9.30pm.

Banana Leaf Apolo 56–58 Race Course Rd ☏62938682; also at Little India Arcade; see map, pp.68–69. Pioneering banana-leaf-meal restaurant with a wide selection of Indian dishes, including fish-head curry ($22–30 depending on size of serving) plus chicken, mutton and prawn curries ($10–12). The "South Indian veg meal" is a steal, comprising rice, pappadums, two main curries and several side ones, plus a dessert, for just $6. Daily 10am–10pm.

Bombay Café 332–334 Tanjong Katong Rd ☏63450070; see map, p.94. Flash-looking restaurant that serves up terrific vegetarian food. Bollywood dance sequences showing on various TV screens makes it popular with young locals at weekends. $7–12 a dish. Daily 11am–2.45pm & 6pm–10.15pm.

Islamic 745 North Bridge Rd ☏62987563; see map, pp.68–69. Only the photos of functions this restaurant catered for in the 1920s give away its pedigree – certainly not the bland, modernized shophouse premises of today. Biriyanis are their trademark offering ($6) though they also do a huge range of north Indian chicken, mutton, prawn, squid and veg curries, with good-value set meals at $8. Daily 10am–10pm (closed Fri 1–2pm).

Kinara 57 Boat Quay ☏65330412; see map, pp.54–55. Exquisite restaurant boasting antique fittings imported from the subcontinent; a marvellous view of the river from upstairs, and elegantly presented Punjabi dishes. $60–70 for two. Daily noon–2.30pm & 6.30–10.30pm.

Komala Vilas 76–78 Serangoon Rd ☏62936980 & 12–14 Buffalo Rd ☏62933664; see map, pp.68–69. A well-established though cramped vegetarian establishment with more than a dozen variations of dosai at just

a few dollars each, with fresh coconut to wash it down with ($3). They also do more substantial rice meals upstairs at Serangoon Rd (11am–4pm). Daily: Serangoon Rd 7am–10.30pm; Buffalo Rd 8am–10.30pm.

Madras New Woodlands 12–14 Upper Dickson Rd ☏62971594; see map, pp.68–69. A simple affair serving up decent vegetarian food. House specialities are the dosais ($2–4) and thali set meals (around $7), and there's a good-value daily special too ($7). Daily 7.30am–11.30pm.

New Chettinadu 41 Chander Rd ☏62917161; see map, pp.68–69. Chettinadu is a particular place in Tamil Nadu state, southern Indian, and while nobody seems to be able to explain precisely what distinguishes Chettinadu from general Tamil cuisine, it hardly matters when the curries are as good as those served up in this tiny diner. Idlis, dosais and so forth are available in addition to biryani rice. You can eat well for $8. Daily 8am till late.

Orchard Maharajah 25 Cuppage Terrace, Cuppage Rd ☏67326331; see map, pp.78–79. Set in a wonderful old Peranakan house, this splendid north Indian restaurant has a large terrace and a tempting menu that includes the famous Goa fish curry – boneless fish in a coconut flavoured sauce ($18). Mains $17–22. Daily 11am–11pm.

Our Village 5th floor, 46 Boat Quay ☏65383092; see map, pp.54–55. A hidden gem, with fine north Indian and Sri Lankan food, and peachy views of the river, city and Colonial District from its lamplit roof terrace. Try the rich murgh makhanwala (butter chicken) or the malai kofta (paneer balls in a creamy sauce), and finish with a spicy palate-cleansing masala tea. $20 per head. Mon–Fri noon–1.45pm & 6–11.30pm, Sat & Sun 6–11.30pm; reservation recommended.

Samy's Blk 25 Dempsey Rd ☏64722080. Bus #7 from Orchard MRT; alight when you see Pierce Rd to the left; see map, pp.78–79. Having sunk a few Tigers in one of Dempsey's many happening bars, you'll be ready for a wonderfully spicy Samy's curry, served on a banana leaf and best enjoyed overlooking the trees at a table on the fairy-lit veranda. Around $15 for two people. Daily 11am–3pm & 6–10pm.

Malay and Nonya

Though Malays form the largest minority in Singapore, the Malay eating scene is disappointingly one-dimensional, mainly because the Malays themselves don't have a tradition of elaborate eating out. Every hawker centre has several Malay stalls, but these tend to serve fairly basic rice and noodle dishes. It's a shame, because **Malay** cuisine is a spicy and sophisticated affair with interesting connections to Indian, Indonesian, Thai and Chinese cooking. It's notable for its use of coconut milk and ingredients such as galangal (a root similar to ginger), coriander and lemon grass. Another common feature is sambal, a condiment comprising pounded chillies blended with belacan (shrimp paste), onions and garlic. The most well-known dish is satay, but it's worth trying at least one other classic, namely a *rendang* – beef, chicken or mutton stewed with lemon grass and coconut.

Pork, of course, doesn't feature in Malay food but is prominent in **Nonya** or **Peranakan** cuisine which, like the Peranakan community itself, is a blend of Malay and Chinese. A popular dish is *laksa*, noodles in spicy coconut soup served with seafood and chopped beansprouts. Other popular dishes include *ayam buah keluak*, chicken cooked with "black" nuts; and *otak-otak*, fish mashed with coconut milk and chilli paste and steamed in a banana leaf.

328 Katong Laksa 216 East Coast Rd; see map, p.94. This humble outdoor eatery has a loyal following among locals for its deliciously rich and creamy *laksa*. $5–9 a dish. Daily 8am–10pm.

Briyani Bistro 742 North Bridge Rd; see map, pp.68–69. The food at this friendly, open-fronted place is probably more Malay than anything else, though you're initially asked to choose from supposedly Afghan (yellow-grained), Turkish "dum" (yellow/orange) or Iranian (with flecks of colour) biriyani rice; the next step is to select a curry or stew made from fish, chicken or mutton. Your choices are then heaped on your plate along with *achar* (pickle) for the princely sum of $8 or so. Daily 11am–8pm.

Blue Ginger 97 Tanjong Pagar Rd ☎ 62223928; see map, pp.54–55. Housed in a renovated shophouse, this trendy Peranakan restaurant is a yuppy favourite, thanks to dishes such as *ikan masal assam gulai* (mackerel simmered in a tamarind and lemon-grass gravy), and that benchmark of Nonya cuisine, *ayam buah keluak* – braised chicken with Indonesian black nuts. $25–35 per head. Daily noon–2.15pm & 6.30–10pm.

Chilli Padi 11 Joo Chiat Place ☎ 62751002; see map, p.94. Red batik ceiling drapes and tablecloths bring homely warmth to this family-run restaurant, whose Nonya dishes, like spicy chilli fish and *popiah*, have justly won it plaudits. The jars of kaya and curry paste for sale make unusual gifts to take home. $10–15 per dish. Daily 11.30am–2.30pm & 5.30–10pm.

Guan Hoe Soon 38/40 Joo Chiat Place ☎ 63442761; see map, p.94. After fifty years, chef Raymond Ou Yong is still turning out fine cuisine; try the amazing *mee* (fried noodles), *ayam buah keluak* (chicken marinated in shrimp paste and shallots) and the succulent crackling roast pork. Around $30 for two. Daily 10.30am–3pm & 6–9.30pm.

▲ Preparing murtabak

Haji Maimunah **11 & 15 Jalan Pisang** ⊤62913132, **51 Bencoolen St #01-06** ⊤63385684; see map, pp.68–69. Despite the workaday feel, this inexpensive Malay diner serves good breakfasts (including *nasi lemak*) and dishes such as *ayam bakar Sunda* (Sundanese-style barbecued chicken) and *siput lemak sedut* (snails in coconut milk). Mon–Sat: Jalan Pisang 7am–8pm; Bencoolen St 11am–9pm.

Kampong Glam Café **17 Bussorah St; see map, pp.68–69.** Unpretentious and convivial roadside coffee shop serving the usual rice and noodle dishes, cooked to order, plus a range of curries. Come not just for the food but for a good chinwag with friends over *teh tarik* late into the evening. Daily 8am–1am.

Peranakan Inn **210 East Coast Rd** ⊤64406195; see map, p.94. As much effort goes into the food as went into the renovation of this immaculate, bright-green shophouse restaurant, which offers authentic Nonya favourites at reasonable prices; around $10 a dish. Try the *babi chin* (stewed pork flavoured with miso). Daily 11am–3pm & 6–10.30pm.

American, North and South

Bedrock Bar & Grill **#01-05 Pan Pacific Service Suites, 96 Somerset Rd** ⊤62380054; see map, pp.78–79. Classic American steakhouse with an atmosphere straight out of *The Sopranos*. The steaks are juicy (from $55) and the cocktails stiff. Mon–Sat noon–3pm & 6.30pm–midnight (last order 10.30pm).

Bobby's **#B1-03, CHIJMES, 30 Victoria St** ⊤63375477; see map, pp.68–69. With an atmospheric setting around the basement fountain courtyard, *Bobby's* specializes in barbecue beef rib and other meaty delights, including steaks and burgers, with pizzas and pasta dishes also available. Mains from $25. Mon–Fri 3pm–1am, Sat & Sun noon–1am.

Café Iguana **#01-03 Riverside Point, 30 Merchant Rd** ⊤62361275; see map, pp.54–55. Riverfront Mexican restaurant and bar situated within colourful walls. Tortillas, chilli, quesadillas and all the usual favourites feature on the menu, plus a huge selection of tequilas. $20–30 for a main course. Mon–Thurs 6pm–1am, Fri 6pm–3am, Sat noon–3am, Sun noon–1am.

Cha Cha Cha **32 Lorong Mambong, Holland Village** ⊤64621650; see map, p.104. A vibrantly coloured restaurant offering the full range of Mexican favourites – tacos, burritos, enchiladas etc – starting at around $15. Reliable and consistently busy. Daily 11am–11pm (Fri & Sat until midnight).

Chili's Grill & Bar **#02-23 Tanglin Mall, 163 Tanglin Rd** ⊤67333317; see map, pp.78–79. Popular Tex-Mex chain famed for its excellent service, baby back ribs and fresh fajitas. With six types of margarita on offer, it's a popular choice for an evening drink. Sun–Thurs 11am–10pm, Fri & Sat 11am–11pm.

Lawry's The Prime Rib **#04-01/31 Mandarin Gallery, 333A Orchard Rd** ⊤68363333; see map, pp.78–79. Superior ribs, served with Yorkshire pudding, mashed potato and whipped cream horseradish. Plan on $70 a head. Daily 11.30am–2.30pm & 5–10pm.

Seah Street Deli **North Bridge Rd end of Raffles Hotel** ⊤64121816; see map, p.40. The soda and root beer signs, jukebox and outsized Americana on the walls make this

Cookery classes

Should the fine dining that Singapore offers leave you wanting to replicate some of it back home, you could give yourself a head start by booking onto a cookery class.

At-Sunrice **Fort Canning Centre, Fort Canning Park** ⊤68776990, ⓦwww.at-sunrice .com. Their "Morning Gourmet" sessions (Thurs & Sat; $110; 4hr) offer demonstrations of Asian cooking plus the chance to prepare three dishes. Alternatively, learn about Asian herbs and spices in their spice garden, with morning tea to follow ($40).

Coriander Leaf **See p.136.** Their Streets of Singapore and Singapore Classics courses ($130) are half-day sessions featuring thorough demonstrations of how to cook the likes of Hainanese chicken rice and chilli crab, though note you don't get to cook anything yourself.

the most un-colonial establishment at *Raffles Hotel*. A great place for burgers, pizzas, mountainous sandwiches and barbecued ribs; most mains are in the $20–30 range. Daily 11am–10pm (Fri & Sat till 11pm).

European

Black Sheep Café 35 Mayo St ☎62925772; **see map, pp.68–69.** The idea of a French meal prepared by a Singaporean Indian chef may sound droll, but this low-key, simply decorated restaurant in Little India is where to come for just that. Proprietor Rathakrishnan does a competent job with the limited menu and daily specials he offers; the tender lamb shank is probably the best-known dish. Reckon on $30 per person. Mon–Sat 11.30am–3pm & 6.30–10pm.

Broth 21 Duxton Hill ☎63233353; **see map, pp.54–55.** Superb dishes such as deep sea perch fillet with lentils, tomato coulis and crisp pancetta ($35) in an old shophouse on a delightfully quiet, tree-shaded Chinatown back street. A charming oasis. Mon–Fri noon–2.30pm, 6–10.30pm, Sat 6–10.30pm.

Club 211 (aka 211 Café) Holland Rd Shopping Centre #04-01 ☎64626194; **see map, p.104.** This café-restaurant is a real hidden gem, serving a great range of pizza and pasta dishes, as well as snacks and cakes. The lovely roof garden offers a quirky view of residential tower blocks looming all around. Much cheaper than similar places downtown, with mains from $15. Daily 9am–10.45pm.

Da Paolo Il Ristorante 80 Club St ☎62247081; **see map, pp.54–55.** Great home-made pasta, or splash out on the authentic Sicilian meat and fish dishes, best washed down with one of the Italian wines. $55–60 per head. Open Mon–Fri 11.30am–2.30pm, Sat 6.30–11.30pm.

De Sté #01-25, Discovery Walk at 313@Somerset, 313 Orchard Rd ☎68365344; **see map, pp.78–79.** This Italian cake and coffee shop serves up gorgeously decadent desserts, such as dark chocolate custard choux buns and a wicked truffle cake; perfect after a day lugging shopping bags. Cakes from $5. Daily 9am–11pm.

The French Kitchen #01-03 Central Mall, 7 Magazine Rd ☎64381823; **see map, pp.54–55.** Classic French food beautifully executed. The scallops and mussels in béchamel sauce is exquisite and the seared cod with truffle mashed potato is cooked to perfection. Best value for money is the $88 five-course degustation menu, otherwise mains are around $38. Mon–Fri noon–2.30pm & 6.30–10pm, Sat 7–9.30pm.

The Lighthouse The Fullerton, Level 8, 1 Fullerton Square ☎68778933; **see map, pp.54–55.** Excellent Italian fine dining restaurant in a former lighthouse, which affords breathtaking views of the city. The pork cheek with pumpkin purée is melt in the mouth. You can also opt to enjoy a glass of bubbly on the roof beforehand. Around $120 per person. Mon–Fri noon–2.30pm & 6–10.30pm, Sat & Sun 6.30–10.30pm.

Original Sin #01-62 Blk 43, Jln Merah Saga ☎64755605; **see map, p.104.** Quality Mediterranean and Asian vegetarian food, from Thai green curry to mushroom and asparagus polenta with truffle oil. Despite being pricey for what it is – mains start at $25 – it's often busy. Mon 6–10.30pm, Tues–Sun 11.30am–2.30pm & 6–10.30pm.

Oso Ristorante 46 Bukit Pasoh Rd ☎63278378; **see map, pp.54–55.** With sculpted red sofas, black leather dining chairs and interesting works of art, diners flock to this Italian restaurant. Expect classics such as Parma ham mousse, green asparagus soup and gnocchi in gorgonzola; a meal for two will cost around $70. Mon–Fri noon–2.30pm & 6–10.30pm, Sat 6–10.30pm.

Pasta Fresca 30 Boat Quay ☎65326283; **see map, pp.54–55.** Match up fresh pasta (made at the owner's factory) and a sauce from the menu, and sit out on the riverside terrace. Around $30 a head. Daily 11am–10pm.

Paulaner Bräuhaus #01-01 Millennia Walk, 9 Raffles Blvd ☎68832572; **see map, p.40.** The menu of Bavarian delights is impressive, but the best reason to come here is the terrific Sunday brunch spread, including superb pork knuckle, a range of sausages and salads, and desserts like strudel and cheesecake ($39 with unlimited soft drinks, or $51 with unlimited beer from their micro-brewery). Mon–Fri noon–2.30pm & 6.30–10.30pm, Sat 6.30–10.30pm, Sun 11.30am–2.30pm & 6.30–10.30pm.

Spizza 29 Club St ☎62242525; see map,
pp.54–55. Homely, rustic and affordable
pizzeria, whose menu boasts a tempting
A–Z of thick-crust pizzas (around $20),
cooked in a traditional wood oven. Daily
noon–2pm & 6–10pm.
Swensen's Level 1, Bugis Junction, 200 Victoria
St (See map, pp.68–69); #03-23 Plaza

Singapura, 68 Orchard Rd (see map, pp.78–79);
251/253 Holland Ave (see map, p.104); and other
locations. This ice-cream parlour chain wins
no prizes for atmosphere or decor, but it
does offer affordable Western food, from
spaghetti to burgers with chips. Daily
10.30am–10.30pm; the Holland Ave
branch is 24hr.

Indonesian

Similar to Malay cuisine (see p.132), **Indonesian** cookery is characterized by its
use of fragrant, aromatic spices and sweet, peanut-based sauces. Look out in
particular for *nasi padang* – a style of cooking that comes from Sumatra, which can
encompass anything from fish-head curry with tamarind to veg stir-fries.

Cumi Bali 66 Tanjong Pagar Rd ☎62206619;
see map, pp.54–55. Jolly *nasi padang* joint
whose walls are strung with Indonesian
fishing nets, puppets, instruments and
batiks. The beef *rendang* and *ikan bakar*
(barbecue fish) both hit the spot; or try one
of the generous set lunches. Around $20
per person. Mon–Sat 11.30am–3pm &

6–9.00pm. Sunday lunch must be reserved
in advance.
Pepes #04-16 Ngee Ann City, 391 Orchard
Rd ☎68363456; see map, pp.78–79. The
modern glass walls and geometric patterns
mixed with colourful Indonesian artwork
reflect the traditional food with a modern
twist on offer here. The *udang pepes*

High tea and dessert

Many of Singapore's swisher hotels advertise that most colonial of traditions, **high tea**.
Typically, a Singapore high tea comprises local and Western snacks, both sweet and
savoury. There are also a few specialist **dessert** places, ranging from ice-cream parlours
to places rooted in the weird and wonderful world of local sweets, where beans, corn
and root vegetables like sweet potato are standard ingredients of stews and slushy ice
concoctions – both of which you can also get at any hawker centre or food court.

2am Dessert Bar 21a Lorong Liput; see map, p.104. Hidden down a Holland Village
side street, this upstairs venue features sleek decor and a slew of sinful puddings
(from $17), plus simpler delights such as Spanish *churros* dunked in hot chocolate.
There's a full range of wines to wash them down with, too. Mon–Sat 4.30pm–2am.

Ah Chew Desserts 1 Liang Seah St #01-11 ☎63398198; see map, pp.68–69. Taking
up two restored shophouses, this is as good a place as any to start your appreciation
of local desserts. The cashew-nut paste is not bad if you like the sound of a broth made
of peanut butter; also available are the likes of *pulot hitam*, made with black sticky rice
and better warm than with the optional ice cream. Order the small portions to
cautiously sample a few items; hardly anything costs more than $4 a bowl. Mon–Thurs
12.30–11.30pm, Fri 12.30pm–12.30am, Sat 1.30pm–12.30am, Sun 1.30–11.30am.

Café l'Espresso *Goodwood Park Hotel*, 22 Scotts Rd ☎67301743; see map, pp.78–79.
A legendary array of English cakes, pastries and speciality coffees. Daily 2–5pm.

Swensen's A well-established, affordable chain of ice-cream parlours with regular
flavours as well as odd Far Eastern ones such as yam (actually rather nice). Sizeable
sundaes and other concoctions weigh in at a reasonable $8. See above for locations
and opening times.

Tiffin Room *Raffles Hotel*, 1 Beach Rd ☎64121816; see map, p.40. High tea here
(daily 3.30–5.30pm) is a buffet of local dishes plus servings of English scones,
pastries, cakes and sandwiches – come here for a blowout at $58.

(shrimp in a spicy sauce), grilled in a banana leaf, is juicy and tangy, while the *sambal kangkong* (water spinach sauteed in sambal paste) is a fiery delight. Reckon on $30 a head. Daily noon–2.30pm & 6–9.30pm.

Rendezvous #02-02 Hotel Rendezvous, 9 Bras Basah Rd ☏63397508; see map, pp.68–69. The spicy *nasi padang* here was once served out of a revered coffee shop on the very spot now occupied by the hotel. Thankfully, the curries have stayed the same over the decades, in particular the superb chicken korma, made with coconut milk rather than cream or yoghurt. Reasonably priced – a couple of curries with some side dishes and rice are unlikely to set you back more than $25 a head. Daily 11am–9pm.

Rumah Makan Minang 18a Kandahar St; see map, pp.68–69. A street-corner place serving a superb range of *nasi padang*, including the mildly spiced chicken *balado* and more unusual curries made with tempeh (fermented soybean cakes) or offal. For dessert there are freshly made sweet pancakes stuffed with peanuts and corn – much better than they sound. Just $5 per head for a good feed. Daily 8am–8pm.

Warung M Nasir 61 Circular Rd ☏65367998; see map, pp.54–55. A no-frills affair at the back of Boat Quay serving up quick Indonesian dishes, such as beef *rendang*, *sambal goreng* and *nasi goreng*. With dishes priced around $5 you can't go wrong. Mon–Fri 11am–8pm.

International and eclectic/fusion

Blu Shangri-La Hotel, Orange Grove Rd ☏62134598; see map, pp.78–79. One of Singapore's most exquisite dining experiences: California fusion cuisine of the highest quality, overlooking downtown Singapore from the *Shangri-La*'s 24th floor. Dishes include a delicious Thai crab ravioli. Pricey at $180 a head. Daily 7–11pm.

Blu Jaz Café 11 Bali Lane ☏62923800; see map, pp.68–69. Chilled-out café-restaurant stretching between Bali and Haji lanes, and easily spotted with its gaudy decor. They do reliable local and Western food, and at affordable prices; fish and chips costs around $10, for example. Live jazz Mon, Fri & Sat eves. Mon–Fri 11am–midnight, Sat 5pm–1am.

Buko Nero 126 Tanjong Pagar Rd ☏63246225; see map, pp.54–55. Japanese/Italian fusion food is the order of the day here in the simple yet chic interior. Try the aromatic pan-fried Scottish salmon with black olive crust ($35) – it's no wonder there's a three-week waiting list. Bookings essential. Set menu $48. Tues–Thurs 6.30pm–9.30pm, Fri & Sat noon–2pm & 6.30–9.30pm.

Colours by the Bay Esplanade, 8 Raffles Ave; see map, p.40. Like a very posh food court with restaurants rather than stalls as tenants. You can't go wrong here with *Thai Express* (see p.139) or the Italian *Al Dente* (☏63419188), both mid-priced chain restaurants.

Coriander Leaf Block A, Clarke Quay #02-03 ☏67323354; see map, p.40. In elegant upstairs premises, *Coriander Leaf* offers

pan-Asian and Mediterranean food, encompassing everything from Lebanese mezze to Vietnamese spring rolls. Main courses start at $25, or you can order a good-value sampler platter for $20. Mon–Fri noon–2.30pm & 6.30–10pm, Sat 6.30–10.30pm.

Eight Café & Bar 8 Bukit Pasoh Rd ☏62204513; see map, pp.54–55. This relaxed, retro-inspired café serves up Asian-Western fusion food that gets the cool kids clamouring for more. Try the *laksa* pasta with king prawns – a house favourite. Expect to pay around $28 per person. Happy Hour 7–9pm. Daily noon–2pm & 6.30–11pm. Drinks Fri–Sat 10pm–1am.

Flutes at the Fort 23B Coleman St ☏6338770; see map, p.40. If you think Singapore's colonial architecture is all about grand Palladian buildings, you'll be pleasantly put right at this restaurant, in a beautiful black-and-white wooden colonial house on the leafy slopes of Fort Canning Hill. You can sit indoors or out on the veranda to enjoy two- or three-course set lunches ($33 or $38 respectively), and there's a full menu of modern European and fusion fare too. Best to reserve ahead. To get there, take the little path through the car park by the Masonic Lodge. Mon–Fri noon–3pm & 6.30–10pm, Sat 11.30am–2.30pm (brunch) & 6.30–10pm.

Food #03 107 & 109 Rowell Rd ☏63967980; see map, pp.68–69. Associated with the independent art gallery next door, this is as close as Singapore gets to an alternative café – they sell ethically sourced coffee and serve an offbeat but tasty range of light veggie meals, including concoctions like pizza topped with pak choy and petai, a jungle legume much beloved of Malays. Ever so cool, despite the lack of a/c and the brothels nearby. Around $20 per head for two courses. Tues–Thurs 5–10pm, Fri 5pm–midnight, Sat noon–midnight, Sun noon–10pm.

Halia Singapore Botanic Gardens, 1 Cluny Rd ⓣ64766711; see map, pp.78–79. Moon- and candlelit after dusk, *Halia*'s magical garden-veranda setting whisks you a world away from downtown Singapore. The East-meets-West lunch menu spans sandwiches, pasta and *laksa*; at night, there are more substantial dishes such as rack of lamb and seafood stew. Take along the papers and tuck into the weekend buffet breakfast. $50–60 per person. Daily noon–3pm & 6.30–10.15pm.

Iggy's The Regent, 1 Cuscaden Rd ⓣ67322234; see map, pp.78–79. The minimal decor of this modern fusion restaurant belies the culinary fireworks in the kitchen; expect uncomplicated but very flavoursome food, including a great signature burger with truffle and sabayon sauce. Set menus only: two-course lunch $55, four-course lunch $65, evening gastronomica menu $195. Mon–Fri noon–2pm & 7–10pm, Sat & Sun 7–10pm.

Mezza9 Grand Hyatt, 10 Scotts Rd ⓣ67381234; see map, pp.78–79. Popular with local celebrities, this buzzing top-floor restaurant has remained at the top of the eat-and-be-seen lists. The impressive buffet encompasses sushi, a European deli, Thai, and a grill and rotisserie, or add champagne for the boozy Sunday brunch (11.30am–3pm; $138). $35–45 per head. Mon–Sat noon–2pm, & 6–10.30pm, Sun 6–10.30pm.

The Moomba 52 Circular Rd ⓣ64380141; see map, pp.54–55. Contemporary Australian restaurant named after the Aboriginal saying "let's get together". Great salads and the grain-fed Aussie beef steaks ($50) are cooked to perfection. Mains start from $16. Mon–Fri 11.30am–2.30pm & 6.30–10pm, Sun 6.30–10pm.

Perle Noir Oyster & Grill Bar 687 East Coast Rd ⓣ64481732; see map, p.92. Diners can eat on the leafy outdoor patio or inside a dimly lit, sail-bedecked wooden interior with blue fish tanks. Live oysters are $15 for half a dozen, and the "classic lunch" menu is a surprisingly low $10. Mon, Wed–Sat noon–3pm & 6–11pm, Sun 4–11pm.

PS Café 28B Harding Rd, Tanglin Village (Dempsey) ⓣ64793343; see map, pp.78–79. A glass-walled box acts as the food and bar space here, with a slightly shabby-chic interior design, serving up comfort food classics such as eggs benedict, French onion soup and club sandwiches. But what makes it special is the gorgeous leafy green garden out front, perfect for lunch or whiling away a balmy evening under the stars. $30–40 a head. Mon–Fri 11.30am–5pm & 6.30–10.30pm (Fri till 1am), Sat 6.30pm–1am, Sun 6.30–10.30pm.

Quentin's 139 Ceylon Rd ⓣ62544556; see map, p.94. Don't be surprised if you see the prime minister of Singapore eating here – it's just round the corner from his house and he's a frequent patron. Try the Devil Curry – stewed chicken in a sour red curry sauce. Mains from around $13. Daily 11.30am–2.30pm & 6.30–10pm.

Wild Rocket Hangout @ Mount Emily, 10A Upper Wilkie Rd ⓣ63399448; see map, pp.68–69. This cosy restaurant is run by a lawyer-turned-chef who hates being associated with fusion food, though that is pretty much what he does. The three-course set lunches (from $32) and dinners (from $50) are a reasonable deal, but going à la carte is pricey, and service could be sharper. Better to take a taxi here than trek uphill. Tues–Sat noon–3pm & 6.30–11pm, Sun 11.30am–3pm & 6.30–10.30pm.

Japanese and Korean

Both Japanese and Korean food aren't hard to find in Singapore, though neither tends to be cheap. If you're being budget-conscious, head to the Japanese deli-style counters in the basement of the Bugis Junction mall.

Beppu Menkan #01-19 China Court, 20 Cross St ⓣ64380328; see map, pp.54–55. Choose from grilled eel, ramen noodle soup and other Japanese favourites, eaten amid Japanese lanterns and cartoons of noodle-slurpers. Around $20 a head. Mon–Fri

11.30am–3pm & 6–10pm, Sat & Sun noon–10pm.

Ippudo #04-02/03/04 Mandarin Gallery, 333A Orchard Rd ⊤62352797; see map, pp.78–79. Bustling joint in the shiny, upmarket Mandarin Gallery rustling up ramen noodles double quick. $20–30 a head. Daily 11.30am–11pm.

Sakae Sushi #02-18 Wheelock Pl, 501 Orchard Rd ⊤67376281; see map, pp.78–79. One of a popular chain, this sushi and sashimi bar, bang in the centre of Orchard Road, has set lunches that start from $15. Diners choose to sit up at the conveyor-belt bar, or in diner-style booths around the venue's outer walls. Sun–Thurs 11.30am–10pm, Fri & Sat 11.30am–10.30pm.

Seoul Garden #02-52 Bugis Junction, 200 Victoria St ⊤63343339; see map, pp.68–69; **#03-119 Marina Square, 6 Raffles Blvd** ⊤63391339; see map, p.40. Entertaining, busy restaurant popular for its "all you can eat" Korean barbecue – a buffet of seasoned meats, seafoods and vegetables which you cook at your table ($22 at lunch, $26 dinner, $4 extra at weekends). Daily 11.30am–10.30pm.

Tonkichi #04-24/24A Ngee Ann City, 391 Orchard Rd ⊤67357522; see map, pp.78–79. A cosy place famed for its excellent *tonkatsu* (breaded deep-fried pork cutlets); the pork belly and *rosu katsu toji* (battered pork loin in claypot) are also recommended. $20–30 a head. Daily 10.30am–10pm.

Middle Eastern

Middle Eastern food is best sampled in the Arab Street area – which is not as trite a claim as it may sound. The first Arab restaurants here opened only a decade ago, soon followed by a wave of copycat establishments, some diversifying into Iranian and Turkish food. At least all this has reminded Singaporeans of their historical ties with the Arab world, though, ironically, there's scarcely anything on offer from the country where the island's Arab community has its roots – Yemen.

Café Le Caire 39 & 42 Arab St ⊤62920979; see map, pp.68–69. This relaxed diner pioneered Arab cuisine in the area and now has a swanky new outlet opposite the original venue, which remains open. It's a good inexpensive bet for Lebanese and Egyptian specialities – you can get a decent falafel sandwich with chips for just $7 – though one of the main specialities is the Yemeni harissa, a spicy stew of minced lamb and cracked wheat. They do a big range of hubble-bubble tobaccos, too. Daily 10am–3.30am, Fri & Sat till 5.30am.

Cappadocia Café Ground floor, Hotel Rendezvous, 9 Bras Basah Rd ⊤63379982; see map, pp.68–69. A great range of reasonable Turkish food, including *izgara köfte* (cigar-shaped skewerless kebabs) and the pizza-like *pide* and *lahmacun*. There's cherry juice and *ayran*, similar to buttermilk, to wash it all down with. Main courses around $15. Daily noon–11pm.

El Sheikh 18 Pahang St ⊤62969116; see map, pp.68–69. *El Sheikh* has seating on three levels and, along with *Café Le Caire*, has been a stalwart of the Arab St scene. The menu runs the usual gamut of Lebanese specialities, from meze to main courses such as *shish taouk* (filleted chicken on a skewer; $14), backed up by a great selection of juices and desserts. Daily 11am till late.

Shiraz Block A, Clarke Quay #01-06 ⊤63342282; see map, p.40. The best Iranian restaurant in town – not that there's much competition, but the many Iranians among the clientele can't be misguided. *Shiraz* keeps them coming with massive portions of tender kebabs and stews, all served with mounds of fluffy, aromatic saffron rice. Not cheap – main courses start at around $30 – but still better value than most places in overpriced Clarke Quay. Belly-dancing some evenings, too. Mon 6.30pm–1.30am, Tues–Sun noon–2.30pm & 6.30pm–1.30am (later at weekends).

Thai and Indochinese

The cheapest, if rather unexciting, place to sample Thai food is the **Golden Mile Complex** on Beach Road, the main hangout for Singapore's Thai community.

Indochine 49 Club St ☎63230503; see map, pp.54–55; Empress Place ☎63391720; see map, p.40; 44 Lorong Mambong, Holland Village ☎6468 5798; see map, p.104. *Indochine* is one of Singapore's most elegant restaurants, its beautiful fixtures complemented by a truly great menu embracing Vietnamese, Lao and Cambodian cuisine. Try the Laotian *larb kai* (spicy minced chicken salad) or *Nha Trang* roast duck and mango salad. The Indochine restaurant and café on the Singapore River at Empress Place offers great views across to Boat Quay and a slightly different menu, with the *pho bo* (beef noodle soup) particularly highly rated. Pricey but worth it. Club St Mon–Sat noon–2.30pm & 6–11pm; Empress Place Mon–Fri noon–3pm, dinner Mon–Thurs & Sun 6.30–11.30pm, Fri & Sat 6.30pm–12.30am; café daily 11am–11pm; Holland Village Mon–Sat noon–2.30pm & 6–11.30pm.

Bumbu 44 Kandahar St ☎63928628; see map, pp.68–69. Featuring fine Peranakan artefacts amassed by the owner, *Bumbu* is as much a social history document as a restaurant. Happily, the furnishings don't outshine the fine Thai cuisine, with a few Indonesian offerings too. Reckon on $25 per person. Tues–Sun 11am–3pm & 6–10pm.

Jim Thompson 45 Minden Rd, Dempsey Hill ☎64756088; see map, pp.78–79. Housed in one of Dempsey's loftier converted army barracks, decorated with spectacular mirrored mosaics, bird cages housing conical traditional Thai food covers and plush chairs that are more like thrones. Try the delicious *tom ka gai* (spicy coconut and chicken soup) or the hearty massaman curry (dishes from $18). Daily noon–midnight.

Madam Saigon 30 Liang Seah St ☎63339798; see map, pp.54–55. Affordable, if unremarkably appointed, restaurant whose Vietnamese chef knocks out tasty *pho* and *com tam* (broken rice with chicken), both around the $12 mark. Daily 11.30am–2.30pm & 6–10.30pm.

Patara #03-14 Tanglin Mall, Orchard Rd ☎67370818; see map, pp.78–79. Refined dining room, where the tasting menus (around $40) are a good way of acquainting yourself with Thai flavours. Daily noon–3pm & 6–10pm.

Sukhothai 47 Boat Quay ☎65382422; see map, pp.54–55. Chef's recommendations include fried cotton fish topped with sliced green mangoes, but you can't go far wrong whatever you choose as it's all great. The dining room is rather understated, so take advantage of the riverside tables. Mon–Fri 11.30am–3pm & 6–11pm, Sat & Sun 6–11pm.

Thai Express 16 Lorong Mambong ☎64666766; see map, p.104; Colours By The Bay, Esplanade ☎65336766; see map, p.40. A modern chain with plenty of wood and chrome fittings and where everything is chop-chop. The menu is packed with Thai rice and noodle standards (from $12) plus a good range of desserts. Daily 11.30am–10pm.

Yhingthai Palace 36 Purvis St #01-04 ☎63371161; see map, pp.68–69. A smart Chinese-influenced Thai restaurant, where you can't go wrong with their deep-fried pomfret served with Thai-style dressing, fried chicken wings with prawn filling, and Thai fishcakes. Around $40 per head, excluding drinks. Daily 11.30am–2pm & 6–10pm.

Nightlife

S ingapore's nightlife has gone from strength to strength over the past decade. The island's well-developed bar and pub scene means there is now a vast range of drinking holes to choose from. The Colonial District, Emerald Road and the converted barracks area of Dempsey close to The Botanic Gardens, as well as the toytown-like Clarke Quay and quaint Boat Quay all offer good pub-crawl potential. With competition so hot, bars are increasingly turning to live music to woo patrons.

Clubs also do increasingly brisk business. Glitzy and vibrant, they feature the latest imported pop, rock and dance music, and many frequently book the trendiest DJs from London, New York and Sydney.

Bars and pubs

With the bars and pubs of Singapore ranging from slick cocktail joints and elegant colonial chambers to boozy dives, you're bound to find a place that suits you. Establishments open either in the late morning (to catch the lunchtime trade) or in the early evening, closing anywhere between midnight and 3am. Most serve snacks throughout the day, and many offer more substantial dishes. It's possible to buy a small glass of beer in most places for around $12, but prices can be double that amount in swankier joints. A glass of wine usually costs much the same as a beer, and spirits a dollar or two more. One way of cutting costs is to arrive in time for happy hour in the early evening, when bars offer local beers and house wine either at half price, or "one for one" – you get two of whatever you order, but one is held back for later. The happy hours mentioned in the listings are daily unless otherwise stated.

The Colonial District and Marina Bay

Axis Mandarin Oriental, 5 Raffles Ave ☎68853098. A plush red and mahogany bar with to-die-for views over Marina Bay. Try the zingy sweet and sour Adam's Apple Martini ($24). Happy hour from 5–7pm. Mon–Thurs 10am–1am, Fri & Sat 10am–2am, Sun 10am–midnight.

Balaclava #01-01b Suntec City Convention Centre, 1 Raffles Blvd ☎63391600. Perennially popular bar that buzzes with an eclectic mix of straight-from-the-office suits and the cocktail-sipping fashion pack. The interior is

brooding, with masculine leather chairs, sassy red lamps and dark-wood veneers, while the large outdoor smoking area offers a more laidback vibe. Happy hour from 3–9pm, and live music Wed, Thurs and Fri from 8.30pm. Mon–Thurs 3pm–1am, Fri 3pm–2am, Sat 6pm–2am.

Bar Opiume Asian Civilisations Museum, 1 Empress Place ☎63392876. Cool-as-ice cocktail bar, ideal for a classy aperitif before dining at adjacent *Indochine* (see p.139). The barmen mix a mean Singapore Sling and there are stunning views of the waterfront from the outside terrace. Inside, the

sundowners (5–9pm). Sun–Tues 3pm–1am, Wed–Thurs 3pm–2am, Fri & Sat 3pm–3am.

▲ Bar at Indochine

Orgo Roof Terrace, The Espanade, 8 Raffles Ave ☎63369366. Rooftop bar that serves scrumptious fresh fruit cocktails blended by Japanese mixologists. While you drink, admire the striking silhouette of the city's skyline from every photographers' favourite vantage point. A hidden gem. Happy Hour 5–8pm. Daily 5pm–2am.

Chinatown and the CBD

Bar Savanh 49 Club St ☎63230145. You know a bar means business when it counts a six-metre waterfall and a koi carp pond among its fixtures and fittings. Candlelit, and crammed with Buddha effigies, scatter cushions and plants, *Savanh* ("Heaven" in Lao) is the epitome of a chilled-out bar. Upstairs is sister establishment, *Indochine* restaurant (see p.139). Happy hour 5–8pm. Mon–Thurs 3pm–2am, Fri & Sat 3pm–3am.

BQ Bar 39 Boat Quay ☎65369722. Arguably Boat Quay's most popular venue, thanks to its chilled dance music, comfy sofas and outgoing staff. The second level affords memorable views of the river. Tues–Sat 11am–1am, Sun & Mon 11am–midnight.

Harry's Quayside 28 Boat Quay ☎65383029. Always a hive of activity, especially with the expat crowd, this is a more upmarket branch of the now ubiquitous chain. Serves light food, and there's live jazz and R&B from Tues to Sat. Happy hour is from 11am–8pm. Sun–Thurs 11am–1am, Fri & Sat 11am–2am.

Molly Malone's 56 Circular Rd ☎65362029. With Kilkenny and Guinness ($14/pint) on tap, sounds courtesy of Van Morrison and the Pogues, and a menu offering Irish stew and fish and chips, this is hardly your quintessential Singaporean boozer, but good craic nonetheless, when full. Pints are cheaper during happy hour (11am–8pm). Sun–Thurs 11am–1am, Fri & Sat 11am–2am.

Screening Room Rooftop Bar 12 Ann Siang Rd ☎62211694. Terrific open-air bar situated in a characterful corner of Chinatown. With views over the red-tiled rooftops of the surrounding former shophouses, and soaring skyscrapers in the distance, you can contemplate the city's eclecticism over a mojito. Mon–Thurs 6pm–1am, Fri & Sat 6pm–3am.

sophisticated bar is graced by huge crystal chandeliers, modish, square-cut leather furniture and a lordly standing Buddha statue. Mon–Sat 5pm–2am, Sun 5pm–1am.

The Clinic 3C River Valley Rd, #01-03 The Cannery, Clarke Quay ☎68873733. At this kooky bar, staff dress up in doctors' scrubs and serve cocktails from IV drips, which can be sipped from the comfort of a gold spray-painted wheelchair. Certainly not everybody's cup of tea, but a popular alternative to the city's Identikit chain bars. Daily 5.30pm–1am.

The Long Bar Raffles Hotel, 1 Beach Rd ☎64121816. Indulge in the iconic Singapore Sling, invented here in 1915, while antique fans spin overhead and peanut shells, casually slung over the shoulder by patrons, crunch underfoot. Sun–Thurs 11am–12.30am, Fri & Sat 11am–1.30am.

Lot, Stock and Barrel Pub 30 Seah St ☎63385540. Frequented by an early office crowd and a late backpacker crowd (the guesthouses of Beach and North Bridge roads are just around the corner), who come for the rock classics on the jukebox; happy hour 4–8pm. Daily 4pm–midnight.

New Asia Bar Swissôtel The Stamford, 2 Stamford Rd ☎64315672. With jaw-dropping views from the angled floor – on a clear evening you can see all the way to Malaysia – this sleek bar is the perfect choice for

Speakeasy 54 Blair Rd (off Spottisewoode Park Rd) ☏97595111. A pearl of a bar on a quiet, beautifully maintained Peranakan street. Themed around 1920s Prohibition America, with black-and-white films flickering on the wall and cocktails drawn from the era that are both old-fashioned and satisfyingly stiff. Small but tasty plates of food are also available. Wed–Sat 6pm–late.

Bras Basah, Little India and The Arab Quarter

Divine Parkview Square, 600 North Bridge Rd ☏63964466. All the decadence and excess of 1920s café society comes outrageously to life at *Divine*, a big, bonkers bar whose adoption of a wine angel (a waitress, kitted out in wings and harness, who is winched up and down the 40ft wine rack) might just be the most politically incorrect thing you'll ever see. This is supposed to be a member's-only establishment, but dress sharp and you'll have no trouble getting in. Daily 11am–1am.

Loof #03-07 Odeon Towers, 331 North Bridge Rd ☏6338 8035. Effortlessly cool rooftop bar overlooking *Raffles*, with screens depicting finger shadow puppets and menus that fold out into "makeshift shelters" in case the heavens open – hope that they do, as drinks are two for one. The pizzas aren't bad either. Sun–Thurs 5pm–1.30am, Fri–Sat 5pm–3am.

Prince of Wales 101 Dunlop St ☏62990130. Scruffy backpackers' boozer also popular with expats that offers good live music every night (Mon–Sat from 9pm; Sun from 4pm). Mon–Thurs 9am–1am, Fri–Sun 9am–2am.

Wild Oats 11 Upper Wilkie Rd ☏63365413. Housed in a huge white colonial-style building atop Mount Emily, this charming bar with potted plants on outdoor decking feels a world away from the city's hustle and bustle – and serves cocktails the size of your head. Happy hour 6–9pm. Tues–Thurs & Sun 6pm–midnight, Fri & Sat 6pm–1am.

Orchard Road and around

Alley Bar 2 Emerald Hill Rd ☏67388818. Stand at the counter and you'll swear you're drinking under the stars, such is the ingenuity of the decor in this well designed joint. The candlelit seated area behind the bar is cosier and it's best to take advantage of their happy hour (daily 5–9pm) when it's

2 for 1 on selected drinks. Sun–Thurs 5pm–2am, Fri & Sat 5pm–3am.

Astor Bar St.Regis, 29 Tanglin Rd ☏65066888. Swanky joint with original Picasso prints and an Edward Hopper-esque bar. Famous for its cocktails, in particular the fiery chili padi Mary (a local interpretation of a bloody Mary) – lemon grass, Chinese ginger, tomato juice, vodka and fiery bird's eye chilli. Daily 3pm–2am.

Bar Stop 6 Devonshire Rd ☏67356614. Trendy bar with exposed brick walls, red leather sofas and a killer whisky selection. Ask the friendly bartenders to knock you up a cocktail off the cuff. Live music Mon–Wed (8/8.30pm). Mon–Thurs 5pm–1am, Fri & Sat 5pm–2am.

The Dubliner Windsland Conservation House, 165 Penang Rd ☏67352220. Set up in a colonial-era mansion, this is not your typical Irish pub. The grub is a notch above as well, and there are sometimes live bands on offer. Enjoying a beer on the veranda may be the best seat in the house. Sun–Thurs 11am–1am, Fri & Sat 11.30am–2am.

Hacienda 13A Dempsey Rd ☏94762922. One of Dempsey's nicest bars, with an elegant outside area surrounded by swaying trees that twinkle with fairy lights. Magical. Mon–Thurs 5pm–midnight, Fri & Sat 5pm–2am, Sun 11am–midnight.

Ice Cold Beer 9 Emerald Hill Rd ☏67359929. Noisy, hectic and happening place where the beers are kept on ice under the glass-topped bar. There are regular drinks promotions and two pool tables upstairs. Happy hour 5–9pm & 1–3am. Sun–Thurs 5pm–2am, Fri & Sat 5pm–3am.

KPO 1 Killiney Rd ☏67333648. Sister to *Bar Stop*, this former post office is now a chilled-out bar offering all-day dining and live DJs on Wed–Sat evenings. Happy hour from opening until 8pm. Mon–Thurs & Sat 9.30am–1am, Fri 9.30am–2am, Sun 10.30am–11pm.

No. 5 Emerald Hill 5 Emerald Hill Rd ☏67320818. A pleasant Peranakan-style bar-restaurant with an unpretentious feel. Kick back and join the rest of the cheery crowd in tossing a peanut shell or two on the floor. Happy hour Sun–Thurs noon–9pm & 1–2am, Fri & Sat 1–3am. Sun–Thurs noon–2am, Fri–Sat noon–3am.

Observation Lounge 38th floor, Mandarin Orchard, 333 Orchard Rd ☏68316288. Swanky cocktail bar offering awesome views over downtown Singapore. Mon–Thurs & Sun 5pm–1am, Fri & Sat 5pm–2am.

Que Pasa 7 Emerald Hill ☏62356626. Brooding tapas-themed bar featuring a creaky wooden staircase and scattered with wine bottles. A bit rough around the edges, which helps lend it an old-fashioned European character. Sun–Thurs 1.30pm–2am, Fri & Sat 1.30pm–3am.

Red Dot Brewhouse #01-01 25A Dempsey Rd ☏64750500. Mesh lanterns light up the large and leafy outdoor space like fireflies in this microbrewery and restaurant. Try the green spirulina lager for a health-infused kick at the end of a long day. Happy hour noon–6pm. Sun–Thurs noon–11pm, Fri & Sat noon–1am.

Eastern Singapore

1 TwentySix #01-26 Playground@Big Splash, 902 East Coast Parkway ☏63482126. With its lush alfresco area and expertly mixed-to-order cocktails, this beachfront bar is well

worth the trek. Excellent service with an atmosphere that melts all your cares away. Recommended. Daily 6.30pm–2am.

Western Singapore

Wala Wala Café Bar 31 Lorong Mambong, Holland Village ☏64624288. Rocking Holland Village joint serving Boddington's, Stella and Hoegaarden and featuring a generous happy hour (4–9pm). A live band plays upstairs in *Bar Above*. Mon–Thurs 4pm–1am, Fri & Sat 4pm–2am, Sun 3pm–1am.

Sentosa

Bellini Room at St James Power Station 3 Sentosa Gateway ☏62707676. Dark bar sporadically lit with strips of neon green, which plays Motown classics, swing and jazz tunes. Live music Mon–Sat from 10pm. Mon–Thurs 8pm–3am, Fri & Sat 8pm–4am.

Discos and nightclubs

Singapore's **nightclub scene** has transformed itself over the last few years. Clubs are far more self-aware, the dance music they feature is far more cutting-edge than previously, and the cult of the **celebrity DJ** has taken a firm hold. Happily, Singaporean clubbers themselves remain, on the whole, more intent on having fun than on posing. European and American dance music dominates (though some play Cantonese pop songs, too), and many feature live bands playing cover versions of current hits and pop classics.

Clubs tend to open around 9pm, though some start earlier in the evening with a happy hour. Indeed, the difference between bars and discos has recently begun to blur, and some now include bars or restaurants that kick off at lunchtime. Most have a cover charge, at least on busy Friday and Saturday nights, which fluctuates between $15 and $30, depending on what day it is and what sex you are (women are generally allowed in for less – especially on "ladies' nights"), and it almost invariably entitles you to a drink or two. It's worth checking the local press to see which venues are currently in favour; a scan through *8 Days*, *I-S* or *Juice* magazines will bring you up to date. Singapore also has a plethora of extremely seedy hostess clubs, in which Chinese hostesses working on commission try to hassle you into buying them an extortionately expensive drink. Fortunately, they are easy to spot: even if you get beyond the heavy wooden front door flanked by brandy adverts, the pitch dark inside gives the game away. For a **beach party**, head to Sentosa (see p.109).

Attica + Attica Too Clarke Quay, #01-03, 3A River Valley Rd ☏63339973. Attracts a mixed crowd of expats, locals and "working girls", and has a reputation for being "utterly shameless". Hip-hop on the ground floor, laser lights on the top floor. Sun–Tues

5pm–2am ($12), Thurs 5pm–3am, Wed, Fri & Sat 5pm–4am ($28).

Brix Grand Hyatt Singapore, 10–12 Scotts Rd ☏67381234. This large basement bar has a reputation for being a pick-up joint, but the in-house live band, Shades, are pretty good

(11)

(Mon–Wed 9.30pm, Thurs–Sat 10pm). Monday is your best bet if you want to boogie to r'n'b and disco tunes. $25 cover charge after 9pm. Thurs–Sat 9pm–4am, Sun–Wed 9pm–3am.

Butter Factory #01-06 One Fullerton, 1 Fullerton Rd ☎63338243. Situated on the riverfront, this new addition to the nightlife scene has two rooms: the electro playing Fash, and Bump, which churns out r'n'b/hip-hop for an increasingly younger crowd. $10–25. Wed 10pm–3am, Thurs 9pm–2am, Fri & Sat 10pm–4am.

Home Club #B1-01/06 The Riverwalk, 20 Upper Circular Rd ☎65382928. A little more off the radar than the city's other clubs, *Home Club* plays host to local band album launches, as well as international DJs like Goldie. Throw yourself around in its living room-like space to hip-hop, deep house, techno, indie, electro and drum'n'bass. $12–15. Tues–Fri 9pm–3am, Sat 10pm–4am.

Powerhouse@StJames Power Station 3 Sentosa Gateway ☎62707676. Huge space with three separate sound-proofed rooms offering Latin, radio friendly r'n'b and "house pop" (pop songs given a clubby spin). $15–20, ladies free on Wed. Wed, Fri & Sat 8pm–4am.

Stereolab & Stereobar Ground floor, Pan Pacific Singapore, 7 Raffles Blvd ☎63370800.

Restaurant and house music club designed to look like a recording studio, with a custom-built state-of-the-art sound system. Over-21s only. Stereobar: Mon & Tues 5pm–1am, Wed & Thurs 5pm–3am, Fri & Sat 5pm–4am. Stereolab: Wed 9pm–3am, Fri & Sat 10pm–4am.

Zirca Mega Club Block C, #01-02/05 & #02-01/08, The Cannery, Clarke Quay ☎63334168. Huge dance club that also comprises *Rebel!* and *Yello Jello*, complete with aerialists and fire twirlers. Popular with gay men on "Fabulous Sundays". $15–28, ladies free on Wed. Wed–Sat 9.30pm–late.

Zouk 17 Jiak Kim St ☎67382988. Singapore (and arguably Southeast Asia's) trendiest club, fitted out with palm trees and Moorish tiles to create a Mediterranean feel. World famous DJs like Paul Oakenfold, Judge Jools and Carl Cox guest regularly. As well as *Zouk* itself, the warehouse is also home to *Phuture* (Wed, Fri & Sat 9pm–4am) a dark, smoky joint with futuristic decor and harder hip-hop, break beat and drum'n'bass, and *Velvet Underground* (Wed–Sat 9pm–late), which is favoured by a slightly older, more chilled-out crowd. Wed 10pm–4am; Fri & Sat 10pm–4am. $15–28, ladies free on Wed.

Gay and lesbian nightlife

Singapore's **gay scene**, though modest, is one of the liveliest in Southeast Asia. That said, attitudes to homosexuality remain a bit schizophrenic. Colonial-era legislation banning sex between men remains on the statute book following a failed attempt in 2007 to get parliament to repeal it, though the government has said it will continue not to enforce the law and has no intention of compelling gay venues to go underground. Despite the generally tolerant atmosphere, it makes sense to be discreet: gay issues are seldom discussed in public, and open displays of affection, whether gay or straight, aren't really the done thing in Singapore.

At night, the scene centres on Chinatown and Tanjong Pagar, where there are a fair number of bars. In addition to those places listed below, *Zirca* (see above) is popular with gay men on its "Fabulous Sundays", while the mixed-crowd scene of *Zouk/Velvet Underground* (see above) is popular with both gay and lesbians.

The best way to keep abreast of the current hotspots is to go online. A portal for gay men in Singapore ⓦ www.trevvy.com, details all the best bars and clubs of the moment, as well as cruising hotspots, including MRT stations, shopping centres and swimming pools. The website ⓦ www.fridae.com is a pan-Asian portal aimed at both gay men and lesbians.

Backstage 13a Trengganu St ☎62271712. Gay-friendly bar plastered with posters of *The Sound of Music* and other musicals, and

with a small balcony over the hustle and bustle of Chinatown. Happy hour 7–9pm. Sun–Thurs 7pm–2am, Fri & Sat 7pm–3am.

Singapore food

Singaporeans live to makan ("eat", in Malay), and the island's ethnic diversity is reflected in its culinary offerings. From southern China, there are all the classics of Cantonese cuisine and less familiar provincial dishes; the Malay kitchen offers curries that are at once spicy and subtly flavoured with herbs; and you'll also find yet more curries, plus pancakes and griddle breads, in the fiery style of south India. There's even a local fusion cuisine, called Nonya or Peranakan cooking, created by a community with a mixed Chinese and Malay heritage.

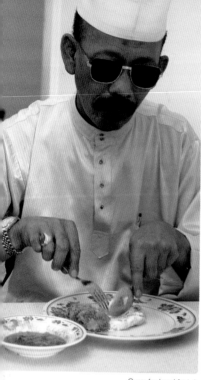

Breakfast

No meal demonstrates the multicultural nature of Singapore better than breakfast. Chinese residents often favour **congee**, a rice gruel either cooked plain and served with salt fish and omelette strips, or else boiled up with chicken or fish. Malay mornings typically begin with **nasi lemak**, rice fragrant with coconut milk and served with *ikan bilis* (dried anchovies), sliced omelette and cucumber. A favourite breakfast with locals of all hues is **roti prata**, a layered and griddle-fried south Indian bread dipped in curry gravy. For something a little more familiar to western taste buds, try **kaya toast**, *kaya* being a local jam made from coconut, sugar and egg.

Curry for breakfast ▲

Barbecuing satay ▼

Unofficial national dishes

You could stay in Singapore for a month and never eat the same meal twice. That said, some dishes have attained iconic status, and locals return to them time and again.

Chilli crab Whole crabs wok-fried with garlic, chilli and tomato paste.

Chicken rice Hainanese dish of poached chicken, served on rice cooked in chicken stock.

Char kway teow Flat rice noodles stir-fried with sweet soy sauce, Chinese sausage and prawns.

Murtabak A thick Indian griddle bread stuffed with minced meat, onion and egg.

Laksa Noodles, prawns and other morsels steeped in a hot chilli-coconut soup.

Satay Meat skewers roasted over coals and dipped in a sweet peanut sauce, served with cucumber and *ketupat* (rice cakes).

Fish head curry A fiery, tangy stew containing a large fish head – eyes and all; the cheeks are the best bits.

Entertainment and the arts

Singapore offers an excellent range of cultural events in all genres, drawing on both Asian and Western traditions, and even on a brief visit it's hard not to notice how much money has been invested in the arts. Prime downtown property has been turned over to arts organizations in areas like Waterloo Street and Little India, and prestige venues like Theatres On The Bay bring in world-class performers – at top-dollar prices.

This isn't to say that all is hunky-dory: questions linger over whether creativity is truly valued when censorship still lingers, if not as overtly as in the 1970s and 1980s, then in terms of there being well-established red lines concerning party politics, ethnicity and religion which no one dare cross. More cynically, some say that arts funding is a way to keep Singapore attractive to expats and its own sometimes restless middle class. All this means that the local scene can seem unusually low-key.

Events are widely advertised in the press and in listings magazines such as the weekly *I-S* (free in print, and at Ⓦ is-magazine.com). Tickets can be obtained directly from venues or through **ticketing agencies** such as SISTIC (the largest, with outlets in many downtown malls; Ⓣ 63485555, Ⓦ www.sistic.com.sg), Tickets.com (Ⓣ 62962929, Ⓦ www.tdc.sg) and Gatecrash (Ⓣ 61002005, Ⓦ www .gatecrash.com.sg).

There are two major international arts festivals annually: the **Singapore Arts Festival** (four weeks in May & June; Ⓦ www.singaporeartsfest.com), running the gamut from theatre through dance and film to concerts; and the **Singapore Fringe Festival** (Jan; Ⓦ www.singaporefringe.com), which concentrates on theatre, dance and the visual arts.

Arts centres and general-purpose venues

In addition to the venues listed here, the two casino-resorts of *Marina Bay Sands* (see p.51) and *Resorts World* (see p.107) also play host to some concerts and musical extravaganzas. For details of smaller, independent venues where you can catch live rock, jazz and blues music, see p.145.

The Arts House 1 Old Parliament Lane, near Empress Place Ⓣ 63326919, Ⓦ www.thearts house.com.sg. Plays, concerts, films and art exhibitions.

DBS Arts Centre 20 Merbau Rd, Robertson Quay Ⓣ 67323266. Plays and concerts.

Hawker food

For the most authentic Singapore eating experience, visit a **hawker centre**, cooked-food markets with rows of shared tables and scores of stalls allowing punters to mix and match from a huge range of inexpensive meals, snacks, desserts and drinks. Hawker centres were originally set up for practical reasons, to take the food vendors off the streets and ensure consistent levels of hygiene, and, at their best, they offer a glimpse of the old street life, with smoke, steam and aromas mingling and the air ringing to the clatter of spatula on wok and the cries of coffee-sellers calling out orders. Among the best downtown are those at Tekka Market, Maxwell Road and Lau Pasat Festival Market (see pp.123–124).

▲ Busy stall at a food court

▼ A simple Indian meal

Fruits

Somewhat surprisingly, tropical fruits often tend to be available seasonally rather than year-round. Listed below are a few to look out for, with their approximate seasons.

Jackfruit Huge, sack-like fruit with coarse green skin and sweet lumps of flesh inside (March–September).

Starfruit Starry in cross-section, and vaguely appley in taste; also called the carambola (March–July).

Durian A spiky large fruit whose notoriously smelly, custardy flesh has notes of garlic, almond and caramel (April–July).

Mangosteen The segmented flesh is sweet and also slightly tangy, but beware the crimson rind, which can stain clothes indelibly (May–September).

Rambutan Beneath the bright red, hairy peel is a fruit with sweet translucent flesh and a single stone (June–September).

▼ Jackfruit

Jellied desserts ▲

Fresh sugar cane juice ▼

Liquid pleasures

Nothing kick-starts a Singapore day better than a hot mug of **kopi see** – strong black coffee served with a huge dollop of evaporated milk. Tea-lovers may prefer **teh halia**, a rich, sweet tea infused with ginger, or a milky **teh tarik** (in Malay, "pulled tea"), which is poured repeatedly from one beaker to another to create a frothy tea milkshake. Another treat available at hawker centres is **sugar cane juice**, pressed on the spot by forcing the canes through a mangle. If you want a drop of the hard stuff, a **Singapore Sling** – a heady blend of gin, cherry brandy, pineapple and lime juices and cointreau – is practically de rigueur, but for most Singaporeans nothing beats an ice-cold bottle of **Tiger beer**.

Nonya cuisine

The closest Singapore comes to an indigenous cuisine is the food of the Straits Chinese, or Peranakans – descendants of early Chinese settlers in Penang, Malacca and Singapore who, in many cases, married Malay women. The resulting cuisine (known as Nonya after the local word for Peranakan women) blends Chinese and Malay ingredients, cooking techniques and dishes to mouth-watering effect. Most Nonya menus are framed around a handful of classic dishes. **Otak-otak**, fish mashed with coconut milk and chilli and steamed in banana leaf, makes a piquant starter. Next, you could try **ikan assam pedas** (a spicy fish stew), **itek tim** (duck and salted vegetable soup) or **babi pongteh** (pork braised in soy sauce). For the quintessential taste of Nonya food, order **ayam buah keluak**, chicken cooked with black nuts. The traditional dessert of **bubur cha-cha** – yam, sweet potato, tapioca flour and coconut milk – rounds a meal off in style.

Play #01-02-04 21 Tanjong Pagar Rd ☎62277400. Graffitti-scrawled walls with boys in tight tops dancing to deep house and poppy remixes. $15. Wed & Thurs 9pm–3am, Fri 9pm–3am, Sat 9pm–4am.

Tantric 78 Neil Rd ☎64239232. Double shot drinks at no extra charge makes this a popular choice. More chilled during the week, it's standing-room only at the weekends. Free. Sun–Fri 8.30pm–3am, Sat 8.30pm–4am.

Taboo 65–67 Neil Rd ☎62256256. Sweaty bodies dominate the dance floor, gyrating popular house music. Attracts a straight crowd too. Drag performances and fashion parades take place throughout the month. $20 including two drinks. Wed & Thurs 8pm–2am, Fri 10pm–3am, Sat 10pm–4am.

Why Not? 56 Tras St ☎63233010. Pumping gay club awash with young male Chinese revellers. Karaoke nights Mon–Thurs 8pm–3am, disco nights Fri 11pm–3am, Sat 11pm–4am.

Live music

Singapore is an established part of the East Asian circuit for **Western stadium-rock outfits** as well as indie bands, though gigs can be marred by a rather staid atmosphere as locals are often still uncomfortable about letting their hair down. **Local bands** do exist and some aren't at all bad, but these are more likely to perform in community centres, rather than decent venues. Rivalling Western music in terms of popularity in Singapore is **Canto-pop**, a bland hybrid of Cantonese lyrics and Western disco beats whose origins lie in the soundtracks of 1950s Cantonese movie musicals; Hong Kong Canto-pop superstars visit periodically, and the rapturous welcome they receive make their shows quite an experience.

No matter who else is in town, you can always catch a set of cover versions at one of Singapore's bars and clubs; the main venues are picked out below. Jazz and blues ensembles are also popular.

The most exhaustive lists of what's on are to be found in the weekly magazine, *8 Days*, the fortnightly *I-S* and monthly *Where Singapore*, though the "Life!" section of the *Straits Times* is also worth a scan. The best music festival is **Mosaic** (March; ⊛ www.mosaicmusicfestival.com), showcasing an excellent range of jazz and rock acts at Theatres On The Bay.

Balaclava See p.140. Live torch song (love songs), rock and jazz sets nightly.

Bar Opiume See p.140. Modern and Brazilian jazz. Mon–Sat 9pm–12.30am.

Bellini Room at St James Powerstation See p.143. Swing and jazz Mon–Sat from 10pm.

Blu Jaz Café See p.136. Live jazz music every Wed, Fri & Sat 9.30pm–midnight.

Brix See p.143. Live music from Monday to Saturday from local band Shades.

Crazy Elephant 3E River Valley Rd, #01-03 Clarke Quay ☎63377859. Bar playing decent rock music on the turntable between live sessions by the house blues band. The decor is an interesting mix of wood panelling and graffiti, but regulars prefer the tables out by the water's edge. Happy hour 5–9pm. Sun–Thurs 5pm–2am, Fri & Sat 3pm–3am.

Southbridge Jazz @ 7atenine 8 Raffles Ave ☎63380789. Mellow jazz played live nightly from about 9pm. Sun–Thurs 5pm–1am, Fri & Sat 5pm–2am.

The Pump Room @ Clarke Quay 3B River Valley Rd, The Foundry, Clarke Quay ☎63342628. Local band Jive Talkin' play pop, R&B and jazz Tuesday to Saturday from 10.45pm.

Singapore Indoor Stadium Stadium Rd ☎63442660. The usual venue for big-name bands in town; tickets are available through SISTIC (see p.146).

Timbre Substation, 5 Armenian St; The Arts House, 1 Old Parliament Lane; 11A Mount Sophia ☎63380789. Open-air venues with local bands and singer-songwriters serving up their own material, though it can be a little derivative. Daily from 6pm, music from 9pm (Arts House venue closed Sun).

Yello Jello Block C, #01-06, The Cannery, Clarke Quay ☎68873733. Originally meant as a retro-themed bar, *Yello Jello* has become more of a live music venue with local band John Molina & Krueger thrashing out rock classics Mon–Sat. Mon–Sun 6pm–late.

Drama Centre Level 3, National Library, 100 Victoria St ☎68378400. Mainly plays by local companies.

Esplanade – Theatres on the Bay 1 Esplanade Drive ☎68288222, ⓦwww.esplanade.com.sg. Sucks up most of the high-profile events.

Jubilee Hall Raffles Hotel, 1 Beach Rd ☎64121340. Plays and other performances are occasionally staged here; check the press for details.

MAX Pavilion Singapore Expo, 1 Expo Dr ⓦwww.singaporeexpo.com.sg. Big-name concerts at this huge hall, inconveniently located out by Changi Airport.

NAFA Lee Foundation Theatre Campus 3, Nanyang Academy of Fine Arts, 151 Bencoolen St ☎65134000. Plays and other performances.

Singapore Indoor Stadium 2 Stadium Walk, Kallang ⓦwww.sis.gov.sg. The usual venue for big-selling bands in town.

Substation 45 Armenian St ☎63377535, ⓦwww.substation.org. One of the oldest independent arts organizations in Singapore, presenting drama and dance in their multipurpose hall, as well as art, sculpture and photography exhibitions in their gallery.

Victoria Concert Hall and Theatre 11 Empress Place ⓦwww.vch.org.sg. Concerts and plays, though closed until 2013 for a major refit.

Theatre

Singapore's arts scene is probably at its best when it comes to **drama**: a surprising number of small theatre companies have sprung up over the years, performing works by local playwrights which dare to include a certain amount of social commentary. Foreign theatre companies tour regularly too, and lavish Western musicals are staged from time to time.

Companies

Action Theatre 42 Waterloo St ☎68370842, ⓦwww.action.org.sg. Stages work by Singaporean playwrights as well as the standard repetoire, with its own 100-seater venue on site.

The Necessary Stage Marine Parade Community Building, 278 Marine Parade Rd ☎63380611, ⓦwww.necessary.org. Pioneering socially conscious theatre group. Their premises are out near Katong but some of their productions are staged downtown.

Singapore Repertory Theatre DBS Arts Centre (see opposite); ⓦwww.srt.com.sg. English-language theatre, performing more than just the most obvious British and American plays.

Theatreworks #72-13 Mohamed Sultan Rd ☎67377213, ⓦwww.theatreworks.com.sg. Another of the early pioneers of the Singapore stage.

Street theatre

If you walk around Singapore long enough, you're likely to stumble upon some sort of streetside cultural event, most usually a **wayang** – a Malay word used in Singapore to denote Chinese opera. Played out on outdoor stages next to temples and markets, or in open spaces in the new towns, wayangs are highly dramatic and stylized affairs, in which garishly made-up characters enact popular Chinese legends to the accompaniment of the crashes of cymbals and gongs. They're staged throughout the year, but the best time to catch one is during the Festival of the Hungry Ghosts, when they are held to entertain passing spooks, or during the Festival of the Nine Emperor Gods (see p.152). Another fascinating traditional performance, lion-dancing, takes to the streets during Chinese New Year, and puppet theatres may appear around then, too. Chinatown and the Bugis/Waterloo Street area are good places in which you may catch performances.

Classical and traditional music and dance

At the heart of Singapore's Western classical music scene is the **Singapore Symphony Orchestra**, whose concerts often feature guest soloists, conductors and choirs from around the world.

Companies and orchestras

Chinese Opera Teahouse 5 Smith St ☏63234862, ⓦwww.ctcopera.com.sg. For an interesting culinary and musical experience, come here for the *Sights and Sounds of Chinese Opera* (7pm), a set dinner followed by performances of excerpts from Chinese operas. The package costs $35, though you can watch the opera selections alone for $20 (includes tea and snacks; admission at 7.50pm).

Nanyang Academy of Fine Arts City Chinese Orchestra ⓦwww.cityco.com.sg. Chinese classical and folk music recitals.

Singapore Chinese Orchestra ⓦsco.com.sg. Performances of traditional Chinese music through the year, plus occasional free concerts.

Singapore Lyric Opera ⓦwww.singaporeopera .com.sg. Western opera and operetta.

Singapore Dance Theatre ☏63380611, ⓦwww .singaporedancetheatre.com. Contemporary and classical works, sometimes in the open-air at Fort Canning Hill.

Singapore Symphony Orchestra ⓦwww.sso.org .sg. Performances throughout the year at Esplanade – Theatres on the Bay and other venues. Occasional free concerts at the Botanic Gardens too.

Temple of Fine Arts ☏65350509, ⓦwww .templeoffinearts.org. This Indian cultural organization puts on occasional shows of classical music and dance.

Film

As explored in the National Museum's film gallery (see p.48), postwar Singapore was the nexus of the Malay-language movie industry, with some films in Chinese also shot here. That flowering lasted all of twenty years until, following independence, Malay film-making drifted off to Kuala Lumpur while in Singapore censorship grew more problematic as tastes were, in any case, gravitating away from locally made films towards slicker efforts from the West and Hong Kong. It wasn't until the 1990s that local film-making saw a renaissance, and today a thriving independent scene releases full-length features, shorts and documentaries.

The best time to appreciate locally made movies is at the annual **Singapore International Film Festival** (two weeks in April; ⓦwww.filmfest.org.sg). If you intend to be in Singapore for a while, you might want to join the Singapore Film Society (ⓦwww.sfs.org.sg), which puts on its own monthly screenings of films (members-only) and mounts occasional film festivals (with discounts for members).

Otherwise, Singapore's cinemas offer up all the latest blockbusters from Hollywood, Bollywood and Hong Kong, with English subtitles as appropriate. Turn up early or book in advance to secure tickets (seldom more than S$10) if the film is newly released – and take a sweater, as the air-conditioning units are perpetually on full blast. Note also that Singaporeans often chat incessantly at the cinema.

Multiplex chains

Cathay Cinemas include: Cathay Cineplex, 2 Handy Rd (near Dhoby Ghaut MRT); Cineleisure Orchard, 8 Grange Rd (near Somerset MRT); ☏62351155, ⓦwww.cathay.com.sg. The Art Deco Cathay Cineplex is a city landmark and includes a gallery of memorabilia from Cathay's own involvement in local film-making in the mid-twentieth century (Tues–Sun noon–8pm; free).

Eng Wah Downtown at #03-51 Suntec City Mall, 3 Temasek Blvd, Marina Centre ☏68369074, ⓦwww.ewcinemas.com.sg.

Golden Village Cinemas include: Level 7, Plaza Singapura, 68 Orchard Rd; Levels 2 & 3, VivoCity, Harbourfront; #03/04-01 Marina Leisureplex, near the Mandarin Oriental hotel, Marina Centre; ☎1900/912 1234, ⓦwww.gv.com.sg.

Shaw Cinemas include: Lido 8 Cineplex, levels 5 & 6, Shaw House, 350 Orchard Rd; Bugis Cineplex, Bugis Junction, 200 Victoria St; ☎67380555, ⓦwww.shaw.sg.

Independent cinemas

Alliance Française 1 Sarkies Rd (10-min walk from Newton MRT) ⓦwww.alliancefrancaise .org.sg/cineclub.html. Weekly French-language films with English subtitles; tickets through SISTIC.

National Museum Cinematheque National Museum, 93 Stamford Rd ⓦwww.national museum.sg. The museum mounts its own laudable programme of films from around the world. Tickets from the museum itself or SISTIC.

Omni-Theatre See p.103. Singapore's IMAX cinema.

The Picturehouse Cathay Building, 2 Handy Rd ☎62351155, ⓦwww .thepicturehouse.com.sg. Part of the Cathay empire but, unlike its multiplexes, devoted to art-house films.

The Screening Room 12 Ann Siang Hill ☎62211694, ⓦwww.screeningroom.com.sg. "Where food meets film" is the motto of this complex, incorporating a basement lounge, restaurant, gallery space and a cinema screening the relatively intellectual end of Hollywood's output plus the odd Asian film.

Sinema #B1-12 Old School, 11B Mount Sophia ☎63369707, ⓦwww.sinema.sg. Excellent venue screening work by home-grown talent plus some foreign art-house films, and hosting forums involving local film personages. It's one of many arts organizations at Old School, a rather confusing complex that was once the Methodist Girls' School; you can reach it via the long flight of steps up from Handy Rd near the back of Plaza Singapura.

Festivals

With so many ethnic groups and religions present in Singapore, you'll be unlucky if your trip doesn't coincide with some sort of **festival**, either secular or religious. Religious celebrations range from exuberant, family-oriented pageants to blood-curdlingly gory displays of devotion; secular events tend to comprise a carnival with a cast of thousands. Below is a chronological round-up of Singapore's major festivals, with suggestions of where best to enjoy them. Most have no fixed **dates**, but change annually according to the lunar calendar. We've listed rough timings, but for specific dates each year it's a good idea to check with the STB, which produces a monthly round-up of festivals in Singapore, or check out the calendar of events to be found on many Singapore tourism websites such as Ⓦwww.yoursingapore.com.

Some, but by no means all, festivals are also **public holidays**, when many shops and restaurants may close. For a full list of public holidays, see p.34.

January–March

Thaiponggal

Mid-Jan A Tamil thanksgiving festival marking the end of the rainy season and the onset of spring. In Hindu homes, rice is cooked in a new pot and allowed to boil over, to symbolize prosperity. At the Sri Srinivasa Perumal Temple on Serangoon Road, food is prepared against a cacophony of drums, bells, conch shells and chanting, offered up to the gods, and then eaten by devotees as a symbol of cleansing.

Chinese New Year

Jan–Feb Singapore's Chinese community springs spectacularly to life to welcome in the new lunar year. The festival's origins lie in a Chinese legend telling of a horned monster that was awoken by the onset of spring, terrorizing nearby villagers until they discovered it could be held at bay by noise, light and the colour red. Essentially, Chinese New Year is a family affair – old debts are settled, friends and relatives visited, mandarin oranges exchanged, red envelopes (*hong bao*) containing money given to children, and red scrolls and papers bearing the character *fu* pasted to front doors as a sign of good fortune. Even so, there's still plenty to see in Chinatown, whose streets are ablaze with lanterns and fairy lights. Mediacorp's annual televised Lunar New Year Countdown is broadcast live from an outdoor location in the city, and is well worth looking out for in the press to ensure you can take part in the festivities.

Thaipusam

Jan/Feb Not for the faint-hearted, this Hindu festival sees entranced penitents walking the three kilometres from Little India's Sri Perumal Srinivasa Temple to the Chettiar Temple on Tank Road, carrying *kavadis* – elaborate steel arches decorated with peacock feathers and attached to their skin by hooks and prongs – and with skewers spiked through their cheeks and tongues – to honour the Lord Murugan. Some join the procession to pray for assistance, others to give thanks for heavenly aid already granted. Coconuts are smashed at the feet of the penitents for good luck as they set off, and friends and relatives jig around them en route, singing and chanting to spur them on.

NUS Arts Festival

March A month-long event organized by the National University of Singapore, comprising more than fifty concerts covering theatre, dance and music. Tickets are available from SISTIC (☎63485555, ⓦwww.sistic.com.sg).

April–August

Qing Ming

April Ancestral graves are cleaned and restored, and prayers and offerings made of joss sticks, incense papers and food from Chinese families at the beginning of the third lunar month, to remember dead ancestors and mark the beginning of spring.

Vesak Day

May Saffron-robed monks chant sacred scriptures at packed Buddhist temples, and devotees release caged birds to commemorate the Buddha's birth (May), enlightenment and the attainment of Nirvana; in the evening, candlelit processions are held at temples. The Buddha Tooth Relic Temple in Chinatown (see p.61) is a good place to experience this festival.

Dumpling Festival

May/June Stalls along Albert Mall sell traditional pyramid-shaped Chinese dumplings in the run-up to the Dumpling Festival, celebrated on the fifth day of the fifth lunar month. The festival commemorates Qu Yuan, a Chinese scholar who drowned himself in protest against political corruption. Local people, it is said, tried to save him from sea creatures by beating drums, disturbing the waters with their oars, and throwing in rice dumplings to feed them, but to no avail.

Singapore Arts Festival

May/June Annual celebration of world dance, music, drama and art, utilizing venues around the state, with events lasting several weeks.

Dragon Boat Festival

June/July Rowing boats, bearing a dragon's head and tail, their crews spurred on by the pounding of a great drum in the prow, race across Marina Bay to commemorate Qu Yuan (see "*Festive Singapore*" colour section).

Singapore Food Festival

June/July Organized by the STB and lasting a month, this gastronomic festival celebrates Singapore's diverse cuisines. Highlights include cookery workshops, a riverboat tea cruise, street shows in Chinatown – and, of course, ample opportunity to experience the fantastic local cuisine at discounted rates.

Ramadan

July–Aug Muslims spend the ninth month of the Islamic calendar fasting in the daytime in order to intensify awareness of the plight of the poor and to identify with the hungry. Many also abstain from drinking (anything), smoking and sex. The fast is broken nightly with delicious Malay sweetmeats served at stalls outside mosques. The biggest collection of stalls sets up along Bussorah and Kandahar streets, outside the Arab Quarter's Sultan Mosque. Muslims mark Hari Raya Puasa (Eid-al-Fitr), the end of Ramadan, by feasting, donning their best traditional clothes and visiting family and friends.

Singapore National Day

Aug 9 Singapore's gaining of independence in 1965 is celebrated with a national holiday and a huge show at either the Padang or the National Stadium, featuring military parades and fireworks.

Festival of the Hungry Ghosts

Aug/Sept Sometimes called Yue Lan, this festival is held to appease the souls of the dead released from Purgatory during the thirty days of the seventh lunar month, and thereby forestall unlucky events. Chinese street operas and concerts are held for the entertainment of the "wandering spirits", and joss sticks – some the size of a man – red candles and paper money are burnt outside Chinese homes. Paper effigies of worldly goods such as houses, cars and servants are sometimes burnt, too. Elsewhere, marquees are set up in the street to hold festive banquets, followed by auctions of pieces of charcoal, cake and flowers – all thought to be auspicious.

September–December

Birthday of the Monkey God

Sept (also Feb) To celebrate the birthday of one of the most popular deities in the Chinese pantheon, mediums possessed by the Monkey God's spirit pierce themselves

⑬

with skewers and dispense charms written in their own blood at the Monkey God Temple on Seng Poh Road, while a sedan chair possessed by the god himself is carried by worshippers. Elsewhere, street operas and puppet shows are performed – look out for ad hoc canopies erected near Chinese temples.

Mooncake Festival

Sept Also known as the Mid-Autumn Festival (held on the fifteenth day of the eighth lunar month), when Chinese people eat and exchange moon cakes (made from sesame and lotus seeds and stuffed with red bean paste or a duck egg) to honour the fall of the Mongol Empire – plotted, so legend has it, by means of messages secreted in cakes. Another, simpler explanation is that the cakes represent the full moon, at its brightest at this time of year. Moon cake stalls spring up across Singapore two weeks before the festival, but particularly in Chinatown.

Lantern Festival

Sept Strictly speaking a subset of the Mooncake Festival (see "*Festive Singapore*" colour section), the Lantern Festival is celebrated over two weeks in the Chinese Gardens in Jurong, where children parade with gaily coloured lanterns, and cultural shows – lion and dragon dances in particular – are a common sight.

Navarathiri

Sept–Oct Hindu temples such as the Chettiar Temple on Tank Road, and Chinatown's Sri Mariamman Temple, devote nine nights to classical dance and music in honour of Durga, Lakshmi and Saraswathi, the consorts of the Hindu gods Shiva, Vishnu and Brahma. Visitors are welcome at the nightly performances that take place at temples across the island. On the tenth night, a silver horse is carried at the head of a procession that begins at the Sri Thandayuthapani Temple on Tank Road.

Thimithi

Sept–Nov Another dramatic Hindu ceremony, this one sees devotees proving the strength of their faith by running across a four-metre-long pit of hot coals at the Sri Mariamman Temple in Chinatown. Outside the temple, devotees in their hundreds line up awaiting their turn, and building up their courage by dancing, shouting and singing.

Birthday of the Third Prince

Around Oct On the ninth day of the ninth lunar month, entranced mediums cut themselves with swords to honour the birthday of the Buddhist child god Nezha, who is said to carry a magic bracelet and a spear, and to ride the wind; their blood is wiped on much sought-after paper charms at temples around the state.

Festival of the Nine Emperor Gods

Oct The nine-day sojourn on earth of the Nine Emperor Gods, thought to cure ailments and bring good health and longevity, is celebrated at the Kiu Ong Yiah Temple on Upper Serangoon Road by Chinese opera and mediums conducting their trade in the streets. Capping the festival is a procession, during which effigies of the nine gods are carried in sedan chairs.

Pilgrimage to Kusu Island

Oct Locals visit Kusu Island (see p.110) in their thousands to pray for good luck and fertility at the Tua Pekong Temple and the island's Muslim shrine. The pilgrimage commemorates the ancient tale of a turtle that turned itself into an island to save two shipwrecked sailors.

Hari Raya Haji

Oct/Nov An auspicious day for Singapore's Muslims, who gather at mosques to honour those who have completed the Haj, or pilgrimage to Mecca (birthplace of Muhammad). Goats are sacrificed, and their meat given to the needy, which is derived from the story of the prophet Abraham who was prepared to sacrifice his son in order to show his devotion to Allah.

Deepavali (Diwali)

Oct/Nov Serangoon Road is festooned with fairy lights during this, the most auspicious of Hindu festivals, celebrating the victory of the Lord Krishna over Narakasura, and thus of light over dark. Oil lamps are lit outside homes to attract Lakshmi, the goddess of prosperity, and prayers are offered at all temples.

Christmas

Dec 25 Singapore's central shopping centres vie annually for the best decorations in town, making Christmas a particularly colourful and atmospheric time for shopping.

Shopping

C hoice and convenience make the Singapore shopping experience a rewarding one, but the island's affluence and the strong Singapore dollar mean most things are priced at Western levels. Perhaps the best time to bargain-hunt is during the annual **Great Singapore Sale** (from late May to late July; Ⓦ www.greatsingaporesale.com.sg), when you'll find prices seriously marked down in many outlets across the island.

Orchard Road, of course, offers the biggest concentration of malls, with multiple outlets selling the top designer labels, clothes by local designers, bespoke suits, sports equipment, electronic goods and so on. There's a smaller peppering of malls in **Chinatown**, the most interesting of which are little more than multi-storey markets, home to a few more traditional outlets stocking Chinese foodstuffs, medicines, instruments and porcelain. Chinatown also has a number of antique and curio shops along South Bridge Road, and there are more knick-knacks on sale around **Arab Street**, where you'll also find textiles and batiks, robust basketware and some good deals on jewellery. **Little India** has various silk stores and goldsmiths as well as Mustafa, a department store that's known all over the island for being open 24/7. South of Little India, the grid of streets between Rochor Road and the Singapore River is home to a few malls specializing in cameras, electronics and computer products.

Typical shopping **hours** are daily from 10am or 11am to 9pm (10pm in some malls, especially along Orchard Road). Note that **haggling** is customary in smaller family-owned or independent shops, but nowhere else.

Tourists flying out of Singapore can claim a refund of the island's goods and services tax (**GST**; seven percent at the time of writing) on purchases over a certain amount (at least $100, though some retailers require a larger outlay and may also charge an administration fee), either through an agency (for stores displaying a Premier Tax Free or Tax Free Shopping sticker) or the retailer directly, though not all shops offer this service. For detailed information, have a look at the GST section of Ⓦ www.iras.gov.sg. Should you have a **complaint** with a particular store that can't be resolved, you can report it to the Singapore Tourism Board on Ⓣ 1800/736 2000 or even go to the Small Claims Tribunal at the Subordinate Courts, 1 Havelock Square (on Upper Cross St near Chinatown MRT; Ⓦ www.smallclaims.gov.sg), which has a fast-track system for tourists; it costs $10 to have your case heard.

Shopping malls

Singapore's malls, the most popular of which are listed below, can't be avoided even if you have no intention of visiting department stores or big retail chains: in this built-up city, plenty of little boutiques and family-run shops find homes in malls too. The addresses here therefore apply to many of the outlets reviewed later in this chapter.

Orchard Road and around

See the map on pp.78–79 for locations.

313@Somerset 313 Somerset Rd (above Somerset MRT) Ⓦ www.313somerset.com.sg. Uniqlo is the star name at this new mall.

Centrepoint 176 Orchard Rd Ⓦ www.frasers centrepointmalls.com. Dependable all-round complex, whose seven floors of shops include Robinsons, Singapore's oldest department store.

Forum the Shopping Mall 583 Orchard Rd (near the Orchard Parade hotel) Ⓦ www.forumthe shoppingmall.com. Plenty of items to pamper the youngsters in your life – upmarket kids' clothes, toys and so forth.

Ion Orchard 2 Orchard Turn (above Orchard MRT). One of the more architecturally striking buildings on Orchard Rd, this cavernous mall tends to be rather quiet as it's largely for those who can afford Prada, Armani, Louis Vuitton and Dior, among other designer names.

Ngee Ann City 391A Orchard Rd Ⓦ www .ngeeanncity.com.sg. A brooding twin-towered complex, home to the Japanese Takashimaya department store and the excellent Kinokuniya bookstore, plus Cartier, YSL and other heavyweights.

Palais Renaissance 390 Orchard Rd. Prada, DKNY and yet more top brands.

Paragon Opposite Ngee Ann City Ⓦ www .paragon.sg. This swanky mall is holding its own despite upstart competition. Come here for Calvin Klein, Gucci, Versace and many more big names.

🎯 **Plaza Singapura** 68 Orchard Rd Ⓦ www .plazasingapura.com.sg. Veteran mall with a bit of everything: Marks & Spencer, the Singapore department store John Little, sportswear and sports equipment, musical instruments, audio, video and general electrical equipment. Always busy.

Tanglin Shopping Centre 19 Tanglin Rd (next to the Orchard Parade hotel) Ⓦ www.tanglinsc .com. Good for art, antiques and curios.

Tangs Junction of Orchard and Scotts Rd Ⓦ www.tangs.com. Tangs looks like a mall but is actually a department store dating back to the 1950s, and the only one to have its own building on Orchard Rd, topped by a pagoda-style construction occupied by the *Marriott* hotel. The store sells a wide range

of reasonably priced clothes and accessories.

Wheelock Place 501 Orchard Rd. This impressive pyramid of a building includes a well-stocked Borders bookshop, Marks & Spencer and a Zara store.

Wisma Atria 435 Orchard Rd (opposite Tangs) Ⓦ www.wismaonline.com. Hosts a good range of middle-market local and inter-national fashion shops, plus the Japanese department store Isetan.

Chinatown

See the map on pp.54–55 for locations.

Chinatown Point 133 New Bridge Rd. One of the two buildings here is a handicraft centre with scores of tourist-oriented businesses.

Hong Lim Complex 531–531A Upper Cross St. Several Chinese provisions stores, fronted by sackfuls of dried mushrooms, cuttlefish, chillies, garlic cloves, onions, fritters and crackers. Other shops sell products ranging from acupuncture accessories to birds' nests.

Lucky Chinatown 211 New Bridge Rd, between Pagoda and Temple streets. Fairly upmarket place with lots of jewellery shops.

Pearl's Centre 100 Eu Tong Sen St. Home to some Chinese medicine clinics, where set-ups such as TCM Chinese Medicines at #02-20 will offer you a consultation for a few dollars, plus a few shops selling Buddhist paraphernalia.

People's Park Centre 101 Upper Cross St. Stall-like shop units selling Chinese handicrafts, CDs, electronics, silk, jade and gold.

🎯 **People's Park Complex** 1 Park Rd. A venerable shopping centre that, like the Hong Lim Complex and adjacent People's Park Centre, is among the most entertaining places to browse in Chinatown because it's so workaday, a place for ordinary folk to buy day-to-day needs. Also here is the Overseas Emporium on level 4, selling Chinese musical instruments, calligraphy pens, lacquerwork and jade.

The Colonial District and Marina Centre

See the map on p.39 for locations.

Funan DigitaLife Mall 109 North Bridge Rd Ⓦ www.funan.com.sg. A variety of stores here sell computer and electronics equipment.

Marina Square 6 Raffles Blvd ⓦwww
.marinasquare.com.sg. Nowhere near as large
as its sprawling neighbour, Suntec City, but
better laid out and with a very diverse range
of outlets.
Raffles City 252 North Bridge Rd (above City
Hall MRT) ⓦwww.rafflescity.com. Home to a
branch of Robinsons department store with
a Marks & Spencer within it, plus numerous
fashion chains.

Bras Basah Road to Rochor Road

See the map on pp.68–69 for locations.

Bugis Junction Junction Victoria St and Rochor
Rd (above Bugis MRT) ⓦwww.bugisjunction
-mall.com.sg. Mall encasing several streets of
restored shophouses, and featuring the
Japanese/Chinese department store BHG.
Sim Lim Square 1 Rochor Canal Rd ⓦwww
.simlimsquare.com.sg. Electronics and
computer equipment.

Little India

Mustafa Syed Alwi Rd ⓦwww.mustafa
.com.sg; see map, pp.68–69. Totally
different in feel to the malls of Orchard Rd,
Mustafa is a phenomenon, selling
electronics, fresh food, luggage, you name it
– and it never closes. See p.73 for more.

Elsewhere in Singapore

Holland Road Shopping Centre 211 Holland Ave,
Holland Village; see map, p.104. The shops

▲ Sim Lim Square

above the supermarket are good places to
browse for curios.

VivoCity Next to HarbourFront Centre and
above HarbourFront MRT ⓦwww.vivocity
.com.sg. A humdinger of a mall, containing a
branch of Tangs department store, Page
One bookstore, a cinema, three food courts
(Food Republic is exceptionally good) and
several restaurants.

Art, antiques, crafts, curios and souvenirs

Singapore bulges with stores selling Asian antiques and crafts, ranging from Chinese
snuff bottles to Malaysian pewter; there are also a few galleries specializing in
artworks by local painters and sculptors. If it's **antiques** you're after, try trawling
through Tanglin Shopping Centre at the western end of Orchard Road, or Holland
Road Shopping Centre in Holland Village (see p.104). Besides the outlets listed
here, it's also worth calling in at the MICA Building, 140 Hill St, which houses as
good a selection of art galleries as you'll find in Singapore; and the Singapore
Handicraft Centre in Chinatown Point, which collects a few dozen souvenir shops
under one roof.

Antiques of the Orient #02-40 Tanglin Shopping
Centre ☏67349351. Antiquarian books, maps
and prints.
Artfolio Level 2, Raffles Hotel Arcade,
328 North Bridge Rd ☏63344677. The works
of contemporary Asian artists are
showcased here.

Eng Tiang Huat 284 River Valley Rd
☏67343738. Oriental musical instruments,
wayang costumes and props.
Far East Inspirations 33 Pagoda St, Chinatown.
The classiest of several antique shops here,
offering Asian furniture, porcelain-based
lamps, prints and watercolours.

House of Zhen 252 South Bridge Rd, Chinatown. This expansive store at the junction with Temple St has a superb range of antiques, collectables and furniture. Members of staff are friendly and knowledgeable.

Jasmine Fine Arts #05-29 Paragon ☎67345688. Appealing artwork from all over the world.

Katong Antiques House 208 East Coast Rd, Katong ☎63458544. Peranakan artefacts and Chinese porcelain; see p.94.

Kwok Gallery #03-01 Far East Shopping Centre, 545 Orchard Rd ☎62352516. A broad, impressive inventory of antique Chinese artwork.

Lim's Arts & Living #02-01 Holland Rd Shopping Centre ☎67326486; **#02-154 VivoCity** ☎63769468. A sort of Asian Conran Shop, packed with bamboo pipes, dainty teapots, cherrywood furniture and lamps crafted from old tea jars.

Little Shophouse 43 Bussorah St, near Sultan Mosque ☎62952328. Well named, this tiny outlet boasts some beautiful examples of Peranakan beaded slippers (from $180), plus replica Peranakan crockery.

Lopburi #01-04 Tanglin Place, 91 Tanglin Rd. Seriously fine – and seriously expensive – antique Buddhas and Khmer sculptures, as well as some old silk textiles.

Malay Art Gallery 31 Bussorah St ☎62948051. Stocks *kerises* (traditional daggers) from Malaysia and Indonesia.

Melor's Curios 39 Bussorah St ☎62923934. Aladdin's cave probably had fewer treasures than this shop, which sells Javanese and other Asian furniture, hangers made of bamboo for displaying fabrics, plus an assortment of batik, silk and *congkak* (mancala) sets.

One Price Store 3 Emerald Hill Rd, off Orchard Rd ☎67341680. Everything from carved camphor-wood chests to Chinese snuff bottles.

Red Peach Level 2, Raffles Hotel Arcade ☎62222215. A repository of Asian art, incense sticks, tea sets, fabrics and chopsticks.

Rishi Handicrafts 5 Baghdad St, close to Arab St ☎62982408. Leather sandals, necklaces, briefcases, belts and knick-knacks.

Royal Selangor #03-33 Raffles City Shopping Centre ☎63393958. Pewter tankards, plates and more elaborate items, worthy if a little dull.

Rumah Bebe 113 East Coast Rd, Katong ☎62478781, ⓦwww.rumahbebe.com. Peranakan products; see p.93 for more.

Singapore Tyler Print Institute 41 Robertson Quay ☎63363663. In a nineteenth-century godown, the STPI is a state-of-the-art print- and paper-making workshop and art gallery.

Sun Craft #02-08 Tanglin Shopping Centre ☎67371308. Work by well-known local artists, using a range of different media.

TeaJoy #01-05 North Bridge Centre, North Bridge Rd ☎63393739. Close to the National Library, this sells Chinese tea sets with special attention paid to oolong accoutrements.

Zhen Lacquer Gallery 1 Trengganu St, Chinatown ☎62222718. Specializes in lacquerware boxes and bowls.

Books

Singapore's bookshops are as well stocked as many in the West; all the larger outlets carry a good selection of Western and local fiction, plus books on Southeast Asia and a range of magazines.

BooksActually 5 Ann Siang Hill ⓦwww.booksactually.com. In a tidy restored shophouse, this small independent retailer takes pride in its literary selection and its central display devoted to the shop's cat.

Borders Ground floor, Wheelock Place ⓦwww.borders.com.sg. Always reliable. Open till 11pm most nights, Fri & Sat till midnight.

Earshot See listing under "CDs and DVDs".

Kinokuniya Level 3, Ngee Ann City; branches at Liang Court near Clarke Quay, and at Bugis Junction ⓦwww.kinokuniya.sg. The main outlet is one of Singapore's largest and best bookshops, with titles on every conceivable subject and some foreign-language literature too.

MPH Level B1, Raffles City ⓦwww.mph.com.sg. Veteran of the local book trade, though not as comprehensive these days as it should be.

Page One Level 2, Vivocity ⓦwww.pageone group.com. Similar in feel to Kinokuniya, Page One started out as a publisher of art and architecture books and stocks plenty of titles on these areas, along with books on most other subjects.

Select Books #03-15 Tanglin Shopping Centre ⓦ www.selectbooks.com.sg. Tiny shop packing in a great range of books on Singapore, Malaysia and the rest of the region. A great resource.

Times Bookstores Level 4, Centrepoint; Level 4, Plaza Singapura; ⓦ www.timesbookstores .com.sg. A well-stocked local chain.

Jewellery

⑭

Singapore isn't a bad place to buy jewellery, particularly if you share the Chinese affection for jade or the local fondness for high-purity gold (22 or 24 carat).

Chu's Jade Centre #01-53/54 Chinatown Point, 133 New Bridge Rd Ⓣ 65344868. Semiprecious stones, huge clusters of freshwater pearl necklaces, and exquisite jade sculptures.
CT Hoo #01-22 Tanglin Shopping Centre Ⓣ 67375447. Specializing in pearls.
Flower Diamond #03-02 Ngee Ann City Ⓣ 67341221. Contemporary designs as well as more traditionally styled bling, at sensible prices.

Poh Heng Level 1, People's Park Complex Ⓣ 65350960. Old-fangled Chinese jewellers dating back to 1948, though now housed in modern premises.
Risis National Orchid Garden, see p.81. Singaporeans tend to regard gold-plated orchids as clichéd, but tourists snap them up here as well as at a few malls and at Changi Airport.

CDs and DVDs

Plenty of Western CDs and DVDs are available in Singapore. If you want to buy Asian material, you'll find Chinese music and DVDs widely available; for Indian releases, there are several outlets in Little India, including Jothi Music Corner in the Little India Arcade at the start of Serangoon Rd; and for Malay music, head to the Joo Chiat Complex, Geylang (see p.93).

Borders Wheelock Place. Carries the customary selection of pop and classical CDs, though it's not as comprehensive as HMV.
Earshot Arts House, 1 Old Parliament Lane Ⓣ 63340130, ⓦ www.earshot.com.sg. Nothing but CDs, DVDs and books by Singaporean artists and writers.
Gramophone Cathay Building, 2 Handy Rd (where Orchard Rd becomes Bras Basah Rd). Largely mainstream CD releases.

HMV Level 4, 313@Somerset Ⓣ 67331822. A substantial store, your best bet for mainstream releases and with dedicated jazz and classical music sections.
Roxy Records #02-15 Excelsior Shopping Centre (at the Hill St end of the Peninsula Excelsior Hotel) Ⓣ 63377783. A range of imported indie and other hard-to-find releases, and even secondhand vinyl.
That CD Level B1, Raffles City. More chart CDs.

Fabric, clothes, shoes and carpets

The Arab Quarter and Geylang Serai are among the main areas for old-fashioned fabric stores packed with bolts of cloth. Some of these stock Malaysian and Indonesian **batik**, produced by applying hot wax to a piece of cloth with either a pen or metal stamp; patterns appear when dye is applied as it cannot penetrate the waxed areas. Also available is the exquisite style of brocade known as **songket**, made by handweaving gold and silver thread into plain cloth. Not cheap, it's traditionally worn as a *sampin*, a sarong-like garment. Chinese, Japanese and Thai silks are all available, too, and there are multi-hued silk **saris** on sale in Little India.

It might seem odd to look for Middle Eastern **carpets** in Singapore, but this cosmopolitan island has been home to a number of venerable carpet dealers for generations. For different reasons, it might also seem odd to shop for **fashion** items as big-name designer goods are no cheaper in Singapore than elsewhere. The trick is to look out for the best of the local designers, who offer quality clothes and shoes at decent prices.

Aljunied Brothers 91 Arab St ☎62932751. Batik fabric as well as ready-made clothes.

Amir & Sons 36 Kandahar St ☎67349112. One of the oldest carpet sellers in the country, stocking fine Persian carpets and with Iranian staff to advise, too.

Charles & Keith Level 1, Bugis Junction; Level 2, 313@Somerset; and other outlets. Singapore's answer to Malaysia's Jimmy Choo, the brothers Charles and Keith Wong design stylish, surprisingly affordable women's shoes and handbags too.

Dakshaini Silks 164 Serangoon Rd ☎62919969. Premier Indian embroidered silks.

GG<5 Level B1, Wisma Atria, and other outlets. Reasonably priced designer clothes for women.

Jim Thompson Silk Shop Level 1, Raffles Hotel Arcade, 328 North Bridge Rd ☎63365322. Though businessman Jim Thompson disappeared under mysterious circumstances in Malaysia's Cameron Highlands

in 1967, his name is still a byword for quality silk.

Justmen's Level 1, Tanglin Shopping Centre ☎67374800. Bangkok is still the place to go in Southeast Asia for inexpensive bespoke suits, but if you have the cash to shell out for one in Singapore, this shop is among the most reliable places to do it.

M)phosis #B1-09 Ngee Ann City, 391 Orchard Rd. Chic, glamorous women's eveningwear and shoes by Singaporean designer, Colin Koh.

Malay Art Gallery See p.156. *Songket* cloth, suitable for wearing or framing.

The Orientalist Level 1, 50 Cuscaden Rd, behind the Orchard Parade Hotel ☎67320880. Slick emporium piled high with carpets and kilims from Iran and South Asia.

Rossi Apparel Level 1, Millenia Walk, Marina Centre ☎63362818. For the male executive who just has to have bespoke shirts, starting at $120 apiece in high-quality cotton.

⑮

Sports

S
ingapore may be the gastronomic capital of Southeast Asia, but its range of affordable **sports facilities** means there is no excuse for running to fat during your stay. Whether your recreational leaning is towards racquet sports, watersports, golf, or less energetic pastimes such as snooker and darts, you'll find ample opportunities. We've listed alphabetically the main possibilities below, along with advice on whom to contact. Armchair sports fans will find some scope too for **spectator sports**, but don't expect your fixture list to be as congested as it is back home. Should sporting activities not be your idea of a holiday, you might consider a day's pampering at one of Singapore's many **spas**.

International events do crop up periodically, some even attracting the odd household name, but on the whole, you'll have a simple choice between horse racing and football. The listings magazine *8 Days* details all forthcoming events, big and small, while the STB will fill you in on all major events in the Singaporean sporting calendar. Online, the best resources are Ⓦ www.singaporesport.com.sg and the Singapore Sports Council's site Ⓦ www.ssc.gov.sg.

Cricket

The Singapore Cricket Club hosts **cricket** matches, from March to October, on Saturday afternoons and Sunday mornings; spectators are welcome to watch from the Padang (see p.39), though entry into the club itself is restricted to members only.

Football

The number of column inches set aside for **football**, both local and international, in the *Straits Times* and *New Paper*, testifies to the huge interest taken in the sport over here. English and European league and cup matches are shown weekly on TV, and there are occasional visits from world-famous teams such as Liverpool and Arsenal. Many pubs and bars advertise live sports screenings via satellite – British and Irish pubs are your best bet.

Singapore's national side draws crowds large enough to fill the 55,000-capacity National Stadium in Kallang. Until 1995, the team played in the Malaysia Premier League and the Malaysia Cup, but in 1995, the Football Association of Singapore (FAS) pulled out of both, possibly motivated by a desire to disassociate itself from the bribes scandal that rocked Malaysian soccer in 1994. Since then, the FAS has set up the S.League, Singapore's first ever professional league, which features twelve teams, including Chinese club Sinchi FC, and the Singaporean national under-23 team. The S.League season runs from February to October and a game is shown live on Singaporean TV's Channel i every Saturday night. In addition, the league's twelve teams battle for the Singapore Cup every year. For a current fixture list and ticketing details, check out the local press or go to Ⓦ www.sleague.com.

Tickets for **national fixtures** normally go on sale on match day, at the National Stadium's FAS box office (Ⓣ 62931477). Again, check the local press or Ⓦ www .fas.org.sg for details.

Formula 1

The 61-lap race, which is currently contracted to run until at least 2012, is carried out on a street circuit around the Marina Bay area at night and usually takes place around the third or fourth weekend in September. A wide range of tickets are available on Ⓦ www.singaporegp.sg and via the ticketing hotline Ⓣ 67386738, as well as ticketing website SISTIC (Ⓦ www.sistic.com.sg) and selected SingPost outlets. Tickets cost between $50 for a day pass to $1088 for a three-day premium pass.

Golf

Singapore boasts a number of **golf** courses quite disproportionate to its size, and several of them are truly world-class. All the clubs listed below allow non-members to play upon payment of a green fee, though all will be bulging with members at the weekend. Green fees start from around $90 for eighteen holes, but you'll pay far more than this at the island's poshest country clubs; caddies' fees are around the $25 mark.

If you just want to watch golf, there's the **Barclays Singapore Open Golf Championship**, an annual event that usually attracts some big names. The Johnnie Walker Classic, Southeast Asia's most prestigious golf tournament, was staged here in 1996, and is likely to return in the future.

Changi Golf Club 20 Netheravon Rd Ⓣ 65455133.
Jurong Country Club 9 Science Centre Rd Ⓣ 65605655.
Keppel Club 10 Bukit Chermin Rd Ⓣ 63755569.
Marina Bay Golf Course #01-01 80 Rhu Cross Ⓣ 63457788.

Raffles Country Club 450 Jalan Ahmad Ibrahim Ⓣ 68617655.
Seletar Country Club 101 Seletar Club Rd Ⓣ 64860801.
Sentosa Golf Club 27 Bukit Manis Rd, Sentosa Island Ⓣ 62750022.

Horse racing, riding and polo

The Singapore Turf Club, 1 Turf Club Avenue (adjacent to Kranji MRT station, or bus #170; Ⓣ 68791000, Ⓦ www.turfclub.com.sg), shows live coverage of Malaysian, Hong Kong and Western Australian meetings on a giant screen. The club typically holds twenty or so meets annually, including prestigious events like the Singapore Gold Cup and the Singapore Derby. Otherwise, the Singapore Polo Club, 80 Mount Pleasant Road (Ⓣ 68543999), hosts regular **polo** matches; call ahead for a current fixture list.

Several organizations offer **horseriding** sessions, including the **Bukit Timah Saddle Club**, 51 Fairways Drive (Ⓣ 64662264; $130/hr).

Martial arts

Martial arts are not as evident as you would imagine in a country of such predominantly Chinese stock as Singapore. The best chance of catching any sort of performance is to watch locals practising **t'ai chi** – a series of slow, balletic exercises designed to stimulate mind and body – early in the morning at the Singapore Botanic Gardens or at the East Coast Beach. You'll find details of Singaporean t'ai chi schools and instructors at Ⓦwww.singapore-taiji.com. Singapore Wushu Dragon and Lion Dance Federation lists the places across Singapore offering wushu and qigong Ⓦwww.wuzong.com.

Skiing

Strange though it may sound, **skiing** – along with snowman-building and snowball fighting – is possible at *Snow City*, an indoor snow centre in western Singapore. See p.103 for more details.

Snooker, pool and darts

Snooker and **pool** are hugely popular in Singapore, and there are heaps of clubs from which to choose; all are listed in Singapore's Yellow Pages (Ⓦwww.yellow pages.com.sg). Clubs typically open between 10am and 2am, and an hour's play costs around $10, with rates increasing in the evening. While their dress code doesn't run to bow ties and waistcoats, you may find you are stopped at the door unless you are wearing long trousers, a collar and closed footwear.

As is only proper, a game of **darts** entails a trip to a pub – the Forest Darts Cafe (45 Ann Siang Rd ℡62273522) has seven dart boards both traditional and electronic, while Unca Bunca (47/48 Circular Rd ℡64382282) is a pleasant bar with a dart board and pool table.

Spas

Singapore is awash with luxury spa centres that promise to pamper and indulge to your heart's content. All offer a combination of whirlpools, pools, aromatherapy and beauty treatments, massages, saunas and body scrubs – but at a price. In Willow Stream Spa, for instance, treatments range from $149 to $289. There's also a new-found craze for fish spas – where fish imported from Turkey nibble away the dead skin from your feet ($38 for 40min).

Damai Grand Hyatt, 10 Scotts Rd ℡67381234.
Essence Vale Traders Hotel, Health Club and Spa, #04-1A Cuscaden Rd ℡68314349.
Esthetica #05-15 Far East Plaza, 14 Scotts Rd ℡67337000.

Fish Reflexology Underwater World, 80 Siloso Rd, Sentosa ℡62799229.
Willow Stream Spa Fairmont Singapore, #06-80 Bras Basah Rd ℡64315600.

Swimming

All hotels of a certain size in Singapore have **swimming** pools, but if you're in budget accommodation, you will have to opt either for the beach or for a public pool. The island's longest stretch of beach lies along the East Coast Park, but you'll find the waters off Sentosa's sands much cleaner. Out east, there's the Katong Swimming Complex at 111 Wilkinson Road; while in the west of the island in Holland Village, there's the Buona Vista Swimming Complex, at 76 Holland Drive. More central is the excellent Jalan Besar Swimming Complex near Lavender MRT (100 Tyrwhitt Rd, #01-03; daily 8am–9.30pm; from $1).

▲ Cable-skiing in East Coast Park

Tennis, squash and badminton

Though a number of venues across Singapore offer facilities for racket sports, their popularity means it pays to book well in advance. On average, halls are open daily 7am–10pm, and an hour's **badminton**, **squash** or **tennis** in them costs between $7 and $10. Many will rent out rackets for two or three dollars, but phone ahead to check first.

Kallang Squash & Tennis Centre 52 Stadium Rd ☎63481291.

Toa Payoh Sports Hall 297A Lor 6 Toa Payoh ☎62592916. Badminton courts.

Watersports

Sea-locked Singapore Island offers extensive scope for **watersports**. **Canoeing** is possible at Changi Point, East Coast Park, MacRitchie Reservoir and Sentosa Island, and costs around $10 an hour. For **waterskiing** and wakeboarding, head for East Coast Park, Sembawang or Ponngol. You can expect to pay upwards of $90/100 an hour. Finally, several **scuba** outfits operate out of Singapore; however, for one of their trips into local, Indonesian or Malaysian waters, you'll pay several hundred dollars.

Friendly Waters #01-27-36, 20 Upper Circular Rd, The Riverwalk ☎65570016/8, ⓦ www .friendlywaters.com.sg. Arranges PADI courses and regional diving trips, as well as renting and selling equipment.
The Paddle Lodge MacRitchie Reservoir Park, Lornie Rd (near Thomson Rd) ☎62580057. Kayaking.
Ryders 600 Punggol, 17th Avenue, Marina Country Club ☎63879238. Wakeboarding, waterskiing and kneeboarding.

Ski360 1206A East Coast Parkway ☎64427318. Offers wakeboarding, waterskiing and kneeboarding using a cable system that circuits the lagoon.
Wakepirates SAF Yacht Club, 43 Admiralty Rd West, Sembawang Club House ☎98457452. Wakeboarding specialists.
Wavehouse Sentosa 36 Silosa Beach Walk, Sentosa ☎62381196. Simulated surfing experience.

16

Kids' Singapore

Sleek yet suitably exotic, Singapore can feel like a gigantic theme park to children, and just wandering Little India or even Orchard Road should unearth plenty to interest them. Traditional festivals are generally entertaining too, but Thaipusam (see p.150) is the one event which might freak some kids out. Reactions to the Hindu and Buddhist temples covered throughout this book likewise vary: some children are utterly fascinated by them, while for others the colourful statuary and religious ceremonies just sail over their heads. There are also several theme parks around Singapore, notably on Sentosa, but bear in mind that many rides aren't suitable for young children and so have age or height restrictions.

For **childcare** products, try Mothercare, whose main outlet is on level 1 of the Centrepoint mall on Orchard Road, near Somerset MRT. Upmarket shops geared towards kids cluster within the Forum mall at the Tanglin (western) end of Orchard Road.

Attractions for kids

Where you need to purchase tickets, you can generally expect that children will get in for half or two-thirds the price of adult admission.

Bukit Timah Nature Reserve See p.85. Come for the rainforest trails and macaques – kids love the latter, though note the critters hiss and bare their teeth if you get very close. The trails are probably a bit too strenuous for under-6s.

Cable cars to Sentosa See p.101. Not only is this the way to arrive in style at Sentosa, but the vertiginous views always go down well.

Ducktour and river cruises See p.28. Children love the amphibious Ducktour; the Singapore River cruise is fun but unlikely to make quite such an impression.

E2Max At the Cathay cinemas at Grange Rd and Handy Rd, both off Orchard Rd. Computer gaming might save the day if there's a tropical downpour that just won't blow over, but, annoyingly, when Singapore schools are in session, children aren't allowed in on weekdays until 6.30pm. Daily: Grange Rd noon–midnight, Handy Rd 11am–10pm

(11pm at weekends). PC games cost $2–4/hr to play while Playstation, Xbox and other consoles cost $10–30/hr.

East Coast Park See p.91. Kilometres of sand, biking and rollerblading tracks and barbecue pits. Bus #401 from Bedok MRT.

Escape Theme Park Pasir Ris Close ☏65819112, ⓦ www.escapethemepark.com.sg. More than a dozen fairground-style rides, but miles from downtown: Pasir Ris is the nearest MRT, from where the site is a 10-min walk (or catch bus #354 from the station). Sat, Sun & public holidays 10am–8pm. Tickets $18, children $9.

Go-Go Bambini Block 8, Dempsey Rd ☏64744176, ⓦ www.gogobambini.com. Part of the Dempsey Village complex near the Botanic Garden, this indoor playground features lots of bouncy playpens, climbing walls etc. Best reached by taxi. Mon–Thurs & Sun 10am–6pm, Fri & Sat 10am–8pm;

▲ Singapore Science Centre

children pay $17 for unlimited play ($6 for kids aged 1 or 2) while accompanying adults get in free.

Haw Par Villa See p.98. No rides at this Buddhist theme park, where lurid statues, murals and dioramas dramatize Chinese myths. The occasional shock-horror touch tends to amuse rather than scare.

Jacob Ballas Garden Northern edge of the Botanic Garden. Under-12s will appreciate splashing about in and around the fountains of the water-play area (bring swimming gear), and there's a treehouse and maze to explore, too. Botanic Garden MRT or head up Bukit Timah Rd on bus #171 from Orchard Rd or bus #170 from Little India, getting off just after Evans Rd, when you see the National University of Singapore running track. Tues–Sun 8am–7pm; free.

Jurong Bird Park See p.102. Penguins and flamingos are among the obvious highlights, but do catch at least one bird show – the ones featuring birds of prey are especially good.

MacRitchie Reservoir Park See p.87. A wooded park with easy trails and a boardwalk across the water from where you can spot turtles and fish.

Sentosa Island See Chapter 8. One big playground, boasting Universal Studios and numerous other rides, plus beaches and an aquarium with dolphin shows.

Singapore Flyer See p.50. This is a space-age experience for kids, even though they're just being raised aloft in a glass-and-metal cage. The views are incidental.

Singapore Science Centre See p.103. Uncover your children's latent scientific bent by setting them loose amid zillions of interactive displays.

Singapore Zoo and Night Safari See p.88. Animal exhibits aside, the zoo also has a Rainforest Kidzworld section featuring pony rides and a water-play area, but it's the night safari that some young 'uns find magical.

Snow City See p.103. Hi-tech machines let it snow year-round in this corner of equatorial Singapore, though the slope at this indoor centre is just 60m long and less than three storeys high, leaving scope only for tobogganing on rubber rings.

Superbowl #03-200 Marina Square, Marina Centre. Yet another option in wet weather – ten-pin bowling, costing $4 ($3 for kids) per game on weekdays, a tad more at weekends.

Wild Wild Wet Pasir Ris Close ☎65819112, Ⓦwww.wildwildwet.com. Water slides and more water slides, next door to the Escape Theme Park. Mon & Wed–Fri 1–7pm, Sat & Sun 10am–7pm. Adults $15.50, children $10.50.

Contexts

Contexts

History..167

Religion...173

Singaporean recipes...177

Singapore in literature..181

Books..188

Glossary..192

History

N
ot much is known of Singapore's pre-colonial history. Third-century Chinese sailors could have been referring to Singapore in their account of a place called Pu-Luo-Chung, a corruption of the Malay for "island at the end of a peninsula". In the late thirteenth century, **Marco Polo** reported seeing a place called Chiamassie, which could also have been Singapore. By then the island was known locally as Temasek and was a minor trading outpost of the Sumatran Srivijaya empire. According to the *Sejarah Melayu* (or *Malay Annals*, a historical document commissioned by the Malay sultans in the seventeenth century), by the late fourteenth century the island was called **Singapura**, meaning "Lion City" in Sanskrit, though the origins of the name are mysterious. The annals mention a Sumatran noble who saw what he took to be a lion while sheltering on the island from a storm, but this must be regarded as legend.

Around 1390, a Sumatran prince called **Paramesvara** broke with the Majapahit empire of Java and escaped to what is now Singapore. There he ruled until a Javanese offensive forced him to flee up the Malay Peninsula, where he and his son, **Iskandar Shah**, founded the **Malacca sultanate**. With the rise of Malacca, Singapore declined into a low-key fishing settlement and remained so after the Portuguese and then the Dutch took Malacca in 1511 and 1641 respectively.

The founding of Singapore

In the late eighteenth century the **British East India Company** embarked on a drive to establish ports along the strategic Straits of Malacca. Penang was secured in 1786 and Malacca taken in 1795 at the request of the Dutch Republic (whose government was in exile in London after being brought down by French-backed revolutionaries), but a port was needed further south to counter the Dutch presence in what is now Indonesia. Enter the visionary **Thomas Stamford Raffles** (see p.42), the British lieutenant-governor of Bencoolen in Sumatra. In 1818 he was tasked with setting up a colony at the southern tip of the Malay Peninsula, and the following year he stepped ashore on the northern bank of the Singapore River, accompanied by Colonel William Farquhar, a former senior British official in Malacca who was fluent in Malay.

Swampland and tiger-infested jungle covered Singapore, and its population was probably no more than a thousand, but Raffles recognized that the area at the southern tip of the island could make a superb deep-water harbour. With a view to setting up a trading station, he quickly struck a treaty with Abdul Rahman, *temenggong* (chieftain) of Singapore and a subordinate of the sultan of Johor, the region occupying the southern part of the Malay Peninsula. Raffles also exploited a succession dispute in the ruling house of Johor, bypassing the man who had until then been ruling as sultan, and who was sympathetic to the Dutch. Instead Raffles recognized his half-brother as sultan and signed a second treaty with both him and the *temenggong*. This riled the Dutch, for whom Singapore was part of their domain, but Farquhar managed to divert a contingent of British troops to Singapore and an immediate confrontation was averted. The matter was settled by the **Anglo–Dutch treaty** of 1824, a classic colonial carve-up in which the Dutch let the British keep Malacca and Singapore in exchange for Bencoolen and British recognition of the Riau Archipelago, the islands just south of Singapore, as being part of the Dutch sphere of influence.

The early boom years

With its duty-free stance and ideal position at the gateway to the South China Sea, Singapore experienced a meteoric expansion. The population had reached ten thousand by the time of the first census in 1824, with Malays, Chinese, Indians and Europeans arriving in search of work and commercial opportunities.

Two years earlier, Raffles had begun dividing up what is now downtown Singapore, earmarking the area south of the Singapore River for the Chinese, while Muslims were settled around the Sultan's palace near today's Arab Street. Sultan Hussein and the *temenggong* were bought out in 1824, and Singapore ceded outright to the British. Three years later, the fledgling colony united with Penang and Malacca to form the **Straits Settlements**, which became a British crown colony in 1867. Singapore's laissez-faire economy boomed throughout this time, though life was chaotic and disease was rife. By 1860 the population had reached eighty thousand; Arabs, Indians, Javanese and Bugis (from Sulawesi) all came, but most populous of all were the Chinese from the southeastern provinces of China.

The advent of steamships and the Suez Canal made Singapore a major staging post on the Europe–East Asia route at the close of the nineteenth century. Singapore had also become a world centre for rubber exports thanks to **Henry Ridley**, who led a one-man crusade to introduce the rubber plant to Southeast Asia. As all of the Malay Peninsula gradually fell into British clutches, the island benefitted further from its hinterland's tin- and rubber-based economy.

The Japanese occupation

Singapore's Asian communities began to find their political voice in the 1920s, but pro-independence activity had not gone far when the spectre of war reared its head. Within the space of a few hours in December 1941, Japan had bombed Pearl Harbor and landed on the Malay Peninsula, whose raw materials were vital for the Japanese war effort. By the end of January 1942 they were at Johor Bahru, facing Singapore across the Straits of Johor. But the guns of "Fortress Singapore" pointed south from what is now Sentosa island; received wisdom had it that a Japanese attack would come from the sea. The view of one British intelligence officer that "the Japanese are very small and short-sighted and thus totally unsuited physically to tropical warfare" embodied the complacency of the Allied command under Lieutenant-General Arthur Percival.

After a week's bombing, on February 7 the Japanese General Tomoyuki Yamashita launched his invasion of Singapore with an attack on Pulau Ubin, northeast of the main island. More landings from the north followed, and between February 11 and 14 the Japanese won decisive victories at Bukit Timah and Pasir Panjang, the site of today's museums at the former Ford car factory (see p.86), and Bukit Chandu (see p.100). On February 15, Percival went to Yamashita's new base at the Ford factory and surrendered. Winston Churchill called it "the largest capitulation in British history"; later, it transpired that the Japanese forces had been outnumbered and their supply lines hopelessly stretched prior to the surrender. Three and a half years of brutal Japanese rule ensued, during which Singapore was renamed Syonan, or "Light of the South", and Europeans were either herded into Changi Prison or sent to work on Thailand's infamous "Death Railway". Less well known is the vicious **Operation Sook Ching**, mounted by the military police force, or **Kempeitai**, during which upwards of 25,000 ethnic Chinese men were executed at Singapore's beaches as enemies of the Japanese.

Postwar transformation

Even though the island was back in British hands following the end of World War II in 1945, the aura of colonial supremacy had gone and Singaporeans were demanding a say in the island's administration. The subsequent quarter-century would be a time of enormous political upheaval in Singapore, whose resolution laid the foundations for the regimented and wealthy city-state of today.

Though Britain was beginning to divest itself of its colonial possessions, it was unsure what to do with Singapore. One "obvious" option, for Singapore and the Malay Peninsula to become a new state together, was fraught with difficulty: Singapore had so many Chinese that its inclusion would have led to the politically awkward result of Malays being in a minority in the new state. So it was that when the Straits Settlements were dissolved in 1946, Malacca and Penang joined the newly formed **Malayan Union** together with the rest of the Peninsula, while Singapore became a crown colony in its own right. However, even the Singapore-less union was opposed by Malay nationalists, who did not want the Chinese and Indian communities to be afforded citizenship under the terms of the union, arguing that the Malays should retain special privileges. The British caved in and reinvented the union in 1948 as the **Federation of Malaya**, with rights for the Chinese and Indians to be decided later. Now it was leftists that were disgruntled, and that same year a communist insurgency was launched in Malaya by largely Chinese guerrillas, who had gained experience of jungle warfare in resisting the Japanese. This created another area of potential friction between the two territories: Malayan Chinese politicians tended to be conservative and looked askance at Singapore, where many Chinese were developing leftist sympathies.

In April 1955, Singapore held elections for the newly created legislative assembly, 25 of whose 32 members were directly elected. The **Labour Front** emerged as the biggest party and its leader, **David Marshall**, an idealistic, British-trained lawyer of Iraqi Jewish stock, became the island's first chief minister. The elections were also notable for the emergence of the brand-new **People's Action Party (PAP)**, which came third. Led by another British-qualified lawyer, the shrewd, calculating **Lee Kuan Yew**, a Peranakan, the party had at its core several more graduates of British universities who were generally of the centre left. Lee's key insight was that to take power, the party had to reach out beyond the English-speaking elite. He steered the PAP into absorbing new members further to the left, chiefly trade unionists as well as Chinese activists who were unhappy over the lack of support for Chinese-language education.

Just before the elections, the PAP's left wing had been involved in mass action by ten thousand Chinese high-school students demanding recognition for their union. The following month the bus workers' union, led by two PAP activists, was embroiled in a strike that descended into violence, with a number of deaths. Marshall made concessions to restore order while attacking the PAP for fomenting disorder, but just a year later, he resigned over differences on defence after talks with the British on further constitutional reform. He was replaced by his deputy, **Lim Yew Hock**, who confronted the unions and the students and, in 1957, arrested several PAP left-wingers. Ironically, this aided his political rivals by strengthening the hand of the moderates in the PAP.

Marriage with Malaysia, and divorce

Malaya achieved independence in 1957, and two years later Singapore achieved full self-government, with the PAP winning 43 of the 51 seats in the newly enlarged, totally elected legislative assembly. Lee became Singapore's first prime minister and quickly looked for a merger with Malaya, with a high degree of autonomy for the island. The talk was of Singapore playing New York to Kuala Lumpur's Washington DC, and it made sense: Singapore was Malaya's financial hub and main port, as well as a centre for publishing and the arts. For its part, Malaya, still recovering from the communist insurgency, feared that PAP leftists could yet turn Singapore into an extremist hotbed and so wanted the island under its wing, though with its Chinese element diluted by having Sarawak and British North Borneo (now Sabah) join as well. That was duly achieved in September 1963 with the proclamation of a new country, the **Federation of Malaysia**. Soon afterwards Singapore went to the polls, with the PAP again winning despite a major challenge from ex-PAP left-wingers.

Singapore's presence within Malaysia, was, however, an uneasy one, with the PAP challenging the mainstream Malaysian parties over their ethnically based politics. Racial incidents in Singapore developed into full-scale riots, with several deaths. Within two years Singapore was given its marching orders from the federation, in the face of outrage in Kuala Lumpur at the PAP's attempts to break into Peninsular politics in 1964.

The new nation takes shape

On August 9, 1965, hours after announcing that Singapore would be going it alone as an **independent state**, a tearful Lee Kuan Yew appeared on local TV and called the event "a moment of anguish". With no natural resources, the tiny island seemed destined to fade into obscurity. Against all the odds, the PAP's vision transformed Singapore into an Asian economic heavyweight, but this also meant the government orchestrating seemingly every aspect of life on the island as it saw fit, brooking little opposition.

While the port and shipyards were thriving, the first task was for Singapore to diversify economically and lessen its dependence on Malaysia. For all its leftist credentials, the PAP went all-out to seek **foreign investment**, and new industries sprang up in Jurong and other areas. The government also clamped down on union militancy, a process that had begun in 1961 when it formed the National Trades Union Congress to replace a leftist union grouping; now the unions were told to swallow a **no-strike philosophy** in return for government intervention in resolving industrial disputes fairly.

Soon after the split with Malaysia, Singapore set up military **conscription**, modelled in part on the Israeli system (and, indeed, with Israeli help), but the stakes were raised after the surprise announcement, in 1968, that the British were to close all their military bases east of Suez. Singapore was still a major British outpost, an arrangement which boosted both the island's security and the local economy. While the vacuum left by the British was cushioned by new industries and American investment, conscription has remained a fundamental element of Singapore life ever since, with a sizeable chunk of the budget spent on defence.

There was also the pressing matter of the country's high birth rate and lack of decent housing. In 1966 the Land Acquisition Act was passed, enabling the government to buy land compulsorily for minimal compensation. This allowed the building of **new towns** all over the island, where people from kampongs (villages) or the slums of Chinatown could be resettled in affordable apartments within uniform concrete towers. However, ethnic quotas in each town, meant to prevent ghettoes forming, had the effect of breaking communities apart and of making one area much like another demographically – with electoral implications.

The 1970s and 1980s

Over the next two decades, the PAP consolidated its grip on Singapore as its project for the nation continued to roll. The economy largely enjoyed healthy growth, and by 1980 Singapore was practically an industrialized country. The opposition was moribund: between 1968 and 1980, the PAP held every seat in parliamentary elections, and when the opposition Worker's Party unexpectedly won a by-election in 1981, the new MP, **J.B. Jeyaretnam**, found himself charged with several offences and chased through the Singaporean courts for the next decade. The government was also not averse to using the colonial-era **Internal Security Act**, which allows detention without trial, and used it to keep the leftist Chia Thye Poh either in jail or under some form of detention from 1966 until 1998, longer than Nelson Mandela's imprisonment, for allegedly advocating violence.

Having changed the trade unions, the government now turned its attention to the **press**, which they felt should articulate the policies of the party that the electorate had voted for rather than offering an independent perspective. Press reform culminated in the early 1980s with a wholesale restructuring of the industry: two established Chinese newspapers were closed and two new ones created out of their ashes, while papers in all languages were brought under the umbrella of a new company whose chairman, **S.R. Nathan**, was once a civil servant in charge of Singapore's national security agency.

Another significant development of the time was in **education**. Back in the 1950s, the PAP had appeased Chinese-speaking voters by permitting the launch of a Chinese-language university, Nantah, but thirty years on the public had largely decided that English offered better prospects, and Chinese-language institutions were in decline. In 1980 the government absorbed Nantah into the new National University of Singapore, which used English, and a few years later the remaining state schools that taught mainly in Chinese were switched to English. Though most Singapore students still learn Chinese, Malay or Tamil as a subsidiary language, it is English that now reigns supreme – with all the potential implications that has for the island's identity, cultures and values.

New leaders

As the 1990s began, Singapore was an obvious economic miracle, yet it was also bland and rigid, a consumerist showcase where the historic Chinatown had been partly demolished and the remnants sanitized, and where patronizing state campaigns exhorted citizens to, among other things, be nice to each other and not spit in the street. So when Lee Kuan Yew stepped down in 1990 in favour of his deputy, **Goh Chok Tong**, Singaporeans hoped for a degree of loosening up. Goh promised to lead in a more consultative way, and there were some liberalizing changes: films began to be rated so that they could be viewed intact instead of being cut to shreds in order to be family-friendly, and the arts scene began to take off, though there were still written and unwritten rules curbing freedom of expression. However, the government kept a lid on the press and on the few opposition figures prepared to stick their heads above the parapet, and little changed when Lee's eldest son, **Lee Hsien Loong**, took over as prime minister in 2004. This continuity in approach was no surprise, with Lee Kuan Yew continuing to play an influential role throughout as so-called "senior minister" or "minister mentor".

Prospects

Singapore today feels more at ease with itself and is a great deal more culturally rich than a generation ago. And yet there are a few clouds on the horizon. The island has not truly established itself as the research hub it would like to be, and the wisdom of its reliance on **financial services** was questioned when Singapore suffered a sharp recession in the wake of the global banking crisis of 2008. In this light, government approval for two **integrated resorts** – as the casinos at Sentosa and Marina Bay are euphemistically termed – was not only controversial with the public but was viewed by some as a sign that the country lacked new economic avenues. Other observers single out the country's record on **human rights** and press freedom, but international scrutiny is limited to rare episodes such as in 1994 when the American teenager Michael Fay, then at school in Singapore, was flogged for minor crimes. In general, Western countries prefer to view Singapore as a wealthy trading partner and a useful little ally in the so-called war on terror.

Nor is there much internal pressure on the government: in recent times the opposition has managed at most four directly elected MPs in a parliament of at least eighty members. A further challenge for the opposition is that many seats are part of "group representation constituencies" or **GRCs**, essentially winner-takes-all super-constituencies where only one party succeeds, by gaining the largest share of the combined vote. The system was brought in during the late 1980s apparently to make parliament more diverse (candidates for a GRC must form an ethnically balanced slate), but given that the opposition can barely take ordinary constituencies, it is no surprise that they have not captured one GRC to date.

Nonetheless, occasional expressions of public disquiet suggest that Singaporeans are more sceptical about the system that envelopes their lives than media coverage or elections might reveal. One notable example was when **Temasek Holdings**, the state-owned company that helps manage Singapore's huge foreign reserves, saw a chance to grab stakes in two global banking firms as the recent world financial crisis broke, only to see their shares continue to sink in value. After public disquiet over the losses, it was announced in 2009 that the company's head, Ho Ching – who is also the prime minister's wife – was to step down, though the move was later postponed. Another example is the ongoing public unease over **immigration**. Singapore has long taken in low-paid Asian workers as maids and labourers, plus Malaysian and expat professionals, but numbers have soared in recent times: now a fifth of the population of five million are workers on temporary contracts. Singaporeans complain that the influx is squeezing them out of jobs at all levels and making state housing unaffordable. They also complain that the island's property boom and economic achievements are mainly benefitting the rich, and statistics do show that Singapore has a more unequal distribution of wealth than, for example, Australia or the UK, neither of which is a beacon in this regard. Singapore approaches its sixth decade of independence as a nation of prosperity tempered by internal contradictions. The government rules paternalistically, yet complains that citizens do not show more originality and initiative; capitalism appears to have triumphed over the welfare state, yet the state owns eighty percent of the land and state-dominated institutions play a crucial role in shipping, property, banking and other key sectors of the economy. It remains to be seen if places like Singapore and China truly present some kind of **"neo-Confucian"** alternative to liberal Western democracy, or if Singapore, always a hybrid of East and West, might one day soon embark on a more tolerant and pluralistic path.

Religion

T otal **freedom of worship** is enjoyed in Singapore, whose multicultural society is reflected in the wide range of creeds that it supports. Over half of the population follow Chinese religions – mostly Buddhism, but with elements of Taoism and Confucianism. Malays, who make up fourteen percent of the population, are predominantly Muslim, while the nation's Indians are either Hindu, Muslim or Sikh. In addition, one in ten Singaporeans are Christian: most are Protestants, though all denominations are represented, and there's a large enough Jewish community to support two synagogues.

Below are overviews of the three main strands of belief in Singapore today: Chinese religions, Islam and Hinduism.

Chinese religions

Most Singaporean Chinese are **Buddhist**, **Taoist** or **Confucianist**, although in practice they are often a mixture of all three. These different strands of Chinese religion ostensibly lean in very different directions, but in practice the combination of the three comprises a system of belief that is first and foremost pragmatic. The Chinese use religion to ease their passage through life, whether in the spheres of work or family, while temples double as social centres, where people meet and exchange views.

Buddhism

Buddhism states that the suffering of the world can only be achieved by attaining a state of personal enlightenment, or Nirvana, through meditation. The founder of Buddhism, **Siddhartha Gautama**, was born a prince in Lumbini in present-day Nepal, around 500 BC. Shielded from knowledge of suffering and death for the first decades of his life, he subsequently renounced his pampered life and spent years in meditation, before finding enlightenment under a bodhi tree. At this point he became the Buddha or "Awakened One". (In Singapore and Southeast Asia he is called *Sakyamuni*, or "Holy Man of the Sakya tribe".) In his first sermon, Buddha taught the four noble truths: that suffering exists; that its source should be recognized; that one should strive for a cessation of suffering; and that this can be achieved by following the **Eightfold Path** – practising right views, intentions, speech, action, livelihood, effort, mindfulness and concentration. The Buddhist faith is split into two schisms: **Hinayana** (Lesser Vehicle) Buddhism, which teaches individuals how to attain enlightenment for themselves, and **Mahayana** (Greater Vehicle) Buddhism – favoured in Singapore – which teaches that, having reached enlightenment, followers should help others to do the same.

Taoism

Unity with nature is the chief tenet of Taoism, a philosophical movement dating from the sixth century BC, and propounded by the Chinese scholar **Lao Tze**. Taoism advocates that people follow a central path or truth, known as *Tao* or "The Way", and cultivate an understanding of the nature of things. This search for truth has often expressed itself in Taoism by way of superstition on the part of its devotees, who engage in fortune-telling and the like. The Taoist gods are mainly legendary figures – warriors, statesmen, scholars – with specific powers that can generally be determined by their form; others represent incarnations of the forces of nature.

Confucianism

Confucianism began as a philosophy based on piety, loyalty, humanitarianism and familial devotion. In the 2500 years since **Confucius**, its founder, died, it has transmuted into a set of principles that permeate every aspect of Chinese life. A blueprint for social and moral harmony, the Confucian ideology stresses one's obligation to family, community and the state, hinging on the individual's need to recognize his or her position in the social hierarchy and act accordingly – son must obey father, student must obey teacher, subject must obey ruler.

Chinese temples

The rules of **geomancy**, or **feng shui** (wind and water), are rigorously applied to the construction of **Chinese temples**, so that the buildings are placed to render them free from evil influences. Visitors wishing to cross the threshold of a temple have to step over a kerb that's intended to trip up evil spirits, and walk through doors painted with fearsome door gods; fronting the doors are two stone lions, providing yet another defence. Larger temples typically consist of a front entrance hall opening onto a walled-in courtyard, beyond which is the hall of worship, where joss sticks are burned below images of the deities. The most important and striking element of a Chinese temple is its roof. They are grand, multi-tiered affairs, with low, overhanging eaves, the ridges alive with auspicious creatures such as dragons and phoenixes and, less often, with miniature scenes from traditional Chinese life and legend. Temples are also normally constructed around a framework of huge, lacquered timber beams, adorned with intricately carved warriors, animals and flowers. More figures are moulded onto outer walls, which are dotted with octagonal, hexagonal or round grille-worked windows. Feng shui comes into play again inside the temple, with auspicious room numbers and sizes, colour and sequence of construction. Elsewhere in the temple grounds, you'll see sizeable ovens stuffed constantly with slowly burning fake money, prayer books and other offerings. Pagodas – tall, thin towers thought to keep out evil spirits – are common too.

Chinese temples play an important part in Chinese community life, and some hold occasional musical and theatrical performances, which can be enjoyed by visitors as well as locals. Temples are open from early morning to early evening and devotees go in when they like, to make offerings or to pray; there are no set prayer times. Visitors are welcome and larger temples have janitors who will show you round, though few speak good English.

Islam

Islam ("submission to God") was founded in Mecca in present-day Saudi Arabia by Muhammad (570–632 AD), the last in a long line of prophets that included Abraham, Moses and Jesus. Muhammad transmitted Allah's final and perfected revelation to mankind through the writings of the divinely revealed "recitation", the **Koran**. The official beginning of Islam is dated as 622 AD, when Muhammad and his followers, exiled from Mecca, made the **hijra**, or migration, north to Yathrib, later known as Medina, "City of the Prophet". The *hijra* marks the start of the Islamic calendar, 1 AH (Anno Hijra). All the central tenets of Islam are embodied in the Koran, with the most important known as the **Five Pillars of Islam**. The first pillar is *shahada* – the confession of faith, "There is no god but God, and Muhammad is his messenger." The *shahada* is recited at the *salat*, the second pillar, which enjoins the faithful to kneel five times daily and pray in the direction of Mecca. The other three tenets are: alms-giving to the local Muslim community (*zakat*); fasting during the ninth month of the Muslim lunar calendar, **Ramadan** (*saum* – see p.151); and the pilgrimage (**haj**) to Mecca, money and health allowing.

The first firm foothold made by Islam in Southeast Asia was the conversion of the court of Melaka, in modern-day Malaysia, in the early fifteenth century. One after another, the powerful Malay court rulers took to Islam, adopting the title sultan (ruler); nearby Singapore couldn't help but feel its influence. Today, almost all of Singapore's Malays are Muslims, as well as a proportion of its Indian population. The form of Islam practised is fairly liberal. Some, but not all, women wear long dress and headscarves, and certain taboos – like not drinking alcohol – are ignored by a growing number of Muslims.

Mosques

While only a small proportion attend the mosque every day, all Muslims converge on their nearest **mosque** on Friday – the day of prayer. Once there, the men wash their hands, feet and faces three times in the outer chambers, before entering the prayer hall to recite sections of the Koran. After this initial period, an **imam** will lead prayers and, on occasions, deliver a sermon, in which the teachings of Muhammad will be applied to a contemporary context. Women cannot enter the main prayer hall during prayers and must congregate in a chamber to the side of the hall.

Visitors are welcome at certain times, provided that their shoulders and legs are covered. No non-Muslim is allowed to enter a mosque during prayer time or go into the prayer hall at any time, although it's possible to stand just outside and look in.

Hinduism

Hinduism reached the Malay Peninsula and Singapore long before Islam, brought by Indian traders more than a thousand years ago. Its base of support grew in the nineteenth century, when large numbers of indentured workers and convicts arrived from the subcontinent to labour on rubber estates and in construction.

Hinduism had no founder, but grew slowly over thousands of years. Its central tenet is the belief that life is a series of rebirths and reincarnations (*samsara*) that eventually leads to spiritual release (*moksha*). An individual's progress is determined by his or her *karma*, very much a law of cause and effect, in which negative decisions and actions slow up the process of upward reincarnation and positive ones accelerate it.

A whole variety of deities are worshipped, which on the surface makes Hinduism appear complex, but with only a loose understanding of the **Vedas** (the religion's holy books) the characters and roles of the main gods quickly become apparent. The deities you'll come across most often are the three manifestations of the faith's Supreme Divine Being: **Brahma the Creator**, **Vishnu the Preserver** and **Shiva the Destroyer**. Other enduring favourites among Hindus include: elephant-headed Ganesh, the son of Shiva, who is evoked before every undertaking except funerals; Vishnu's consort, the comely Lakshmi, worshipped as goddess of prosperity and wealth; and Saraswati, wife to Brahma, and seen as a goddess of purification, fertility and learning.

Hindu temples

Visitors are welcome to explore **Hindu temples**, but are expected to remove their shoes before entering. Step over the threshold and you enter a veritable Disneyland of colourful gods and fanciful creatures. The style is typically **Dravidian** (South Indian), as befits the largely Tamil population, with a soaring *gopuram*, or entrance tower, teeming with sculptures, and a central courtyard leading to an inner sanctum (off-limits to tourists) dedicated to the presiding deity.

Singaporean recipes

The most profound pleasures of a stay in Singapore revolve around meal times; eating is a national mania, and locals have some fifty thousand establishments from which to choose. Of course, swanky restaurants abound for gourmands intent on exploring the exclusive end of Asian cooking, but it's far more rewarding to visit a hawker stall, eating house or coffee shop, and sample everyday food as eaten by the Singaporeans.

We can't re-create for you the sensory overload of a busy hawker centre, but **recipes** for three of the island's most popular dishes are given below, representing Singapore's major ethnic groups, the Chinese, Malays and Indians. For the vast majority of visitors, these are a much better reflection of local food than bird's nests and shark's fins.

None of the **ingredients** used should be difficult to find in your local stores, and they don't require specialist equipment to cook.

Hainanese Chicken Rice

You can't walk far in Singapore without stumbling across a coffee shop or stall that serves **Hainanese Chicken Rice**, a deceptively unassuming dish of succulent **boiled chicken** laid on **aromatic rice** that's regarded by many as Singapore's unofficial national dish. The first giveaway is the row of ghostly pale chickens hanging on butcher's hooks along the shop front, the second the ringing noise of metal on butcher's block as the aproned Chinese cook hacks away unceremoniously with his meat cleaver at the chicken carcasses.

Part of the appeal of the dish (which was imported by immigrants from the Chinese island of Hainan, south of China off the north coast of Vietnam) lies in its simplicity and its completeness. Nothing is wasted, with the stock created by boiling the chicken being used to cook rice before finally ending up as a light broth. Hainanese Chicken Rice is traditionally served with chilli and ginger sauce, soya sauce and minced garlic.

Serves 4 people

1.7l or 3 pints chicken stock
Whole 1.5kg or 3lb chicken, giblets removed
1 red chilli, finely sliced
2 cloves garlic, crushed
1cm or half-inch piece ginger, finely grated
1 teaspoon salt
Half teaspoon freshly ground black pepper
400g or 13oz long grain rice
Half cucumber, sliced
3 tomatoes, sliced
2 tablespoons soya sauce

For the chilli and ginger sauce:
8 fresh red chillies, chopped
4cm or 1.5 inch piece ginger, grated
2 cloves garlic, chopped
1 tablespoon vinegar
Sugar and salt to taste

Bring the stock to the boil in a large pan, add the whole chicken, along with the chilli, garlic, ginger, salt and pepper. Cover the pan, and boil the chicken for 45 minutes or until tender. Remove the chicken from the stock and set to one side, reserving the stock. While the chicken is cooling, rinse the rice thoroughly, and cook in the chicken stock. Meanwhile, make the sauce. Pound together the chillies, ginger and garlic in a pestle and mortar. Transfer to a bowl and add the vinegar.

When the rice is cooked, drain, reserving the stock. Pack the rice into cups, and upturn them onto individual plates to form domes.

Cut the chicken into slices, lightly baste them with soya sauce, and lay them around the rice. Garnish with cucumber and tomato. Finally, bring the remaining stock to the boil, season to taste, and serve as a soup.

Satay

If any one Malaysian dish has caught the world's culinary imagination it's surely **satay**, an aromatic snack comprising marinated strips of meat skewered on small sticks, grilled and dipped in a spicy peanut sauce. The sight of the satay man, sporting a *songkok* and fanning the flames of his charcoal barbecue pit with a woven fan, is a reassuringly traditional one in today's high-tech Singapore. **Beef** and **chicken** are the two classic ingredients for Malay satay, though oddities such as fish, seafood and vegetarian satay often crop up on Singaporean menus. The pork satay of the Nonya cook is a variation of the traditional Malay satay, reflecting the Chinese predilection for pork.

There are two styles of satay: **satay terkan**, for which the meat is finely minced and wrapped around a skewer, and the far tastier **satay chochok**, in which whole pieces of meat are used. Nowadays, satay is sold in bunches of five or ten; in days gone by, customers would accumulate skewers during an evening, and the satay man would tally the bill by counting these up at the end of the night.

Makes approximately 20–30 sticks of satay

400g or 13oz beef or chicken, cut into thin strips
Oil for basting

For the marinade:
1 lemon grass stalk, sliced and crushed
8 shallots, finely sliced
2 cloves garlic, chopped
1 teaspoon cumin
1 teaspoon coriander
1 teaspoon turmeric
1 teaspoon sugar
Pinch of salt
2 tablespoons peanut oil

For the sauce:
1 lemon grass stalk, finely grated
2.5cm or 1-inch piece ginger, finely grated
1 onion, finely sliced
10 dried red chillies, soaked and finely chopped
2 cloves garlic
3 tablespoons tamarind juice
250g or 8oz unsalted peanuts, finely chopped

2 tablespoons sugar
Salt to taste
Oil for frying

To make the marinade, mix the lemon grass, shallots, garlic, cumin, coriander, turmeric, sugar and salt in the oil. Mix the strips of meat into the paste and leave for a couple of hours.

Meanwhile, prepare the sauce. Pound the lemon grass and ginger in a pestle and mortar. Fry the onion over a moderate heat for five minutes or until soft, stirring occasionally. Add the lemon grass, ginger, chillies and garlic and mix. Cook for a further two minutes. Now add the tamarind juice, peanuts, sugar, salt and 200ml or 7fl oz water, and simmer for fifteen minutes or until thickened.

Skewer the strips of marinated meat onto small skewers and grill on a barbecue or under a preheated hot grill until crisp, regularly brushing the meat with oil.

Satay is best served hot, dipped in the sauce, with generous chunks of raw cucumber and onion.

Murtabak

The **murtabak** is a thick pancake stuffed with meat, fried onion and egg, and loved by Singapore's Indian population. Half the fun of ordering a murtabak is watching it being made: murtabak cooks have made an art out of spinning their dough dramatically up in the air to stretch it paper-thin, and perhaps it's this process that has earned the dish the otherwise misleading title of Singapore's answer to the pizza. The spectacle is best viewed at one of the Muslim Indian restaurants behind the Sultan Mosque, on North Bridge Road. Murtabaks can be made out of chicken or beef, but more often they feature **minced mutton**. In Singapore, they are cooked on wide griddles, but a frying pan will do. A saucer of curry sauce or daal perfectly complements the dish.

Makes 6 murtabaks

For the dough:
300g or 10oz plain flour
Half teaspoon salt
1 tablespoon ghee (or butter)
Oil to coat dough balls
Flour for rolling

For the filling:
2 tablespoons ghee (or vegetable oil)
2 medium-sized onions, finely sliced
4 green chillies, finely sliced
3 garlic cloves, crushed
5 eggs
400g or 13oz minced meat
1 teaspoon garam masala
Salt and pepper to taste

To make the dough, place the flour, salt and ghee in a mixing bowl and slowly add approximately 8 tablespoons of warm water, mixing together until a stiff dough is formed. Knead until soft. Divide the dough into six balls and leave standing in a covered dish for at least an hour, turning once or twice.

Next, make the filling. Heat the ghee in a pan over moderate heat, add the onion, chilli and garlic, and fry for 5 minutes stirring occasionally. Meanwhile, beat the eggs in a bowl. When the onions are soft, add the meat and garam masala and season. Cook for 20 minutes or until cooked through.

To assemble a murtabak, lift a ball of dough out of the oil and roll out as thinly as possible on a floured surface. Transfer the dough to a greased and pre-heated griddle, or frying pan.

As the dough begins to cook, baste it with beaten egg, and then heap a mound of filling in the middle. Fold in the four corners of the dough to form a parcel, and cook for a couple of minutes on each side, basting with egg to secure the flaps. Serve at once.

Singapore in literature

Since its foundation in 1819, Singapore has provided rich pickings for travel writers, novelists and historians. However, due to the scarcity of indigenous written material, we have to rely almost exclusively on writings by foreign visitors for early depictions of the island.

The one notable exception is the historian **Abdullah bin Kadir**, born in Melaka in 1797 of Malay and Tamil stock, and later employed as a scribe by Sir Stamford Raffles. The first excerpt below comes from his autobiography, the *Hikayat Abdullah*. Published in Malay in 1849, it remains, despite factual inaccuracies, a fascinating social and historic document. It is interesting to contrast Abdullah's squalid portrayal of early Singapore with the altogether more civilized picture painted by English traveller **Isabella Bird** thirty years later. Singapore's contemporary writers are represented first by Lee Tzu Pheng, whose poem *My Country and My People* reflects the cultural disorientation inherent in the establishment of a new nationhood. Finally, R. Rajaram's short story *Hurry* is played out against a Singapore completely remoulded since the days of Abdullah.

Hikayat Abdullah

It was Colonel Farquhar's habit to go for a walk every morning looking round the district. It was all covered with thick scrub. Only in the middle of the open space already mentioned were there no thick bushes, but only myrtle, rhododendron and eugenia trees. On the side nearest the shore were many kinds of trees, *ambong-ambong*, *melpari*, *bulangan* and scattered tree trunks. On the opposite side of the river there was nothing to be seen except mangrove trees, *bakau*, *api-api*, *buta-buta*, *jeruju* and strewn branches. There was no good piece of ground even as much as sixty yards wide, the whole place being covered in deep mud, except only on the hills where the soil was clay. There was a large rise, of moderate elevation, near the point of the headland at the estuary of Singapore River.

In the Singapore River estuary there were many large rocks, with little rivulets running between the fissures, moving like a snake that has been struck. Among these many rocks there was a sharp-pointed one shaped like the snout of a swordfish. The Sea Gypsies used to call it the Swordfish's Head and believed it to be the abode of spirits. To this rock they all made propitiatory offerings in their fear of it, placing bunting on it and treating it with reverence. "If we do not pay our respects to it," they said, "when we go in and out of the shallows it will send us to destruction." Every day they brought offerings and placed them on the rock. All along the shore there were hundreds of human skulls rolling about on the sand; some old, some new, some with hair still sticking to them, some with the teeth filed and others without. News of these skulls was brought to Colonel Farquhar and when he had seen them he ordered them to be gathered up and cast into the sea. So the people collected them in sacks and threw them into the sea. The Sea Gypsies were asked, "Whose are all these skulls?" and they replied, "These are the skulls of men who were robbed at sea. They were slaughtered here. Wherever a fleet of boats or a ship is plundered it is brought to this place for a division of the spoils. Sometimes there is wholesale slaughter among the crews when the cargo is grabbed. Sometimes the pirates tie people up and try out their weapons here along the sea shore." Here-too-was the place where they went in for cockfighting and gambling.

One day Colonel Farquhar wanted to ascend the Forbidden Hill, as it was called by the *temenggong*. The *temenggong*'s men said, "None of us has the courage to go up the hill because there are many ghosts on it. Every day one can hear on it sounds as of hundreds of men. Sometimes one hears the sound of heavy drums and of people shouting." Colonel Farquhar laughed and said, "I should like to see your ghosts," and turning to his Malacca men, "Draw this gun to the top of the hill." Among them there were several who were frightened, but having no option they pulled the gun up. All who went up were Malacca men, none of the Singapore men daring to approach the hill. On the hill there was not much forest and not many large trees, only a few shrubs here and there. Although the men were frightened they were shamed by the presence of Colonel Farquhar and went up whether they wanted to or not. When they reached the top Colonel Farquhar ordered the gun to be loaded and then he himself fired twelve rounds in succession over the top of the hill in front of them. Then he ordered a pole to be erected on which he hoisted the English flag. He said, "Cut down all these bushes." He also ordered them to make a path for people to go up and down the hill. Every day there was this work being done, the undergrowth being slashed down and a pathway cleared.

At that time there were few animals, wild or tame on the Island of Singapore, except rats. There were thousands of rats all over the district, some almost as large as cats. They were so big that they used to attack us if we went out walking at night and many people were knocked over. In the house where I was living we used to keep a cat. One night at about midnight we heard the cat mewing and my friend went out carrying a light to see why the cat was making such a noise. He saw six or seven rats crowding round and biting the cat; some bit its ears, some its paws, some its nose so that it could no longer move but only utter cry after cry. When my companion saw what was happening he shouted to me and I ran out at the back to have a look. Six or seven men came pressing round to watch but did nothing to release the cat which only cried the louder at the sight of so many men, like a person beseeching help. Then someone fetched a stick and struck at the rats, killing the two which were biting the cat's ears. Its ears freed, the cat then pounced on another rat and killed it. Another was hit by the man with a stick and the rest ran away. The cat's face and nose were lacerated and covered with blood. This was the state of affairs in all the houses, which were full of rats. They could hardly be kept under control, and the time had come when they took notice of people. Colonel Farquhar's place was also in the same state and he made an order saying, "To anyone who kills a rat I will give one *wang*." When people heard of this they devised all manner of instruments for killing rats. Some made spring-traps, some pincer traps, some cage-traps, some traps with running nooses, some traps with closing doors, others laid poison or put down lime. I had never in my life before seen rats caught by liming; only now for the first time. Some searched for rat-holes, some speared the rats or killed them in various other ways. Every day crowds of people brought the dead bodies to Colonel Farquhar's place, some having fifty or sixty, others only six or seven. At first the rats brought in every morning were counted almost in thousands, and Colonel Farquhar paid out according to his promise. After six or seven days a multitude of rats were still to be seen, and he promised five *duit* for each rat caught. They were still brought in thousands and Colonel Farquhar ordered a very deep trench to be dug and the dead bodies to be buried. So the numbers began to dwindle, until people were bringing in only some ten or twenty a day. Finally the uproar and the campaign against the rats in Singapore came to an end, the infestation having completely subsided.

Some time later a great many centipedes appeared, people being bitten by them all over the place. In every dwelling, if one sat for any length of time, two or three centipedes would drop from the attap roof. Rising in the morning from a night's sleep one would be sure to find two or three very large centipedes under one's mat and they caused people much annoyance. When the news reached Colonel

Farquhar he made an order saying that to anyone who killed a centipede he would give one *wang*. Hearing this, people searched high and low for centipedes, and every day they brought in hundreds which they had caught by methods of their own devising. So the numbers dwindled until once in two or three days some twenty or thirty centipedes were brought in. Finally the campaign and furore caused by the centipedes came to an end, and people no longer cried out because of the pain when they got bitten.

The above extract is taken from the *Hikayat Abdullah*, by Abdullah bin Kadir, translated by A.H. Hill (1969), with kind permission of Oxford University Press/Penerbit Fajar Bakti.

The Golden Chersonese

Singapore, January 19, 1879.

It is hot – so hot! – but not stifling and all the rich-flavoured, coloured fruits of the tropics are here – fruits whose generous juices are drawn from the moist and heated earth, and whose flavours are the imprisoned rays of the fierce sun of the tropics. Such cartloads and piles of bananas and pineapples, such heaps of gold and green giving off fragrance! Here, too, are treasures of the heated crystal seas – things that one has dreamed of after reading Jules Verne's romances. Big canoes, manned by dark-skinned men in white turbans and loin-cloths, floated round our ship, or lay poised on the clear depths of aquamarine water, with fairy freights – forests of coral white as snow, or red, pink, violet, in massive branches or fernlike sprays, fresh from their warm homes beneath the clear warm waves, where fish as bright-tinted as themselves flash through them "living light". There were displays of wonderful shells, too, of pale rose-pink, and others with rainbow tints which, like rainbows, came and went – nothing scanty, feeble, or pale!

It is a drive of two miles from the pier to Singapore, and to eyes which have only seen the yellow skins and non-vividness of the Far East, a world of wonders opens at every step. It is intensely tropical; there are mangrove swamps, and fringes of coco-palms, and banana groves, date, sago and travellers' palms, tree ferns, india-rubber, mango, custard-apple, jack-fruit, durian, lime, pomegranate, pineapples, and orchids, and all kinds of strangling and parrot-blossomed trailers. Vegetation rich, profuse, endless, rapid, smothering in all shades of vivid green, from the pea-green of spring and the dark velvety green of endless summer to the yellow-green of the plumage of the palm, riots in a heavy shower every night and the heat of a perennial sunblaze every day, while monkeys of various kinds and bright-winged birds skip and flit through the jungle shades. There is a perpetual battle between man and the jungle, and the latter, in fact, is only brought to bay within a short distance of Singapore.

I had scarcely finished breakfast at the hotel, a shady, straggling building much infested by ants, when Mr Cecil Smith, the Colonial Secretary, and his wife called, full of kind thoughts and plans of furtherance; and a little later a resident, to whom I had not even a letter of introduction, took me and my luggage to his bungalow. All the European houses seem to have very deep verandas, large, lofty rooms, punkahs everywhere, windows without glass, brick floors, and jalousies and "tatties" (blinds made of grass or finely split bamboo) to keep out the light and the flies. This equatorial heat is neither as exhausting or depressing as the damp summer heat of Japan, though one does long "to take off one's flesh and sit in one's bones…".

It is all fascinating. Here is none of the indolence and apathy which one associates with Oriental life, and which I have seen in Polynesia. These yellow, brown, tawny, swarthy, olive-tinted men are all intent on gain; busy, industrious, frugal, striving and, no matter what their creed is, all paying homage to Daikoku. In spite of the activity, rapidity, and earnestness, the movements of all but the Chinese are graceful, gliding stealthy, the swarthy faces have no expression that I can read, and the dark liquid eyes are no more intelligible to me than the eyes of oxen. It is the "Asian mystery" all over.

It is only the European part of Singapore which is dull and sleepy looking. No life and movement congregate round the shops. The merchants, hidden away behind jalousies in their offices, or dashing down the streets in covered buggies, make but a poor show. Their houses are mostly pale, roomy, detached bungalows, almost altogether hidden by the bountiful vegetation of the climate. In these their wives, growing paler every week, lead half-expiring lives, kept alive by the efforts of ubiquitous "punkah-wallahs"; writing for the mail, the one active occupation. At a given hour they emerge, and drive in given directions, specially round the esplanade, where for two hours at a time a double row of handsome and showy equipages moves continuously in opposite directions. The number of carriages and the style of dress of their occupants are surprising, and yet people say that large fortunes are not made nowadays in Singapore! Besides the daily drive, the ladies, the officers, and any men who may be described as of "no occupation", divert themselves with kettle-drums, dances, lawn tennis, and various other devices for killing time, and this with the mercury at 80°! Just now the Maharajah of Johore, sovereign of a small state on the nearest part of the mainland, a man much petted and decorated by the British Government for unswerving fidelity to British interests, has a house here, and his receptions and dinner parties vary the monotonous round of gaieties.

The native streets monopolise the picturesqueness of Singapore with their bizarre crowds, but more interesting still are the bazaars or continuous rows of open shops which create for themselves a perpetual twilight by hanging tatties or other screens outside the side walks, forming long shady alleys, in which crowds of buyers and sellers chaffer over their goods, the Chinese shopkeepers asking a little more than they mean to take, and the Kings always asking double. The bustle and noise of this quarter are considerable, and the vociferation mingles with the ringing of bells and the rapid beating of drums and tom-toms, an intensely heathenish sound. And heathenish this great city is. Chinese joss-houses, Hindu temples, and Mohammedan mosques almost jostle each other, and the indescribable clamour of the temples and the din of the joss-houses are faintly pierced by the shrill cry from the minarets calling the faithful to prayer, and proclaiming the divine unity and the mission of Mahomet in one breath.

How I wish I could convey an idea, however faint, of this huge, mingled, coloured, busy, Oriental population; of the old King and Chinese bazaars; of the itinerant sellers of seaweed jelly, water, vegetables, soup, fruit and cooked fish, whose unintelligible street cries are heard above the din of the crowds of coolies, boatmen and gharriemen waiting for hire; of the far-stretching suburbs of Malay and Chinese cottages; of the sheet of water, by no means clean, round which hundreds of Bengalis are to be seen at all hours of daylight unmercifully beating on great stones the delicate laces, gauzy silks, and elaborate flouncings of the European ladies; of the ceaseless rush and hum of industry, and of the resistless, overpowering, astonishing Chinese element, which is gradually turning Singapore into a Chinese city! I must conclude abruptly, or lose the mail.
I.L.B.

Letter VII (Beauties of the Tropics) extracted from *The Golden Chersonese*, by Isabella Bird.

My Country and My People

My country and my people
are neither here nor there, nor
in the comfort of my preferences,
if I could even choose.

At any rate, to fancy is to cheat;
and worse than being alien, or
subversive without cause,
is being a patriot
of the will.

I came in the boom of babies, not guns,
a 'daughter of a better age';
I held a pencil in a school
while the 'age' was quelling riots
in the street, or cutting down
those foreign 'devils',
(whose books I was being taught to read).
Thus privileged I entered early
the Lion City's jaws.
But they sent me back as fast
to my shy, forbearing family.

So I stayed in my parents' house,
and had only household cares.
The city remained a distant way,
but I had no land to till;
only a duck that would not lay,
and a runt of a papaya tree,
(which also turned out to be male).

Then I learnt to drive instead
and praise the highways till
I saw them chop the great trees down,
and plant the little ones;
impound the hungry buffalo
(the big ones and the little ones)
because the cars could not be curbed.
Nor could the population.
They built milli-mini-flats
for a multi-mini-society.
The chiselled profile in the sky
took on a lofty attitude,
but modestly, at any rate
it made the tourist feel 'at home'.

My country and my people
I never understood.
I grew up in China's mighty shadow,
with my gentle, brown-skinned neighbours;
but I keep diaries in English.
I sought to grow
in humanity's rich soil,
and started digging on the banks, then saw
life carrying my friends downstream.

Yet, careful tending of the human heart
may make a hundred flowers bloom;
and perhaps, fence-sitting neighbour,

I claim citizenship in your recognition
of our kind,
my people, and my country,
are you, and you my home.

My Country and My People by Lee Tzu Pheng, reprinted by kind permission of Heinemann.

Hurry

I was running. In the centre of the road. True, I wasn't running like the wind, but my speed was fast enough for beads of perspiration to run down my body and my breath to come in short gasps.

Cars and lorries flashed past me either way. Still I kept running. Somehow it seemed appropriate that I should be running on the white centre line separating the dual carriageway.

Where were the vehicles heading to? I didn't know. Did the drivers in them know where I was running to? No, but there was a possibility that they would think I was a lunatic. So I should not continue to run in this manner.

I would have to cross the road, walk or run the short distance to the MRT station to board a train to Orchard Road. Then I would have to disembark and cross the road to Dynasty Hotel to meet my friend Kamal staying there.

The train would arrive at the station in two minutes' time and I must be in it. I was running in this wild manner all for this. I had crossed half the road. Now running along the white line, I tried desperately to find a way through the thick of the moving traffic to find an opening to make my dash across. Suddenly I spied an opening and lashed across, leaving behind two drivers screeching to a halt as they tried to avoid the collision. One driver even made an obscene gesture with his hands.

I felt a sense of regret. Not at his gesture, but that I had cut his speed of travel. Anyway, there was no time to apologize to him. I had to catch that train or I would really be late.

I must buy a car, I thought to myself. It would be so convenient considering the amount of travelling I have to do. The convenience was more than that. A motorist dares to use foul language and rude gestures because he knows he is safe from the poor pedestrian out on the road. Yes, a car is definitely a convenience in more ways than one.

Miraculously I arrived at the Jurong Station with thirty seconds to spare. From the third level of the station, I could see the sun had half-disappeared in the horizon. When I had left my home in the morning, he had also been half-hidden, but that was the dawn.

Passengers on the platform suddenly moved forward with some standing in the yellow safety line. I could see the train in the distance. This wasn't a bus. There would be ample time for all to board the train before it pulled out. Then why the rush? To ensure that they could get seats? But even if one pushed his way through not everyone could get a seat. I wasn't going to be left out however. I, too, rushed with the crowd and pushed my way to the front.

As the train ground to a halt and the doors slid open we rushed in. I was lucky enough to grab the only seat in my compartment and sank down gladly.

My eyes scanned the passengers. Young, old, middle-aged, they all seemed lost in some thoughts. What were they thinking about, or were they just staring blankly, I wondered.

As the train pulled up at the next station, another human wave entered the train. I noticed my friend Ravi among them in the next compartment. Ravi is a very close friend. Well, at least during our school days. But I still considered him as one. Unfortunately, we had not had many opportunities to meet as often as we used to. As he was staying in the Jurong area, occasionally we met like this in the train.

He had not noticed me. "Hello, Ravi!" I shouted across. He turned, saw me and waved. My voice, however, had shattered the silence in the train and several dozen pairs of eyes bored into me. I turned pink with embarrassment.

Ravi could not come any nearer, the crowd was that thick. No one appeared willing to allow Ravi to walk through to me.

"How is father?" I gestured with my hands. His father had been ill for some time. Ravi answered in a similar manner, giving me the thumbs down sign. His normally cheerful face was tinged with sadness.

As the train sped on, I wondered what I could do. I attempted to convey how I felt with expressions. He was about to say something but changed his mind, pulled out a paper from his pocket and started to scribble something.

The train reached Raffles Place Interchange. Most of us, including me, had to change trains here. In no time, three quarters of the train had emptied. Ravi made his way through the crowd and as I was about to disembark, thrust the paper into my hands. As he didn't need to change trains, I didn't have the time to even exchange a few words.

As the train pulled away my train pulled into the opposite tunnel. Running with the others, I crossed over the platform and boarded it.

Eagerly I opened his note. "We have finalised marriage plans for Chitra. Father insists that he wants to see the marriage before he dies. I'll phone you later."

Chitra marrying. I sat stunned. How could she marry someone when she was my girlfriend...?

Why not? No one, not even Chitra, knew of my love. That's a joke isn't it!

I had wanted to tell Ravi of my love. But the opportunity had never arisen, and being the coward I am I had kept postponing the discussion. Now it was too late. Who could I blame but myself? Anyway, where did I have the time for courtship when I never returned from work till eleven in the night every day.

I crumpled the note and threw it on the floor and looked up. The passenger opposite looked meaningfully at me and the note on the floor. I had littered. Sheepishly I picked up the note and shoved it in my shirt pocket.

Irritated, I reached for a cigarette. My eyes fell on the warning note directly opposite. "No smoking! $500 fine." My hand dropped to the side. I, more than anyone else, knew that every mistake had its penalty.

The train sped on through the tunnels. It was pitch dark outside. I wasn't aware where we were. This is the drawback in travelling by train. A minute's inattention, and one loses track completely of one's whereabouts. The speed with which one was travelling was the only consolation.

Some light pierced the darkness. Instantly the passengers came to life. Orchard Station. I would have to get out here. I glanced at my watch – 7.26pm. I was pleased. Had I come by bus I would not have made it in this short time to keep my 7.30pm appointment with Kamal at Dynasty Hotel's lobby.

I crossed glittering Orchard Road and walked briskly into the hotel. But Kamal was not there. Maybe he was still up in the room. Reception should be able to help.

"Can you give me Kamal's room number?"

"Mr Kamal just vacated his room. His flight was brought forward and he's left for the airport."

If he had just left, he must be waiting for a cab outside the hotel. In my hurry, I must have missed him outside. Maybe, just maybe, I could catch him before he caught a cab, I thought as I dashed out.

Hurry by R. Rajaram, translated by K. Sulosana.

Books

Singapore's bookshops are the best place to get books on the country, stocking imported titles and the output of the island's thriving English-language publishing industry, covering everything from political biographies to encyclopedic tomes on design, though fiction tends to have a low profile. Of the bookshops listed on p.156, the best for more specialist titles is Select Books, which offers a mail-order service. In the reviews below, books marked ☘ are particularly recommended while o/p signifies out of print. Note that authors with Chinese names usually have their surname appearing first, as is the Chinese custom; for Malay and Indian names, the given name is usually followed by the father's name.

Travel writing and memoir

Charles Allen *Tales from the South China Seas*. Recollections of the last generation of British colonists in which predictable Raj attitudes prevail, though some of the drama of everyday lives, often in inhospitable conditions, is evinced with considerable pathos.

Hidayah Amin *Gedung Kuning: Memories of a Malay Childhood*. A simple, heartfelt account of life in the little yellow mansion on Kandahar Street (see p.76), taking in Muslim festivals, family weddings, neighbourhood characters and stories handed down over the generations, culminating with the author's family being pitiably turfed out in 1999 when the state took over the property.

Isabella Bird *The Golden Chersonese*. The intrepid author's adventures in the Malay states in the 1870s ranged from strolls through Singapore's streets to elephant-back rides and encounters with alligators. Periodically reissued, it's also available from various websites as a free download.

Russell Braddon *The Naked Island*. Braddon's disturbing and moving first-hand account of the POW camps of Malaya, Singapore and Thailand displays courage in the face of appalling conditions and treatment.

Eric Lomax *The Railway Man*. An artless, redemptive and moving story of capture during the fall of Singapore, torture by the Japanese and reconciliation with the author's tormentor after fifty years.

☘ **Lucy Lum** *The Thorn of Lion City*. You might think a memoir of a wartime childhood in Singapore would be dominated by the savagery of the Japanese, but for the author that was nothing compared to the torment inflicted on her at the hands of her manipulative and violent mother and grandmother. It's told with zero artifice, which only makes it more compelling.

Michael Wise (ed) *Travellers' Tales of Old Singapore*. A diverse collection of anecdotes and recollections covering the colonial period up to World War II.

History and politics

Munshi Abdullah (aka Abdullah bin Kadir) *The Hikayat Abdullah* (o/p). Raffles' one-time clerk, Abdullah, kept a diary of some of the most formative years of Southeast Asian history, and his first-hand account is crammed with illuminating vignettes and character portraits.

Jim Baker *The Eagle In The Lion City*. About so much more than its declared theme, Singapore–American relations, this entertaining book tells of how British influence fell away in the post-colonial era, allowing common interests in trade and defence to bring the US and Singapore ever closer – hence the somewhat "Californized" (to use the author's term) city-state you see today.

Noel Barber *Sinister Twilight.* Documents the fall of Singapore to the Japanese by re-imagining the crucial events of the period.

🏃 **Maurice Collis** *Raffles.* The most accessible and enjoyable biography of Singapore's founder.

Maya Jayapal *Old Singapore.* Concise volume that charts the growth of the city-state, drawing on contemporary maps, sketches and photographs to engrossing effect.

Patrick Keith *Ousted.* Singapore's unhappy stint as part of Malaysia might seem something from the distant past, but the events of the mid-1960s, recounted in this excellent blow-by-blow account by a former

advisor to the Malaysian government, still shape both countries and their relations today.

Colin Smith *Singapore Burning: Heroism and Surrender in World War II.* Highly detailed, definitive account of the fall of Singapore, written with a journalist's instinct for excitement.

Carl A. Trocki *Singapore: Wealth, Power and the Culture of Control.* A digestible dissection of how the PAP, after co-opting and marginalizing Singapore's Left in the 1960s and then allying "with international capital to create a workers' paradise", acquired its present grip on all aspects of life on the island.

🏃 **C.M. Turnbull** *A History of Modern Singapore 1819–2005.* Mary Turnbull had barely completed a major update of this standard work when she died in 2008, and what a fine legacy: the new edition is lucid, thorough, nearly always spot-on in its analysis and, as always, utterly readable.

Architecture

Julian Davison and Luca Invernizzi Tettoni *Black & White: The Singapore House.* Singapore still has a scattering of colonial "Anglo-Malay" residences – one now houses the *Flutes at the Fort* restaurant (see p.136), and there are more examples lurking in the area around the Botanic Garden. This beautifully photographed study celebrates these strange hybrids of mock Tudor and Southeast Asian elements, which were sometimes raised off the ground on posts like a kampong house.

Ronald Knapp *Chinese Houses of Southeast Asia.* A lavish coffee-table book exploring Chinese mansions and shophouses from Indonesia to southeast China, with coverage of the Tan Yeok Nee mansion and the Baba

House, the latter emblazoned across the jacket. Be warned, though, that it weighs a ton and has a price tag to match.

Peter Lee and Jennifer Chen *The Straits Chinese House.* Packed with old photos, this book on Peranakan homes, domestic artefacts and vanishing traditions makes an excellent memento after you've visited the Baba House or the Peranakan Museum.

Wan Meng Hao and Jacqueline Lau *Heritage Places of Singapore.* A compact, full-colour catalogue of the hugely diverse pre-independence architecture of Singapore, from Palladian colonial buildings to overlooked Art Deco edifices as well as traditional temples and shrines.

Culture and society

James Harding and Ahmad Sarji
P. Ramlee: The Bright Star. An uncritical but enjoyable biography of the singer, actor and director sometimes described as to the Malay world's Harry Belafonte. More importantly, it's a window onto what seems like a different era, only half a century ago, when Singapore was the centre of the Malay entertainment universe.

Leslie Layton *Songbirds in Singapore*. A delightful examination of the local penchant for keeping songbirds, detailing all facets of the pastime, from its growth in the nineteenth century to its most popular birds.

Gerrie Lim *Invisible Trade: High-Class Sex for Sale in Singapore*. This exposé of the local escort industry makes for an entertaining but somewhat unsatisfying read, its basic flaw being the idea that it's a big secret that Singapore might be less squeaky clean than it appears.

Ilsa Sharp *Path of the Righteous Crane*. Eu Tong Sen, after whom one of Chinatown's main thoroughfares is named, was the founder of the Eu Yan Sang emporia of Chinese herbal medicines, and this new biography not only recounts the many successes of this prewar tycoon in Singapore and Malaysia but also unwraps migrant Chinese society of the time.

Food

Aziza Ali *Aziza's Creative Malay Cuisine*. For many years the author ran one of the best Malay restaurants in Singapore, and her recipes are intended more to impress at dinner parties than to reflect what's served on the street. Don't expect Thai-influenced dishes from the northern part of the Peninsula either; the emphasis here is on Singapore and the south.

Sylvia Tan *Singapore Heritage Food*. This book begins a little unpromisingly with passé colonial-era dishes – prawn cocktails and the like – but then comes a romp through all manner of classic Singapore restaurant and hawker food, from Hainanese chicken rice and chilli crab to less familiar standards that visitors seldom notice, such as *oh luak* (scrambled egg with oysters) and *chap chye* (Peranakan mixed veg and fungi braised in soy sauce). Plenty of vintage photos of now-vanished pushcart food stalls, too.

Nature

M. Strange and A. Jeyarajasingam *A Photographic Guide to Birds of Peninsular Malaysia and Singapore*. User-friendly and with oodles of glossy plates, this should help even the bird-blind sort out a black-naped oriole from a white-rumped shama.

Tee Swee Ping (ed) *Trees of our Garden City*. A guide to Singapore's diverse flora is something local publishers haven't properly addressed. This book does at least cover one of the most impressive aspects of that flora, from the majestic rain tree to the red-flowered flame of the forest.

Fiction

Noel Barber *Tanamera*. Romantic saga set in mid-twentieth-century Singapore and dramatized for TV in the 1980s.

Anthony Burgess *The Malayan Trilogy*. Published in one volume, *Time for a Tiger, The Enemy in the*

Blanket and *Beds in the East* provide a witty and acutely observed vision of 1950s Malaya and Singapore, underscoring the racial prejudices of the period.

James Clavell *King Rat*. Set in Japanese-occupied Singapore, a gripping tale of survival in the notorious Changi Prison.

Joseph Conrad *Lord Jim*. Southeast Asia provides the backdrop to the story of Jim's desertion of an apparently sinking ship and subsequent efforts to redeem himself; the main protagonist was modelled on the sailor A.P. Williams, who lived and died in Singapore.

J.G. Farrell *The Singapore Grip*. Lengthy wartime novel, the last of Farrell's empire trilogy, in which real and fictitious characters flit from tennis to dinner party as the countdown to the Japanese occupation begins.

Paul Theroux *Saint Jack*. The compulsively bawdy tale of Jack Flowers, an ageing American who supplements his earnings at a Singapore ship's chandlers by pimping for Westerners. The 1979 movie adaptation, filmed in Singapore behind a smokescreen of subterfuge – the crew knew the sleaziness of the plot would never pass muster with the authorities – has only recently been unbanned on the island.

Glossary

Baba Peranakan male of predominantly Chinese heritage

Bukit Hill

Bumboat Small cargo boat

Cheongsam Tight-fitting Chinese dress with long slit up the side

Expressway Motorway/freeway

Five-foot way Recessed ground-level walkway, substituting for a pavement; a standard feature of rows of shophouses

Godown Riverside warehouse

Gopuram Pyramid of sculpted deities over the entrance to a Hindu temple

Haj Major annual pilgrimage to Mecca

Halal Something permissible in Islam

Hawker centre A cluster of food stalls gathered under one roof and sharing common tables

Istana Palace

Jalan Road or street

Kampong/kampung Village

Kavadi Steel frames hung from the bodies of Hindu devotees during Thaipusam

Keramat Auspicious Malay site

Kongsi Chinese clan association

Kris Wavy-bladed Malay dagger

Lorong Lane

Mahjong A Chinese game with similarities to dominoes

Masjid Mosque

Nonya/Nyonya Peranakan female of predominantly Chinese heritage

Padang Field or square

Pasir Sand, often used in names of areas with beaches

Peranakan Person born in the territories around the Straits of Malacca and of mixed culture and/or race

Pulau Island

Ramadan Muslim fasting month

Rotan Rattan cane used in the infliction of corporal punishment

Sari Traditional Indian woman's garment, worn in conjunction with a choli (short-sleeved blouse)

Shophouse Shuttered building with living quarters upstairs and a shop space at ground level, where the facade is also recessed to create a five-foot way

Songkok Stiff drum-like cap worn by Malay men

Sultan Ruler

T'ai chi Chinese martial art, commonly performed as an early-morning exercise

Tanjong/tanjung Promontory

Telok/teluk Bay

Temenggong Chieftain

Tongkang Chinese sailing boat

Trishaw Three-wheeled cycle-rickshaw

Wayang Theatrical show; in the Singapore context, Chinese opera

Travel store

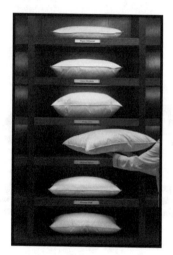

Enriching, exotic and enchanting journeys through South East Asia.

Our itineraries across South East Asia on the Eastern & Oriental Express promise adventure and excitement; discover intriguing destinations and mysterious histories; feast your eyes on ever-changing panoramas and breathtaking landscapes; encounter traditional cultures and ancient ceremonies. Accompanied by local experts from historians to oenologists, and complemented with mouth-watering onboard dining, wooden-panelled cabins and barmen who know how to mix your favourite cocktail, step onboard for an enriching, exotic and enchanting journey.

For further information or to book, contact one of our main reservation offices:

London: Tel: 0845 077 2222 or +44 (0)20 7921 4010
email: oereservations.uk@orient-express.com

Singapore: Tel: +65 6395 0678 email: oereservations.singapore@orient-express.com

United States of America: Tel: 800 524 2420 (Toll Free) or 843 937 9068
email: oereservations@oeh.com

www.orient-express.com/e&o

"The most accurate maps in the world"

San Jose Mercury News

ROUGH GUIDE MAP

France

1:1,000,000 • 1 INCH: 15.8 MILES • 1CM: 10KM

Plastic waterproof map
ideal for planning and touring

CITY MAPS 24 titles
Amsterdam · Athens · Barcelona · Berlin
Boston · Brussels · Chicago · Dublin
Florence & Siena · Frankfurt · Lisbon
London · Los Angeles · Madrid · Marrakesh
Miami · New York City · Paris · Prague
Rome · San Francisco · Toronto · Venice
Washington DC
US$8.99   Can$13.99   £4.99

COUNTRY & REGIONAL MAPS 50 titles
Algarve · Andalucía · Argentina · Australia
Baja California · Brittany · Crete · Croatia
Cuba · Cyprus · Czech Republic · Dominican
Republic · Dubai · Egypt · Greece · Guatemala
& Belize · Iceland · Ireland · India · Kenya
Mexico · Morocco · New Zealand · Northern
Spain · Peru · Portugal · Sicily · South Africa
South India · Sri Lanka · Tenerife · Thailand
Trinidad & Tobago · Turkey · Tuscany
Yucatán Peninsula and more.
US$9.99   Can$13.99   £5.99

waterproof • rip-proof • amazing value
BROADEN YOUR HORIZONS

Small print and
Index

A Rough Guide to Rough Guides

Published in 1982, the first Rough Guide – to Greece – was a student scheme that became a publishing phenomenon. Mark Ellingham, a recent graduate in English from Bristol University, had been travelling in Greece the previous summer and couldn't find the right guidebook. With a small group of friends he wrote his own guide, combining a highly contemporary, journalistic style with a thoroughly practical approach to travellers' needs.

The immediate success of the book spawned a series that rapidly covered dozens of destinations. And, in addition to impecunious backpackers, Rough Guides soon acquired a much broader and older readership that relished the guides' wit and inquisitiveness as much as their enthusiastic, critical approach and value-for-money ethos.

These days, Rough Guides include recommendations from shoestring to luxury and cover more than 200 destinations around the globe, including almost every country in the Americas and Europe, more than half of Africa and most of Asia and Australasia. Our ever-growing team of authors and photographers is spread all over the world, particularly in Europe, the US and Australia.

In the early 1990s, Rough Guides branched out of travel, with the publication of Rough Guides to World Music, Classical Music and the Internet. All three have become benchmark titles in their fields, spearheading the publication of a wide range of books under the Rough Guide name.

Including the travel series, Rough Guides now number more than 350 titles, covering: phrasebooks, waterproof maps, music guides from Opera to Heavy Metal, reference works as diverse as Conspiracy Theories and Shakespeare, and popular culture books from iPods to Poker. Rough Guides also produce a series of more than 120 World Music CDs in partnership with World Music Network.

Visit www.roughguides.com to see our latest publications.

Rough Guide credits

Text editor: Emma Gibbs
Layout: Jessica Subramanian
Cartography: Ashutosh Bharti
Picture editor: Natascha Sturny
Production: Louise Daly
Proofreader: Susanne Hillen
Cover design: Nicole Newman, Dan May, Chloë Roberts
Photographer: Simon Bracken
Editorial: **London** Andy Turner, Keith Drew, Edward Aves, Alice Park, Lucy White, Jo Kirby, James Smart, Natasha Foges, Róisín Cameron, James Rice, Lara Kavanagh, Emma Beatson, Kathryn Lane, Monica Woods, Mani Ramaswamy, Harry Wilson, Lucy Cowie, Alison Roberts, Eleanor Aldridge, Ian Blenkinsop, Joe Staines, Matthew Milton, Tracy Hopkins, Ruth Tidball; **Delhi** Madhavi Singh, Lubna Shaheen, Jalpreen Kaur Chhatwal
Design & Pictures: **London** Scott Stickland, Dan May, Diana Jarvis, Mark Thomas, Nicole Newman, Sarah Cummins, Emily Taylor; **Delhi** Umesh Aggarwal, Ajay Verma, Ankur Guha, Pradeep Thapliyal, Sachin Tanwar, Anita Singh, Nikhil Agarwal, Sachin Gupta

Production: Rebecca Short, Liz Cherry, Erika Pepe
Cartography: **London** Ed Wright, Katie Lloyd-Jones; **Delhi** Rajesh Chhibber, Rajesh Mishra, Animesh Pathak, Jasbir Sandhu, Karobi Gogoi, Swati Handoo, Deshpal Dabas, Lokamata Sahu
Online: **London** Faye Hellon, Jeanette Angell, Fergus Day, Justine Bright, Clare Bryson, Aine Fearon, Adrian Low, Ezgi Celebi; **Delhi** Amit Verma, Rahul Kumar, Narender Kumar, Ravi Yadav, Debojit Borah, Rakesh Kumar, Ganesh Sharma, Shisir Basumatari
Marketing & Publicity: **London** Liz Statham, Jess Carter, Vivienne Watton, Anna Paynton, Rachel Sprackett, Laura Vipond; **New York** Katy Ball; **Delhi** Aman Arora
Digital Travel Publisher: Peter Buckley
Reference Director: Andrew Lockett
Operations Assistant: Becky Doyle
Operations Manager: Helen Atkinson
Publishing Director (Travel): Clare Currie
Commercial Manager: Gino Magnotta
Managing Director: John Duhigg

Publishing information

This sixth edition published November 2010 by
Rough Guides Ltd,
80 Strand, London WC2R 0RL
11, Community Centre, Panchsheel Park, New Delhi 110017, India
Distributed by the Penguin Group
Penguin Books Ltd,
80 Strand, London WC2R 0RL
Penguin Group (USA)
375 Hudson Street, NY 10014, USA
Penguin Group (Australia)
250 Camberwell Road, Camberwell, Victoria 3124, Australia
Penguin Group (NZ)
67 Apollo Drive, Mairangi Bay, Auckland 1310, New Zealand
This paperback edition published in Canada in 2010. Rough Guides is represented in Canada by Tourmaline Editions Inc., 662 King Street West, Suite 304, Toronto, Ontario, M5V 1M7
Cover concept by Peter Dyer.
Typeset in Bembo and Helvetica to an original design by Henry Iles.

Printed in Singapore
© Mark Lewis 200x
Maps © Rough Guides
No part of this book may be reproduced in any form without permission from the publisher except for the quotation of brief passages in reviews.
208pp includes index
A catalogue record for this book is available from the British Library
ISBN: 978-1-84836-561-2

Help us update

We've gone to a lot of effort to ensure that the sixth edition of **The Rough Guide to Singapore** is accurate and up-to-date. However, things change – places get "discovered", opening hours are notoriously fickle, restaurants and rooms raise prices or lower standards. If you feel we've got it wrong or left something out, we'd like to know, and if you can remember the address, the price, the hours, the phone number, so much the better.

Please send your comments with the subject line "**Rough Guide Singapore Update**" to © mail @roughguides.com. We'll credit all contributions and send a copy of the next edition (or any other Rough Guide if you prefer) for the very best emails.

Find more travel information, connect with fellow travellers and book your trip on www.roughguides.com.

Acknowledgements

Richard Lim thanks Valerie Won of the Singapore Tourism Board, Fulvia Wong of the Singapore Flyer and staff at the Peranakan Museum. Thanks also to Marcus "Scubearer" for the wander around Chinatown, to Hidayah Amin and Ameen Talib for the lowdown on Arab Street, and to the late Mary Turnbull. Special thanks to my family in Singapore for helping keep the reviews up to date, and to John Gee and Ooi Kee Beng for feedback on the history section and their continued friendship.

Gemma Sharkey: Tony Tan for his patience and incomparable knowledge of the city and its food, Hau Yin Sau for taking the time to share her foodie passion and knowledge of the city, Diego Marti for his amazing generosity and kindness, Mark Lewis for giving me a great opportunity and being supportive throughout, and Charlene Fang for all her helpful advice when I was feeling overwhelmed.

Readers' letters

Thanks to all the readers who have taken the time to write in with comments and suggestions (and apologies if we've inadvertently omitted or misspelt anyone's name):

James Bunning, Iain Farrow, Marco Mussetta, Patricia Park, Rishi Ramchand, Ryan.

Photo credits

All photos © Rough Guides except the following:

Introduction

The historic villa of Tan Teng Niah Little India Singapore © Travelscape Images/Alamy

Chinatown at dusk Singapore © Peter Adams/Getty Images

Trishaws in streets Chinatown, Singapore © Stephen Shepherd/Alamy

Things not to miss

01 Row of buildings Chinatown, Singapore © Getty Images

02 Clubbing at Zouk Club, Singapore © Eightfish/Alamy

04 Bukit Timah Natural Reserve, Singapore © Richard Lim

05 Chinese opera performance, Singapore © Stock connection/Alamy

06 Thian Hock Keng Temple, Singapore © Wolfgang Kaehler/Alamy

07 Hindu Devotee walks across burning coal © How Hwee Young/Corbis

09 Orchard Road, Singapore © Scott Barbour/Getty Images

11 Universal Studios on Sentosa Island, Singapore © Roslan Rahman/Getty Images

13 Orchid Garden, Singapore © Richard Lim

16 Orang-utan, Singapore Zoo © LOOK Die Bildagentur der Fotografen GmbH/Alamy

17 Baba House exterior, Singapore © Photo courtesy by NUS Baba House

18 Sri Srinivasa Temple, Little India, Singapore © LOOK Die Bildagentur der Fotografen GmbH/Alamy

19 Historic Boat Quay, Singapore © Rob Walls/Alamy

Festive Singapore colour section

Dragon Dance during Chinese New Year, Singapore © Jon Arnold/Alamy

Hindu devotees during Thaipusam festival in Singapore © Geof KirbyAlamy

Dragon Race on the Singapore River © Tim Chong/Corbis

Candles floating in water during Mooncake festival © Justyn Olby/Corbis

Boys dressed for Hari Raya celebration, Singapore © Alamy

Temple celebrations for Chinese New Year in Singapore © Idealink Photography/Alamy

Dancer in the Chingay Parade, Chinese New Year © How Hwee Young/Corbis

Singapore food colour section

Laksa spicy noodle soup, Singapore © Lauryn Ishak/Corbis

Satay barbecue stall, Singapore © Travel Ink/Getty Images

Hawkers at a food court, Singapore © Justin Guariglia/Corbis

Trays with variety of Malay cakes, Singapore © Cn Boon/Alamy

Black and whites

p.62 Buddhas at Buddha Tooth Relic Temple, Singapore © Richard Lim

p.71 Tekka Market, Singapore © Richard Lim

p.109 Sentosa Beach, Singapore © Richard Lim

ROUGH GUIDES

Index

Map entries are in colour.

INDEX

A

Abdul Gaffoor Mosque...72
Abdullah bin Kadir.......181, 188
accommodation 113
addresses.......................23
airlines flying to Singapore
.....................................22
airports 23, 24
Al-Abrar Mosque............53
Albert Street 70
Alexandra Arch.............101
ambulance......................31
Amoy Street....................56
Anglo-Dutch treaty 167
Arab Quarter 75–77
Arab Quarter 68–69
Arab Street 75
Armenian Church of
St Gregory the
Illuminator...................45
arrival.............................23
Arts House......................42
arts, the 146
ArtScience Museum.......51
Asian Civilizations Museum
.....................................43
Baba House....................60
Baba-Nonyas.........47, 132,
Singapore food colour
section
badminton 162
Bali Lane........................75
banks..............................33
bargaining...............31, 153
Barings Bank scandal 64
bars 140
  1 TwentySix.....................143
  Alley Bar 142
  Astor................................142
  Axis 140
  Backstage 144
  Balaclava.........................140
  Bar Opiume.....................140
  Bar Savanh 141
  Bar Stop...........................142
  Bellini Room 143
  Bora-Bora Beach Bar 109
  BQ Bar 141
  Clinic 141
  Divine 142
  Dubliner...........................142
  Hacienda..........................142
  Harry's Quayside..............141
  Ice Cold Beer 142
  KPO..................................142
  Long Bar 141
  Loof..................................142
  Molly Malone's 141
  New Asia Bar 141
  No. 5 Emerald Hill............142
  Observation Lounge 142
  Orgo 141
  Prince of Wales................142
  Que Pasa 143
  Red Dot Brewhouse.........143
  Screening Room Rooftop
    Bar 141
  Speakeasy........................142
  Tantric..............................145
  Wala Wala Café Bar 143
  Wild Oats 142

B

batik..............................157
Battle Box.......................49
Beach Road.....................77
beaches, Changi 95
beaches, Sentosa.........108
bike rental.......................28
Bird, Isabella.........183, 188
birds' nests.....................58
Boat Quay 65
boat trips 28
books............................188
bookshops....................156
Botanic Gardens 81
Bras Basah Road 66
Bras Basah 68–69
breakfast.... 122, *Singapore
food* colour section
Buddha Tooth Relic temple
and museum................61
Buddhism 173
Buffalo Road...................72
Bugis Junction................70
Bugis Street....................70
Bugis Village...................70
Bukit Batok.....................86
Bukit Timah Nature
Reserve.......................85
bus companies (inter-
national routes)............23
buses
  international 24
  local..................................26
Bussorah Street.............76

C

cable cars to Sentosa...101
cafés.............................122
canopy walk (Southern
Ridges)......................100
car rental 28
carpets 157
Cavenagh Bridge............43
Central Business District
.....................................64
Central Fire Station 46
Change Alley Aerial Plaza
.....................................65
Changi Beach.................95
Changi Prison.................94
Changi Village................95
Chettiar Temple 49
Chia Thye Poh..............171
CHIJMES complex 67
children's Singapore.....163
China Street....................56
Chinatown 52–64
Chinatown...............54–55
Chinatown Complex.......61
Chinatown Heritage Centre
.....................................62
Chinese Methodist Church
(Chinatown).................53
Chinese New Year 150,
Festive Singapore colour
section
Chinese Weekly
Entertainment Club......57
Chingay Parade *Festive
Singapore* colour section
cinemas 148
Civil Defence Heritage
Gallery 46
clan associations............56
Clarke Quay....................49
classical music 148
Clifford Pier....................65
climate 9
clinics 30
clothes shops 157
Club Street 56
clubs 143
  Attica/Attica Too...............143
  Azzura Beach Club 109
  Bora-Bora Beach Bar 109
  Brix..................................143
  Butter Factory 143

Café del Mar 109
Home Club.......................... 144
Play 145
Powerhouse 144
Stereolab/Stereobar.......... 144
Taboo 145
Why Not? 145
Zirca 144
Zouk 144
coffee shops (*kopitiams*)
.... 126
Colonial District 39–49
Colonial District 40
Confucianism 174
conscription.................. 170
consulates 32
cookery classes............ 133
costs............................... 31
crafts 155
credit cards 34
cricket............................ 159
crime............................... 31
cruises 28
Cuff Road 73
Cuppage Terrace............ 81
customs formalities 32

D

Dairy Farm Nature Park ...86
darts 161
Deepavali........................ 73
Dempsey Hill 82
dengue fever 30
Desker Road................... 74
desserts 135
Dhoby Ghaut 79
disabled access 35
disabilities, travellers with
.... 35
Diwali 73
doctors 30
Dragon Boat Festival... 151,
Festive Singapore colour
section
driving.............................. 28
drugs 31
Ducktour................. 29, 163
DVD shops 157

E

East Coast Park 91, 163
East India Company....... 42
Eastern and Oriental
Express........................ 21

eating............................. 121
electricity 32
embassies 32
Emerald Hill 81
emergencies 31
Empress Place 43
entertainment 146
Esplanade – Theatres by
the Bay 50
Eu Tong Sen Street 63
Eu Yan Sang Medical Hall
.... 57
exchange........................ 33
EZ-link cards 26

F

Far East Square.............. 56
feng shui 174
ferry operators............... 23
festivals 150
film................................. 148
financial district 64
five-foot way.............. 6, 56
flights to Singapore ... 19–21
food ... 121, *Singapore food*
colour section
food and drink glossary
.... 124
food courts 123
football.......................... 159
Formula 1 159
Fort Canning Park 48
Freemason's Hall............ 46
Fuk Tai Ch'i Street museum
and temple 58
Fullerton Building 65
Fullerton Hotel 65, 114

G

Gateway Building 77
gay Singapore 144
Gedung Kuning 76, 188
Geylang 93
Geylang 94
glossary 192
GMAX 49
Goh Chok Tong 171
Golden Chersonese, the
.... 183, 188
golf................................. 159
Goodwood Park Hotel.... 81
GST 31, 153

guesthouses 114, 116,
117, 120; see also Hostels

H

haggling........................ 153
Haji Lane 75
Hajjah Fatimah Mosque
.... 77
halal food....................... 121
HarbourFront 101
Haw Par Villa 98
hawker centres 123,
Singapore food colour
section
health.............................. 30
Henderson Waves 101
high tea........................... 135
Hikayat Abdullah... 181, 188
Hinduism .... 175, *Festive
Singapore* colour section
history............................ 167
holidays, public 34
Holland Village.............. 104
Holland Village.............. 104
Hong Lim Complex 56
horseracing................... 160
Hort Park 100
hospitals 30
hostels... 114, 116, 117, 120
A Beary Good Hostel....... 114
ABC................................. 116
Ali's Nest 116
Betel Box 118
Checkers Inn 116
Fragrance Hostel 116
G4 Station...................... 117
Hangout @ Mount Emily.. 118
Hive, the......................... 116
InnCrowd......................... 116
Prince of Wales................ 116
Rucksack Inn 114
Sleepy Sam's 116
Tresor Tavern................... 116
Waterloo Hostel 118
Welcome Inn 116
hotels
Albert Court..................... 118
Aliwal Park 117
Amber Hotel..................... 120
Carlton 118
Chinatown........................ 114
Elizabeth.......................... 119
Fortuna............................ 117
Fragrance Imperial 117
Fullerton 115
Gallery 115
Goodwood Park................ 119
Grand Hyatt 119
Grand Mercure Roxy........ 120
Haising 117

Holiday Inn Orchard City Centre 119
Hotel 1929 115
Hotel Michael 120
Hotel Ré! 115
Ibis 118
Inn At Temple Street 115
Intercontinental 118
Kerbau 117
Klapsons 115
Landmark Village 117
Le Peranakan 120
Lloyd's Inn 119
Madras 117
Mandarin Orchard 119
Marriott 119
Metropolitan Y 119
Mövenpick 120
Naumi 118
New Majestic 115
Novotel Clarke Quay 114
Orchard Parade 119
Parkroyal 117
Peninsula Excelsior 114
Perak 117
Raffles 114
Rasa Sentosa Resort 120
Rendezvous 118
Ritz-Carlton Millenia 114
Robertson Quay 114
Santa Grand Bugis 117
Scarlet 115
Sentosa Resort and Spa 120
Shangri-la 119
Siloso Beach Resort 120
Sing Hoe 120
Sloane Court 119
South East Asia 118
St Regis 119
Supreme 119
Swissôtel Merchant Court 115
Swissôtel The Stamford ... 114
Victoria 118
YMCA International House 114
YWCA Fort Canning Lodge 114
House of Tan Teng Niah 72
HSBC TreeTop Walk 87

Images of Singapore 108
information 35
inoculations 30
insurance 32
integrated resorts 51, 107, 172
internet 33
Islam 174

Istana Kampong Glam ... 76
Istana Negara 79

Jacob Ballas Children's Garden 81, 164
Jamae Mosque 59
Japanese occupation 86, 168
Jewel Box 101
jewellery 157
Jewish community 67
Jeyaretnam, J.B. 171
Joo Chiat Complex 93
Joo Chiat Road 93
Jurong 102
Jurong Bird Park 102

Kampong Kapor Methodist Church 73
Kandahar Street 76
Katong 93
Katong 94
Katong Antiques House 94
Kerbau Road 72
Khalid Mosque 93
Kids' Singapore 163
kopitiams 126
Kranji War Cemetery and Memorial 90
Kuan Yim Temple 70
Kusu Island 110
languages 5

Lasalle College of the Arts 67
Lau Pa Sat Festival Market 65
Lee Hsien Loong 171
Lee Kuan Yew 169, 170, 171
lesbian Singapore 144
Lian Shan Shuang Lin Temple 88
Lim Yew Hock 169
literature about Singapore 181, 188

Little India 70–75
Little India 68–69
Little India Arcade 72
live music 145
Luge and Skyride 108

MacRitchie Reservoir Park 87
magazines 29
Maghain Aboth Synagogue 67
mail 33
Majestic Opera House 63
Malabar Mosque 77
Malay Heritage 76
Malay Village 93
Malaysia, union with 169
Mandai Orchid Gardens 89
maps 33
Marina Bay Sands casino 51
Marina Centre 49
Marina Centre 40
Marina South 50
markets, food 122
Marshall, David 169
martial arts 160
masonic lodge 46
media, the 29, 171
medical treatment 30
Megazip 108
Memories at Old Ford Factory 86
Merlion (Sentosa) 108
Merlion 65
MICA Building 49
money 33
Mount Faber 101
MRT 25
music shops 157
Mustafa Centre 73

Nagore Durgha shrine 56
Nanyang Academy of Fine Arts (NAFA) 67
Nathan, S.R. 171
National Archives Building 46
National Museum 47
National Orchid Garden ... 81

New Bridge Road 63
New Supreme Court 41
New Year, Chinese ...... 150, *Festive Singapore* colour section
newspapers 29
Night Safari 88
nightclubs 143
nightlife 140

O

Omni-Theatre 103
One Fullerton 65
opening hours 34
Operation Sook Ching ... 86, 168
Orchard Road 78
Orchard Road 78–79
overland from Southeast Asia 21

P

Padang, the 39
Parkview Square 77
parliament 42
Pasir Panjang 98
People's Action Party ... 169
Peranakan Museum 46
Peranakans .... 132, *Singapore food* colour section
Peranakans 47
pharmacies 30
Philatelic Museum 46
phones 34
Phor Kark See Temple ... 88
police 31
polo 160
postal services 33
pubs 140
Pulau Ubin 96

R

radio 29
Raffles City 44
Raffles Hotel 45, 114
Raffles landing site 41
Raffles Place 64
Raffles, Sir Stamford 167
Raffles, Sir Stamford 42

Rafflesia arnoldii 42
Ramadan .... 151, *Festive Singapore* colour section
recipes, Singaporean ... 176
Reflections at Bukit Chandu 100
religion 173
Resorts World casino ... 107
restaurants 126
　2am Dessert Bar 135
　328 Katong Laksa 132
　Ah Chew Desserts 135
　Annalakshmi 131
　Azzura Beach Club 109
　Banana Leaf Apolo 131
　Bedrock Bar and Grill 133
　Bee Heong Palace 129
　Beng Hiang 129
　Beng Thin Hoon Kee 129
　Beppu Menkan 137
　Black Sheep Café 134
　Blu 136
　Blu Jaz Café 136
　Blue Ginger 132
　Bobby's 133
　Bombay Café 131
　Bora-Bora Beach Bar 109
　Briyani Bistro 132
　Broth 134
　Buko Nero 136
　Bumbu 139
　Café Iguana 133
　Café l'Espresso 135
　Café Le Caire 138
　Cappadocia Café 138
　Cha Cha Cha 133
　Chili's Grill and Bar 133
　Chilli Padi 132
　Ci Yan Organic Vegetarian Health Food 130
　Colours By The Bay 136
　Coriander Leaf 136
　Crystal Jade La Mian Xiao Long Bao 130
　Cumi Bali 135
　Da Paolo II Ristorante 134
　De Sté 134
　Eight Café and Bar 136
　El Sheikh 138
　Fatty's Wing Seong 127
　Flutes at the Fort 136
　Food #03 136
　French Kitchen 134
　Guan Hoe Soon 132
　Haji Maimunah 133
　Halia 122, 137
　Happy Realm Vegetarian Food Centre
　Iggy's 137
　Indochine 139
　Ippudo 138
　Islamic 131
　Jim Thompson 139
　Jing 128
　Kampong Glam Café
　Kinara 131

Komala Vilas 131
Kwan Im Vegetarian 130
Lao Beijing 127
Lawry's The Prime Rib 133
Lee Kui (Ah Hoi) 129
Li Bai 128
Lighthouse 134
Lingzhi 130
Madam Saigon 139
Madras New Woodlands
　.. 131
Magic of Chongqing Hotpot
　.. 129
Majestic 128
Mezza9 137
Min Jiang 129
Mitzi's 128
Mooi Chin Place 129
Moomba 137
Mouth 128
New Chettinadu 131
Orchard Maharajah 131
Original Sin 134
Oso 134
Our Village 131
Pasta Fresca 134
Patara 139
Paulaner Bräuhaus 134
Peach Garden 128
Pepes 135
Peranakan Inn 133
Perle Noir Oyster & Grill Bar
　.. 137
Pine Court 127
PS Café 137
Quentin's 137
Rendezvous 136
Rumah Makan Minang 136
Sakae Sushi 138
Samy's 131
Seah Street Deli 133
Seoul Garden 138
Shiraz 138
Singapura Seafood 130
Soup 128
Spizza 135
Sukhothai 139
Superbowl 130
Swensen's 135
Taste Paradise 128
Teochew City Seafood 129
Thai Express 139
Tiffin Room 135
Tonkichi 138
Trapizza 109
Warung M Nasir 136
Wild Rocket 137
Xu Jun Sheng (Long Ji) Chao Zhou Mei Shi 130
Yet Con Chicken Rice 129
Yhingthai Palace 139
Yum Cha 128
riding 160
river cruises 28
Robertson Quay 49
Rochor Road 66
Rowell Road 74

S

Sago Street 61
Sakaya Muni Buddha Gaya
    Temple 75
sales tax 31
Sam Leong Road 74
Sasanaramsi Burmese
    Buddhist Temple 88
School of the Arts 67
Science Centre 103
Sculpture Square 70
Sentosa 105–109
Sentosa 106
service charge 31
shophouses, Peranakan
    .... 74, 81, 93
shopping 153
Sian Chai Kang Temple ... 56
Singapore Art Museum ... 67
Singapore Chinese
    Chamber of Commerce
    45
Singapore Cricket Club ... 41
Singapore Flyer 50
Singapore Recreation Club
    41
Singapore River 44
Singapore Sling 45
Singapore Tourism Board
    35
Singapore Tourist Pass ... 26
Singapore War Memorial
    45
Singapore Zoological
    Gardens 88
Singapore, eastern 92
Singapore, northern 84
Singapore, western 99
Singlish 7
skiing 161
Sky Park 51
snooker 161
Snow City 103
soccer 159
Song of the Sea 108
songket 157
Sook Ching 168
Sook Ching 86
South Bridge Road 57
Southern Ridges 98
souvenirs 155
spas 161
sports 159
squash 162
Sri Mariamman Temple ... 58
Sri Srinavasa Perumal
    Temple 74
Sri Thendayuthapani
    Temple 49
Sri Veeramakaliamman
    Temple 73
St Andrew's Cathedral ... 44
St James Power Station
    101
St John's Island 110
STB 35
Straits Chinese 47, 132,
    Singapore food colour
    section
Straits Settlements 168
Sultan Mosque 76
Sun Yat Sen Villa 87
Sungei Buloh Wetland
    Reserve 90
supermarkets 122
Supreme Court 41
swimming pools 161

T

table manners 127
Tai Gin Road 87
Tan Yeok Nee mansion ... 80
Tanjong Pagar 59
Taoism 173
taxes 31
taxis 27
teahouses, Chinese 60
Tekka Market 71
telephones 34
Telok Ayer Garden 56
Telok Ayer Street 53
Telok Blangah Hill 101
temples, architecture of
    174
tennis 162
Thaipusam .... 150, *Festive
    Singapore* colour section
theatre 147
Thian Hock Keng Temple
    53
Thimithi .... 152, *Festive
    Singapore* colour section
Thong Chai Medical
    Institute 63
ticket agencies 146

Tiger Brewery 103
Tiger Sky Tower 108
time zone 34
tipping 34, 121
tour operators 22
tourist offices, overseas ... 35
tours 28
trains
    international 24, 25
    MRT 25
trains, Eastern and Oriental
    Express 21
transport 25
travel agents 22
trishaws 28
TV 29

U

Underwater World 107
Universal Studios 107
Upper Dickson Road 73
URA Gallery 59

V

vaccinations 30
Victoria Concert Hall 41
Victoria Theatre 41
visas 32
VivoCity 101

W

Wak Hai Cheng Bio Temple
    56
Wallace Education Centre
    86
Waterloo Street 67
watersports 162
WaveHouse 109
wayangs 147
weather 9

Z

zoo 88

So now we've told you about the things not to miss, the best places to stay, the top restaurants, the liveliest bars and the most spectacular sights, it only seems fair to tell you about the best travel insurance around

✶ WorldNomads.com
keep travelling safely

Recommended by Rough Guides

Map symbols

maps are listed in the full index using coloured text

—·· International border

——— Chapter division boundary

▬▬▬ Expressway

═══ Main road

─── Minor road

▬▬▬ Pedestrianized road

▥▥▥ Steps

—●— Railway

- - - - Footpath

— — Ferry route

●- - -● Cable car

═══ Waterway

)(Bridge/tunnel

⊠ Gate

▲ Peak

☀ Lighthouse

✈ Airport

⊖ MRT station

★ Bus stop

🅿 Parking

♦ General point of interest

ⓘ Tourist office

⊠ Post office

⊞ Hospital/clinic

☺ Swimming pool

⛳ Golf course

☫ Public gardens

◼ Restaurant/café/bar

▲ Hindu temple

✚ Buddhist temple

☪ Mosque

✡ Synagogue

✝ Church

■ Building

▨ Underground mall

◯ Stadium

⊞✝ Christian cemetery

▨ Park

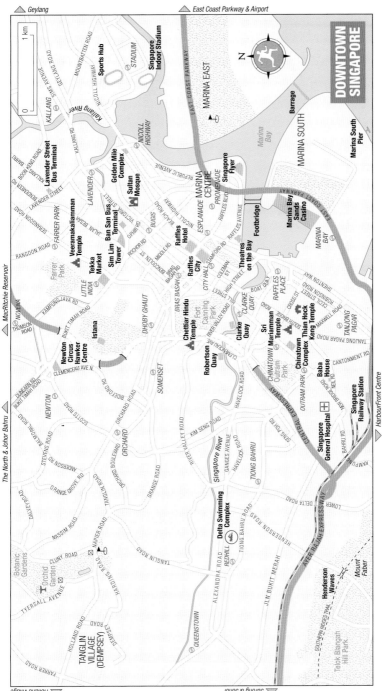

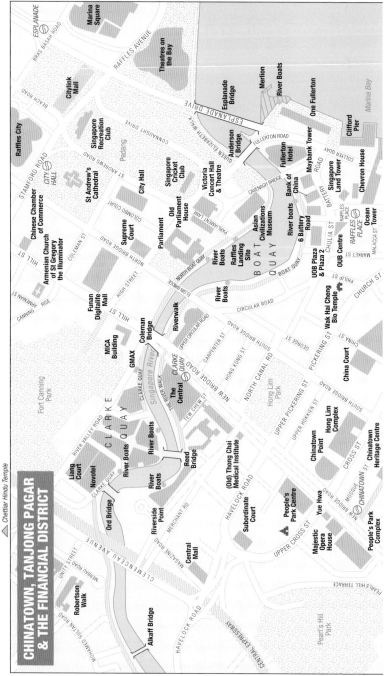

CHINATOWN, TANJONG PAGAR & THE FINANCIAL DISTRICT

△ Chettiar Hindu Temple

Marina Square

Theatres on the Bay

Esplanade

BRAS BASAH ROAD

BEACH ROAD

Citylink Mall

RAFFLES AVENUE

Raffles City

Merlion

River Boats

One Fullerton

Esplanade Bridge

Anderson Bridge

Clifford Pier

Marina Bay

Singapore Recreation Club

CONNAUGHT DRIVE

ESPLANADE DRIVE

QUEEN ELIZABETH WALK

FULLERTON ROAD

Fullerton Hotel

Maybank Tower

COLLYER QUAY

St Andrew's Cathedral

ST ANDREWS ROAD

STAMFORD ROAD

CITY HALL

Chinese Chamber of Commerce

HILL ST

City Hall

Padang

Singapore Cricket Club

Victoria Concert Hall & Theatre

CAVENAGH BRIDGE

Bank of China

ROAD

Singapore Land Tower

Chevron House

BATTERY

Armenian Church of St Gregory the Illuminator

COLEMAN ST

ARMENIAN ST

CANNING RISE

COLOMBO COURT

Supreme Court

Old Parliament House

PARLIAMENT LANE

Asian Civilizations Museum

River boats

6 Battery Road

CHULIA ST

OUB Centre

RAFFLES PLACE

RAFFLES PLACE

MARKET ST

Ocean Tower

MALACCA ST

Parliament

NORTH BRIDGE ROAD

HIGH STREET

Funan Digitalife Mall

Raffles Landing Site

River Boats

NORTH BOAT QUAY

River Boats

BOAT QUAY

UOB Plaza & Plaza 2

ST PHILIP ST

CHURCH ST

Fort Canning Park

MICA Building

GMAX

Coleman Bridge

ELGIN BRIDGE

Riverwalk

UPPER CIRCULAR ROAD

CIRCULAR ROAD

SOUTH BRIDGE ROAD

GEORGE ST

PICKERING ST

Wak Hai Cheng Bio Temple

CHINA ST

B O A T   Q U A Y

The River Walk

Singapore River

The Central

CLARKE QUAY

CLARKE QUAY

CARPENTER ST

HONG KONG ST

NEW BRIDGE ROAD

Hong Lim Park

NORTH CANAL RD

China Court

Liang Court

RIVER VALLEY ROAD

C L A R K E   Q U A Y

River Boats

River Boats

TEW CHEW ST

UPPER PICKERING ST

UPPER HOKKIEN ST

Hong Lim Complex

Chinatown Point

Novotel

Reed Bridge

River Boats

(Old) Thong Chai Medical Institute

HAVELOCK ROAD

Chinatown Heritage Centre

MOSQUE ST

CROSS ST

People's Park Centre

Yue Hwa

CHINATOWN ST

Ord Bridge

Riverside Point

MERCHANT RD

MAGAZINE RD

Subordinate Court

UPPER CROSS ST

People's Park Complex

PEARL'S HILL TERRACE

Central Mall

Majestic Opera House

NEW BRIDGE ROAD

Pearl's Hill Park

Robertson Walk

MOHAMED SULTAN ROAD

MERBAU ROAD

UNITY STREET

C L E M E N C E A U   A V E N U E

Alkaff Bridge

HAVELOCK ROAD

CENTRAL EXPRESSWAY

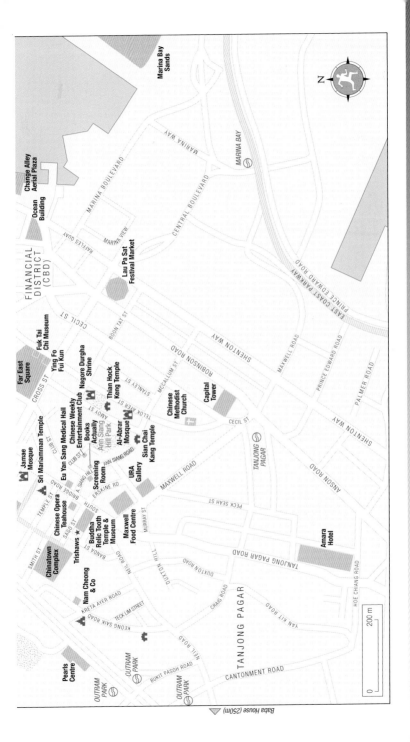

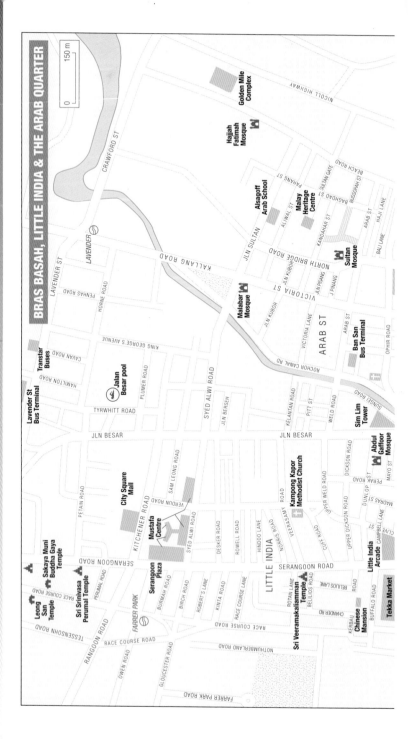

BRAS BASAH, LITTLE INDIA & THE ARAB QUARTER

0   150 m

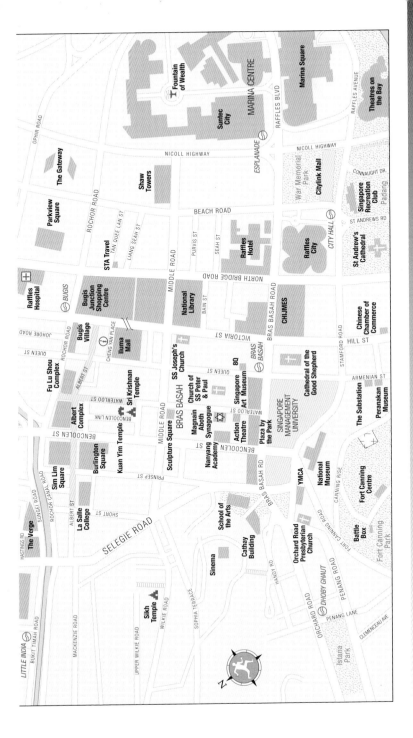

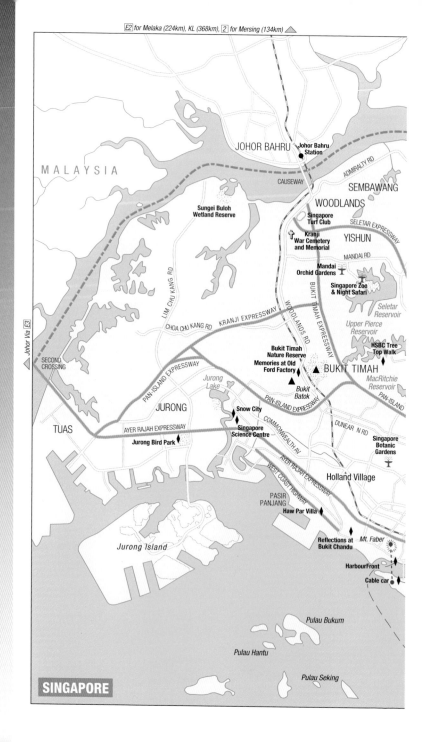

E2 for Melaka (224km), KL (368km), 2 for Mersing (134km)

JOHOR BAHRU
Johor Bahru Station

MALAYSIA

ADMIRALTY RD

CAUSEWAY

SEMBAWANG

WOODLANDS

Sungei Buloh
Wetland Reserve

Singapore
Turf Club

SELETAR EXPRESSWAY

YISHUN

Kranji
War Cemetery
and Memorial

MANDAI RD

Mandai
Orchid Gardens

Singapore Zoo
& Night Safari

LIM CHU KANG RD

Seletar
Reservoir

KRANJI EXPRESSWAY

WOODLANDS RD

BUKIT TIMAH EXPRESSWAY

Upper Pierce
Reservoir

HSBC Tree
Top Walk

Johor Via E3

CHOA CHU KANG RD

SECOND
CROSSING

Bukit Timah
Nature Reserve

BUKIT TIMAH

MacRitchie
Reservoir

Memories at Old
Ford Factory

Bukit
Batok

PAN-ISLAND

PAN-ISLAND EXPRESSWAY

Jurong
Lake

JURONG

Snow City

COMMONWEALTH AV

DUNEAR N RD

TUAS

AYER RAJAH EXPRESSWAY

Singapore
Science Centre

Jurong Bird Park

Singapore
Botanic
Gardens

WEST COAST HIGHWAY

AYER RAJAH EXPRESSWAY

Holland Village

PASIR
PANJANG

Haw Par Villa

Jurong Island

Reflections at
Bukit Chandu

Mt. Faber

HarbourFront

Cable car

Pulau Bukum

Pulau Hantu

Pulau Seking

SINGAPORE

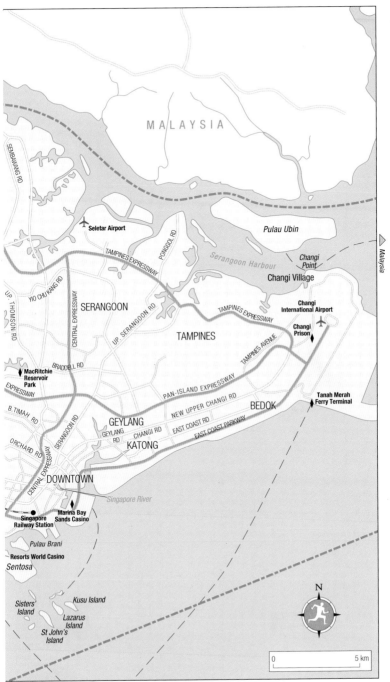

MALAYSIA

✈ Seletar Airport

SERANGAWANG RD

TAMPINES EXPRESSWAY

PONGGOL RD

YIO CHU KANG RD

UP. THOMSON RD

CENTRAL EXPRESSWAY

SERANGOON

UP. SERANGOON RD

BRADDELL RD

MacRitchie
Reservoir
Park

EXPRESSWAY

B. TIMAH RD

ORCHARD RD

CENTRAL EXPRESSWAY

SERANGOON RD

TAMPINES

Pulau Ubin

Serangoon Harbour

*Changi
Point*

Changi Village

TAMPINES EXPRESSWAY

Changi
International Airport

Changi
Prison

TAMPINES AVENUE

PAN-ISLAND EXPRESSWAY

NEW UPPER CHANGI RD

GEYLANG

GEYLANG
RD   CHANGI RD

KATONG

EAST COAST RD

EAST COAST PARKWAY

BEDOK

Tanah Merah
Ferry Terminal

DOWNTOWN

Singapore River

Singapore
Railway Station

Marina Bay
Sands Casino

Pulau Brani

Resorts World Casino

Sentosa

*Sisters'
Island*

Kusu Island

*Lazarus
Island*

*St John's
Island*

N

0   5 km

▷ *Malaysia*

Bintan & ▽ *Batam (Indonesia)*   ▽ *Bintan & Batam (Indonesia)*

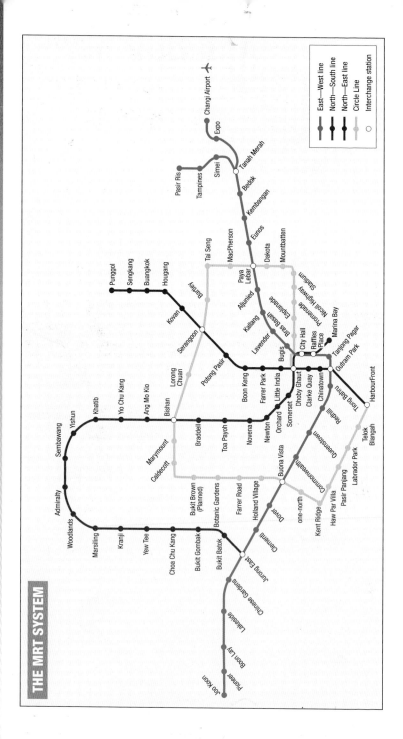

THE MRT SYSTEM

Legend:
- East—West line
- North—South line
- North—East line
- Circle Line
- Interchange station